THE NABOBS OF MADRAS

VIEW OF FORT ST GEORGE FROM ACROSS THE COOUM.

After a water-colour sketch in the Ouseley Collection at the India Office.

Frontispiece.]

THE
NABOBS OF MADRAS

BY

HENRY DODWELL

"I thought at first that the very name of India
sounded hugely; but I do assure you, Sir, that
the ground I tred upon is but dirt still."

LONDON
WILLIAMS AND NORGATE LTD.
14 HENRIETTA STREET, COVENT GARDEN, W.C.2
1926

Made and Printed in Great Britain
by Hazell, Watson & Viney Ld.
London and
Aylesbury

CONTENTS

v

NOTE

Of my illustrations, the second, third, and fifth are reproduced from plates originally prepared for Colonel Love's *Vestiges of Old Madras;* the first is reproduced from an original sketch at the India Office; and the fourth and sixth are reproduced from the India Office copy of Daniell's *Oriental Scenery.* In all these cases, therefore, my very grateful thanks are due to the Rt Hon. the Secretary of State for India.

LIST OF ILLUSTRATIONS

vii

INTRODUCTION

THE nabob, Macaulay tells us, was in the popular conception of the late eighteenth century a gentleman with a tawny complexion, a bad liver, and a worse heart. Clive might describe him in the House of Commons as a hospitable friend, a humane master, and a benevolent citizen, and claim that none was flagitious enough for Mr Foote to mimic at the Haymarket. But he spoke too soon. In a little while that actor was presenting Sir Matthew Mite, surrounded by all the pomp of Asia, profusely scattering the spoils of conquered provinces, committing to memory the latest oaths, and learning to flourish the dice-box with a fashionable air. This caricature was intended to represent the hero of Plassey himself. On the top of this comes the indignation with which Burke and the other managers of Hastings' impeachment pursued the greatest man we ever sent to India. And these fine moral airs sit a little oddly on the age. That virtuous generation tolerated the corruption of Rigby and the debauchery of Old Q. This age of taste could pull down a medieval church in order to build up a Gothic ruin. Why, then, were they so severe upon the nabobs? And what were the nabobs really like? In the following pages I have attempted to answer these questions, in so far as they relate to the particular genus that flourished at Madras. I do not think it was markedly different from the others except in its habitat; but I have been able to observe it much more closely. In such a case the normal individual is what we want much more than any extraordinary specimen. I have therefore given much the greater part of this volume to quite obscure persons, of whom nobody has heard or thought these hundred years, but of whom I found a surprising amount of information among the records of the old Mayor's Court. This I have pieced out with matter from other sources, with an occasional detail about more conspicuous men, whose biographers have neglected it as beneath the dignity of history. But here, where we consort in the main with humble persons, such feelings would be entirely out of place. What I have specially sought to reconstruct is the social background of the events which bulk so large in the second half of the eighteenth century in India. But those events themselves I have carefully avoided, just as I have avoided labelling each of my statements with the source from which it is drawn, though for the benefit of those who would like to see my authorities I have added an appendix, in which they are set out chapter by chapter. As for the nabobs themselves the reader must draw his own conclusions. I have tried to show them as they were, without heightening or obliterating their short-comings. They were very human, and therefore had many failings; they were placed at a critical time in a critical place, and so we owe them a debt of gratitude. A fair estimate must include both their failings and their services.

THE NABOBS OF MADRAS

CHAPTER I

THE VOYAGE TO INDIA

IN the middle of the last century but one, a voyage to India seemed full of perils. You might be taken by the French or the pirates; you might die of the scurvy; you might be wrecked on a desert island or fall into the hands of savages; you might meet contrary winds and die of thirst, or tempests and be drowned. So few young travellers watched without misgiving the English coasts fade behind them into a winter sky. Indeed the first few days at sea must have been peculiarly dismal. There was sea-sickness to reinforce home-sickness; cramped quarters to emphasise the uncertainty of your foothold; the choice of freezing above deck or stifling below. But all the time your vessel was running south; you were getting used to narrow companion-ways, to the conventual regularity of life at sea, to the necessity of lashing things fast, even to the stench of the billage, and your mind itself would turn once more to the contemplation of that golden land to which you were bound. By the time that you had ceased wishing that the voyage was over because it was unpleasant, you had begun to wish it was over because you wanted to be busy making your fortune.

But you were lucky if you sighted Fort St George in the East Indies under four months from the day of your sailing from England. You might easily take six months or eight; and when Clive for the first time sailed eastwards, he was over a year on the voyage. In such conditions very much depended on the character of the ship's officers and of the other passengers. Both were altogether a matter of chance. The captain might be a sprig of fashion, like Augustus Townshend, the son of a lord, or Charles Purvis, nephew of a bishop; or again he might be some rough fellow bred in a chandler's shop in Wapping. The rougher type either predominated in these earlier days, or made a more forcible impression on his passengers. The famous Major Rennell, travelling out to India as a cadet, was pummelled by the commander of the ship, and in revenge perhaps invented and certainly repeated the story that the captain had had his nose tweaked by a common negro in Madagascar. Complaints of ill-treatment were often made by cadets and ensigns; and ships' commanders were excessively conscious of their greatness. A group of youngsters, sailing by a ship that put into the Cape, delayed for some days to pay their respects to the captain ashore; charged with their crime, they pleaded ignorance, but the captain would have none of it. " Every man," said he, " is born with common sense, and one come your length must have known better."

In spite of all his dignity, however, the captain, like every other officer aboard the ship, was much concerned in trade. Each officer was allowed a certain amount of space in the hold, which he might fill with merchandise, carried out, as the phrase went, " on his privilege." By this means the shops (such as they were) of Madras were stocked with those miscellaneous articles that could only be had from Europe—shoes and hats, hams and pickles, buttons and bottled porter. One misanthropic mate carried out a chest of coffin furniture. Others, desiring a higher profit than could be derived from articles of daily use, would bring out a case of portraits, in which a nabob was to recognise his unknown ancestors, or a harpsichord, which unhappily could be neither sold nor kept in tune; or again, toys likely to please an Indian court, looking-glasses, inlaid pistols, and elaborate clocks. Millinery too finds a place; there was a mate of insinuating address who attended every ball at Madras in order to sound the praises of his hats and ribbons in the ears of his partners.

Of the passengers the larger part would always be making their first voyage eastward, as writers or cadets in the Company's service; and even on shipboard these two groups would keep much to themselves, thus antici-pating the perennial rivalry of soldier and civilian in India. Of the two the cadets were much more various and entertaining than the writers. These latter were nearly always youngsters from 16 to 18, fresh from the commercial academy at which they had learnt book-keeping. But the cadets might be boys of 14, or wild rascals like Hickey who had spent in low company the money which he was to have delivered to a client of his father's, or yet wilder bloods who had dissipated their estates, and been obliged to sell their commissions, and were going to India in search of another fortune.

With these " griffins," as new-comers were called at Madras until they had been there a year, would be mingled a few Company's officers or civil servants, who had been home to recover their health or set in order their paternal estates. But in those days there were no leave-rules. A man who wished to go home had to resign whatever post he held, and could only return to India by inducing the Company to restore him to his rank. Accordingly almost every one stayed at Madras till he retired or died, and few but embryo nabobs were to be found on east-bound vessels.

There would be few ladies on board either. Not all

the nabobs were partial to marriage; not all the married ones were partial to their wives; so that the older men were more likely than not to be alone. The young ones, with their fortunes still to make, would almost always be unencumbered. But you might still expect to find some young ladies with one or two married ones on board. The practice of sending girls to India to find husbands was just coming into vogue. The attention which all of them must have received in a ship-load of men must have turned many heads not strong by nature. The distribution of their trivial favours produced more than one duel fought by rival swains at the first convenient landing-place. The publicity of life at sea must have precluded more than sentimental philanderings as a general rule. Nevertheless parents and guardians gave a good deal of sound though very plain advice to young ladies about to embark for India. Here is an example:

" In case of your coming out, I entreat you will be as careful of your conduct on board of the ship as possible. . . . It requires prudence even in young ladys of good families and friends to guard against the ruin of their reputation. . . . You will I hope excuse the advice I give you; but as you have no experience of wily men, you may find this and all you get on this head necessary; and if you was worth £20,000 and lose your character, you will be despised for ever."

As a rule young ladies were entrusted to the care of a friend, but, when none was available, the captain added the duties of chaperon to his other responsibilities. As a rule he discharged them fairly enough; but in at least one instance which remains on record, the Madras Council found itself obliged to investigate a captain's conduct, the young lady in question being nearly related to a Councillor. No criminal charge being substantiated, it was decided to release him from his confinement. He was therefore called in

" and acquainted therewith; but at the same time told that his conduct with relation to this young woman would be a perpetual blot on him, since she was under his care and protection; which he endeavoured to answer by insinuating that she was careless of her reputation before she came on board; but which he had no proof to support, and was therefore stopped from proceeding in this sort of defence."

On the whole the passage to Madras was more likely to produce a certain amount of mild flirtation than romance of a more serious type. But the latter was not always wanting. On occasion, though not very often, you would meet with a Hickey accompanied by his Thais, or Captain Haldane followed by Lauretta who could not bear to be separated from him. It was on the passage to Madras, too, that Warren Hastings first met the handsome German adventuress who was to buy his lifelong devotion on such easy terms. In one way and another straitlaced ladies must have often had to rub shoulders with people very unlike themselves; but they did this the easier because their age never pretended that, because a thing was disapproved, it did not exist.

The organisation of life on board would in any case have made protest difficult and uncomfortable for the protestant. If the passengers were few, they all fed together at the captain's table; if they were too numerous for that, they would be divided into messes. The lady who could not sit down to dinner with the company she found at table would have to take her meals alone in her berth; and that was at once too dull and too ineffective a mark of disapproval to be often employed.

Life was out of all question much simpler on a ship

with no ladies. The following gives an exact idea of the routine of life on a ship that carried none:

"The doctor being appointed caterer, and the purser to preside at the tea-table, we assembled 15 of us . . . at eight every morning to breakfast in the round-house, when we had sometimes tea and sometimes chocolate, with biscuit and butter in plenty; neither did we want milk, having a fine goat that supplied us with it all the voyage. At twelve we dined, the table being always served with four to six dishes of fresh provisions, and equally well with regard to drink, having wine, punch, and beer. In short, we had everything we possibly could have, or the shore could afford, except greens and fruit. At four every afternoon there was tea and coffee. . . . Then at eight we all met again at supper, when we had generally one dish warm with some remains of the dinner; and before we separated from dinner and supper, we drank three toasts—To all our absent friends; To the continuance and increase of the wind if it was fair, or to a fair one if it was not so; and To a happy sight of the next land we intended to make.

"In fair weather (for when it was otherwise I killed it as well as I could) the first thing I did was to walk the deck every morning about two hours, and being a three-decked ship, had the advantage of a very good space from the mizen mast to the main tack, being near 70 feet long; after that I retired to my cabin, and read or wrote till dinner-time, but it was seldom her pitching or rolling would admit the latter with any pleasure. After that [he means dinner] was over, and I had taken two or three turns, I resumed the same employment till tea; from that till six I worked again, finding it very necessary to use much exercise. . . ."

For amusement till supper-time the writer made up a four for whist or else employed himself in brewing a bowl of punch; but sometimes instead of cards they had music, one person having a violin, and others being willing to sing, " and though neither to that perfection as I had heard from Defesch and Beard, yet in our circumstances it was thought very agreeable." This was not a very musical ship; and the writer himself must have been much more studious than the average passenger. In general, cards, music, and liquor furnished the chief pastimes of the voyage; and the enforced intimacy of life commonly produced one of two opposite effects. You probably would make one or two friends and one or two enemies for life. Natural affinities and antipathies had full scope for operation in those months of enforced leisure and inevitable publicity. If two men were inclined to friendliness, they were likely to become bosom-friends; if one jarred on the other, dislike would deepen into hatred, and trifling differences enlarge themselves into questions of honour. It was not unlikely that you would find yourself with a duel on your hands by the end of the voyage, but you would also be provided with a trusty second to back you up.

Meanwhile this microcosm, lacking vegetables and elbow-room, would have been slowly making its way across those many leagues that separated London from Madras. It was a very different business from the voyage of our own time, when you are never more than four or five days without sight of land. In those days ports of call were few. After crossing the Bay, you would continue your steady south-west course, putting into Madeira, if you were going to carry wine, as one ship every season did, to moisten the thirst of India, or passing within sight of Teneriffe. But after that you held on your course for day after day, through the steady region of the trades, until you neared the coast of Brazil. If you needed anything, if you had sprung a mast or run out of provisions, you might then put into Rio de Janeiro; but captains fought shy of that foreign and desperately expensive port, and never put in there if they could help it. As a rule, passengers were limited to telling each other apocryphal stories of the beauty and liberality of the Portuguese ladies of Rio.

Normally then you put about, and, without even sighting land, sailed east by south till you reached the Cape of Good Hope. That would take you between eight weeks and twelve from the time of leaving England. There you often put in. The ship was almost certain to need some repairs; the crew would be showing signs of scurvy after so prolonged a diet of salt junk; the passengers would be irritable with their long confinement. A week's stay there was a welcome break in the long voyage. But it was expensive. You were not allowed to remain on shipboard, eating up the stock of provisions. You had to go ashore, where you found every private house prepared to take in guests for a consideration. What the common rate was at this time I do not know, but a little later people paid a dollar and a half a day.

" In the evening," says the diary of a young cadet, " I went on shore at the Cape Town, and was conducted by some friends to the house of Mr Vanderpool, where we were to lodge. . . . After passing the evening pretty agreeably with our landlord and his four daughters, supper was brought in with greater order than we had been accustomed to see for three months past. Our chief entertainment consisted of a great variety of fruits and abundance of Cape wine.

" No less than nine Scotchmen were at supper, all passengers and officers on board the *Princess Royal*. . . . After some agreeable small talk, we were shown to our apartments where we were to sleep. They were for the most part small and not very elegantly furnished, but they were more agreeable to me than the best-furnished room I had ever seen in Great Britain. . . ."

The Dutch inhabitants seem not to have made a favourable impression on the majority of visitors. They were anxious to please, on condition of being well paid for it. They would sacrifice anything for money, says the cadet quoted above. However, in spite of venal hosts, the stay was always welcome. You would find other ships in the harbour, and meet with a change of company ashore. You could stretch your legs to more purpose than in a space even 70 feet long. You could have a game of billiards, visit the famous Botanical Gardens, or go out to see the Constantia Vineyards. Above all was the change in diet, and the welcome appearance of fruit and vegetables, improving health and temper alike.

The voyage now entered on its final stage. This was the most uncertain of all. You might take the Mozambique Channel, or the outer passage, but in neither case could you be assured of a fair run in the months of April or May when you were generally there. You still had some five thousand miles to go, and might take a long time over it. Sooner or later, however, you would make Ceylon, and enter the Bay of Bengal. Then one morning, when you arose, you would see to port a long, low line of land, rising above the sullen, troubled blue of the sea. That was the Coast of Coromandel. Presently, if you had made a good land-fall, a mate with a telescope would tell you he could see the spire of St Mary's. A line of yellow sand would appear beneath the dark green of the palms, and beneath that again white lines of surf. Then the Fort itself would emerge into view, with its close-built houses, with a dark, low, huddled mass of buildings lying close to it on the north, and another spire rising over the houses of a village farther away to the south. A strange boat, with dark-brown rowers, would be coming out to ask what you were. The ship's guns would begin to salute the fort, which would answer with little puffs of smoke and tiny reports like the sound of toy cannon. The anchor would be let go. The ship would be surrounded by those strange *masula* boats, built of yielding *anjali* planks, sewn together, instead of being nailed to ribs, so as to bear being dashed upon the beach by the unresting surf without instantly breaking to pieces. Into one of these you would jump at the peril of a soaking, and be rowed ashore, deafened by the *ya-li ya-li* of the boat-people; and after passing through the surf with your heart in your mouth, you would be carried to dry land on the back of a wet and slippery fisherman, and make your way through the deep sand up to the Water Gate of Fort St George.

CHAPTER II

MADRAS IN 1750

ON 21 August, 1749, Rear-Admiral Boscawen, followed by a couple of hundred troops of the English East India Company, met M. Barthélemy, Commandant of Madras for His Most Christian Majesty, at St Thomas's Gate, Fort St George. The two exchanged their authorities; the French garrison marched out by the Sea Gate to go on board their vessels in the roads, leaving only the necessary number of guards behind them; the English troops marched in; the blue sentries were replaced by red; the lilies of France were hauled down and the Union Jack hoisted; and so once more Madras lay in English keeping after a French occupation of three years. Indian merchants came crowding back to their old homes, which they had abandoned rather than remain under French government, as joyously as if each man of them had recovered a fortune. But the city which they left had been very different from that to which they returned. Madras had been the home of a solid, continuous prosperity. As a fortress it had always been absurd; well enough to protect the inmates from the attack of pikemen, or afford shelter from a cavalry raid, but never capable of resisting an attack in form, any more than it was when the Frenchman La Bourdonnais appeared before it in 1746. Its garrison had been four weak companies of foot, recruited from the sweepings of London, and officered by men entirely unaccustomed to confront an enemy.   But its trade had been active and prosperous. Up and down the Coromandel Coast it was without a rival. When the French at Pondicherry had a parcel of silver to dispose of, they applied to the bullion-dealers of Madras through the reverend Capuchin fathers at the church of St Andrew.   Madras was the great mart, not only for the cotton stuffs that formed the staple of the exports to Europe, but for every other species of merchandise bought and sold upon the coast.   Its native population was reckoned at 40,000 persons.   Its revenues exceeded 50,000 pagodas, raised almost entirely from its trade; and its credit was so strong that the Government could easily raise as much again at 8 per cent. even in a time of war.   But all this prosperity had vanished after the capture of the place.   In order to render it more defensible, the French had pulled down a considerable part of the native city that had sprung up close under the northern wall of the Fort; they had plundered it with exceeding thoroughness; they had done their utmost to compel the merchants who had made the wealth of Madras to transfer their trade to Pondicherry.   The old inhabitants of the city were thus scattered, impoverished, or dead.   So little value did the place seem to have at the time of its rendition, that the head-quarters of the English were not brought back there until three years later, in 1752.

By then the whole tone of English activities had been transformed.   We had been entirely engrossed in commercial affairs; the ideas and intentions of the native courts had seemed to us so remote from our interests that we had made no endeavour to follow or understand them, and we had never dreamt of using our forces outside the limits of the settlement.   But now political and military business assumed a new appearance altogether. The French were trying to set up one native ruler in Southern India; we were trying to set up another. The native princes who had enjoyed the reputation of irresistible power had lost it, and the Europeans suddenly discovered that their military discipline and tactics could produce great political and great financial results. So it came to pass that military power, politics, finance and the collection of taxes, gradually took the place that had once been occupied by trade. The Nawab of the Carnatic, who had of old lived at Arcot, a mysterious and dreaded prince, came, after our overthrow of the French and the capture of Pondicherry in 1761, to owe his throne to English help. He no longer resided at Arcot, but built for himself a palace at Chepauk on the southern outskirts of the English city. The fort, which had once been so easily captured, was reconstructed, at first of mud faced with turf, so skilfully that it resisted all the efforts of the French to take it in 1759, and on these new lines was rebuilt in brick, and stands to-day a model of the eighteenth-century fortress.

Its surroundings were equally transformed. Whereas the old merchant-governors had been satisfied to live principally in the Fort itself, the new generation that sprang up covered with villas the plain stretching westwards of Madras, called the Choultry Plain, and except in time of war the Fort became for them only a meeting-place or a place of business. The Mount, which had once been a place of retreat and leisure, became an artillery cantonment; the Black Town, to the north, which had once been the exclusively Indian quarter, was invaded by Europeans who could not afford a garden-house on the Plain or a house of business in the Fort. Society lost the village simplicity by which it had once been marked. Every class of society multiplied out of all knowledge, but the soldiers grew faster than any of them; and the four weak companies of 1746 commanded by a dozen officers had swollen by the end of the century into an army that needed over 600 officers for its control. By then Madras had become the capital of Southern India.

The original place had perhaps resembled a little country town more than anything else, though even there we must make large allowances. The European inhabitants all told would amount to upwards of 400 persons. Of these about 300 would be the garrison. Of the remainder you would find some thirty or forty Company's servants, a score of " Freemen inhabitants " or persons permitted to reside there by the Company and occupied in the local trade, perhaps twice as many seafaring men, commanding the ships that plied up and down the coast and might even be encountered at such distant ports as Batavia and Mocha, and ten or twelve military officers. Not half these men would be married; and of the married ones less than half would have European wives. The professions would be represented by a chaplain appointed by the Company and a surgeon.

Of these groups the Company's servants were in every way the most important. They alone could have any share in the government of the place, for from among them were chosen the councillors to whom the Company confided not only the entire management of its commercial affairs, but also the whole administration. Every servant on appointment had to give the Company an indemnity bond and further to find two sureties for his not cheating his employers; so to these covenanted servants, as they were called, the Company felt warranted in extending as much confidence as it gave to anyone in those days and at such a distance from inspection. The extent to which young servants might be punished was uncertain. Governor Thomas Pitt was for vigorous measures. He

would be as glad, he says in one of his letters, to get rid
of certain factors as their friends were when they came
to India,

" more particularly one person, the most incorrigiblest
wrech as ever I knew, who has lately been guilty of such
a piece of insolence as is not to be parrellel'd, whom I
have at this time under confinement, and will severely
punish him, though here is an imbibed notion that no
servant of yours ought to have corporal punishment."

They were paid ridiculously little wages, in spite of the
trust reposed in them. A writer was entitled to only five
pounds by the year. But in the first place the covenanted
servants got a good deal more than their salaries. They
were provided with quarters and servants; they received
diet or an allowance instead of it; they were entitled
to wine out of the Company's warehouse at special rates.
So that their salaries were intended rather as pocket-money
than as maintenance. And in the second place, as Sand-
wich once told Pepys, the value of a place depended not
so much on the salary attached to it as on the opportunities
it offered of making money. Private trade was the great
inducement to join the Company's service. This was
allowed by the Company, which early recognised that it
could not prevent its servants from trading on their own
account, and down to the middle of the eighteenth century
trade offered a secure though not unduly rapid way of
making a fortune. The Company's servants enjoyed the
pick of the trade of all the Company's settlements; and
the higher you rose in the service, the larger the share
which you would get. There was therefore a good deal
of jealousy between the Company's servants and the less-
favoured freemen inhabitants. If, then, early Madras
was to be compared with a little country town, it would

have to be one in which trade filled the place ordinarily occupied by landed property, conferring dignity and accompanying high station.

Next in rank but a long way behind came the military officers. As I have pointed out, they were too few in number to develop much *esprit de corps,* and rather conformed to the general type than displayed a special type of their own. The Company's deliberate policy was to depress them in comparison with its civil servants; and in this it succeeded. In all the four companies there was no higher rank than that of lieutenant, for in earlier times the Governor and the three next civil servants had nominally commanded a company each. That curious practice had died out, and with its disappearance the lieutenants commanding companies had come to receive the courtesy rank of captain; but that did not raise their pay or allowances. Those remained as the Company had fixed them. Six guineas a month was thought sufficient for the lieutenants, and £4 19s. for the ensigns. It is true that for a while the Company had been induced to appoint a major to command the garrison at Madras; but when Major Knipe returned to England, no one was appointed in his place, and, till after the capture of the Fort, the old system had been restored.

As a rule this small band of officers was recruited from the ranks; the sergeants came to look upon promotion to commissioned rank as their due. But this lowered the status of the officer, who was not recognised as at all of equal quality with the governing caste of civilians.

" I could wish," wrote Lieutenant John de Morgan in 1747, " that our governor would vouchsafe a little indulgence to some of our commissioned officers of an inferior rank of this garrison by allowing them sometimes a little admittance to his presence, as all governors of garrisons do in most part of the world. It would very much contribute to increase the respect and submission they are in duty bound to have for their superiors; if some of them by their misbehaviour have deservedly forfeited that remark, let them thank themselves for it; I think it hard a gentleman should suffer for faults committed by others."

Society at Madras was thus topsy-turvy according to the ideas of the day; and it was therefore natural to find officers occupied with pursuits very foreign to the business of a soldier. They had been known to keep punch-houses; they took to trade, and, having no capital of their own, would borrow from the Indian merchants of the place. Lieutenant Edward Amyand, who had been appointed lieutenant of the troops at the Company's factories in Sumatra, in 1738 provided an " adventure " of goods to take with him, but was prevented by an unlucky accident to the ship. The thing was even formally recognised by the Council. The officers are still drawing the same pay as they did many years ago, it informed the Company in 1741,

" when provisions were not half the price they are at now, and our country trade is at so low an ebb that any credit they may have with the merchants can be of no service to them in these days. It is necessary we should have good men here who can be depended upon in case of action, but it may sometimes be difficult to find such without Your Honours shall please to allow of some further encouragement."

The encouragement not being provided, the officers provided for themselves in customary but illicit ways. Some defrauded their men of their pay. " When I came from Madras," wrote one of them in 1741, " there were ten or twelve English soldiers renegadoes, about 30 miles distance, who run away because their pay was taken by their officers." But a more popular and less iniquitous

2

method was to defraud the Company. The commandant of the Madras garrison at the time of its capture, himself described as " an ignorant, superannuated Swede," wrote as follows:

" When Mr Morse came to be governor of Madras, he gave commissions in his name and desired me to keep always the just complement of effective men in the place . . . which I answered was impossible for me to do, as my commission as eldest lieutenant was of no greater force than that of the youngest. . . . Pursuant to Mr Morse's command, I acquainted Captain Hollond and De Gingens with the orders I received from the governor; but Captain Hollond not regarding what I said, went to the governor himself and told him he couldn't live on less than a hundred pagodas a month, and continued 40 ineffective men on the roll, as did the other lieutenants, all but myself, who had only ten and they were able servants."

The method of recruitment, the lack of promotion, the low rate of pay, the trivial nature of the services required, all combined with unmilitary pursuits to render the Company's early officers incompetent. Francis Hugonin, who had long served on the coast, bears emphatic testimony to the fact. Madras, he says prophetically, is not easy to defend, by reason of the great extent of the Black Town, which

" will require a great number of men, with good and experienced officers on which they may depend. This case, Sir, was never duly considered, for during the space of 22 years I have never known but three officers proper to face an enemy, on the wrong notion that being a peaceable country any man will do, which is just the contrary, for as they can learn nothing, so their only aim is to rob the soldiers whom they should protect, so that in time of war, they are incapable to act and afraid to trust their own men."

I fear that the padres, of whom there were two at Madras, one paid by the Company, the other by voluntary contributions, were often as poor in quality as the officers. A really good grade of holy man was not to be expected in such remote and barbarous regions. The motive which carried everyone else to the East Indies, the desire of getting rich, would not automatically select good candidates; and the Company might appeal to the universities for orthodox, godly ministers at £100 a year with accommodation and diet, but it did not always get them. Here, more perhaps than among the military officers, do you find startling contrasts of character. The temper of those early times was naturally devout; everyone was interested in questions of divinity (Captain and Mrs Blifil in the course of their courtship discussed predestination and election by grace), so that even in a money-making place like Madras there was a strong desire for competent divines. Sometimes they were procured. The gentle Padre Isaacson, the zealous Mr Portman who consecrated the church of St Mary's built in 1680 by public subscription, the learned Thomas Consett who left Russian manuscripts in the Library of Fort St George, all fulfilled this condition. But others were more like that minister of the Gospel in Bengal who is described as " a very lewd, drunken, swearing person, drenched in all manner of debaucheries, and a most bitter enemy—note the climax —to King William and the present Government." Such a one must have been the " drunken toss-pot " who held the cure of Madras in 1666; or Francis Fordyce three-quarters of a century later. This latter had first served as chaplain at St Helena, whence he went to Sumatra. Either there were two vicious chaplains at St Helena at about the same time, or Fordyce left in order to escape the vengeance of a planter whose daughter he had debauched. From Sumatra he passed to the Coromandel

Coast. There, having quarrelled with Clive, he was called before the Council to justify his conduct. He refused to attend, but it was declared in evidence that he had vowed he "would pull off his canonicals at any time to do himself justice." He was suspended by the Council, and at last this priest of the Church Militant found a more appropriate cure as chaplain on board the *Harwich* man-of-war.

I do not think that the motives which sometimes inspired applications for the post of chaplain were ever more faithfully revealed than in the following extract from a letter of 1695:

"I am extremely anxious to go as chaplain on the East India fleet. The stipend is small, only £40, but there are many advantages. The last brought home £3,000, and at the last act was made a doctor; his name is Evans. I should expect to be absent two years. I desire also that you would assist me with a sum of money to engage in trade, which is allowed."

The last statement was mistaken. Trading was not allowed, but it was probably winked at often enough by a complaisant Council. Charles Long, for instance, a chaplain at Madras in 1720, was dismissed, not by Council, but by the Company, who wrote:

"We understand Mr Long hath exchanged his study for a counting-house, and is turned supracargo, which in all likelyhood will bring a scandal upon his character, and give the natives and Roman Catholics a handle to depretiate the reputation of a Protestant clergyman. Let him stay no longer in India, but return to England to keep the solemn promise made at his ordination."

The rest of the European population of Madras was too heterogeneous to be easily characterised. They were all traders by profession; and though some traded by land while others traded by sea, the only difference which that could have made was that the first were permanently resident at Madras, and the second only in the intervals between their voyages. Otherwise they were socially indistinguishable. The one curious fact which seems to stand out clearly is that they formed something much more like a colony, in that early factory period which we may regard as ending with the capture of the place by the French in 1746, than one expects to find in European settlements in India. There were families settled at Fort St George, marrying there, bringing up children there, engaged in the country trade and, if they prospered, securing access to the privileged class of the Company's servants. This is quite a different matter from the later monopoly which a group of families established in the Company's services. These latter were settled in England, and sent out their children writers or cadets as they grew up. But the former, such as the Harts, the Powneys, the Boddams, sprang from freemen inhabitants, settled at Madras, acquiring a considerable admixture of Indian blood, and only transferring themselves back to England when the family fortune had been made. Associated with them was a group of families, Portuguese by origin, and coming from the neighbouring Portuguese settlement of St Thomé. These had in general been much longer in the country than had the English families; and in the early days had enjoyed the privilege of providing the sons of the latter with wives of European name and at least something of European blood. Such families were the Carvalhos, the Medeiros, wealthy, dark-complexioned, largely indianised. From this class had sprung that " most deplorable sooty gentlewoman " in whose portrait Horace Walpole with delighted malice recognised the grandmother of Lady Vere of Hanworth.

Another group which gave variety to this section of Madras inhabitants consisted of Jews. They were attracted to the place by the diamond trade, for Madras formed the principal outlet for the stones produced at Golconda, and this traffic flourished far into the eighteenth century, affording a convenient means of remittance to Europe. These Jews seem at first to have been of Spanish or Portuguese birth. De Paiva, Rodrigues, Do Porto, Fonseca—such are the names which occur in the early lists of inhabitants. They had a separate burial ground; and when Mr Bartholomew Rodrigues, Hebrew merchant, died, he was followed to the tomb by the governor and most of the gentry of Madras, with a company of soldiers from the garrison. This Jewish element declined in the eighteenth century, with the decay of the Coast trade and the exhaustion of the Golconda mines; but for long the names of Moses, Salomons, and Franke were familiar in Madras, and in 1756 Solomon Salomons made a resounding bankruptcy.

The last element of this composite society was Armenian. In 1688 special privileges were granted by the Company to Armenians who should settle in their Indian factories. Wherever forty of them were residing, a temporary church was to be built for them, land allotted for a permanent structure, and an allowance of £50 a year paid for seven years for the maintenance of a priest. They became a considerable power in the trading world of Madras, enjoying a monopoly of the early trade with Manila, where Spanish policy admitted them, but would not admit European traders. Their church was built and still survives, though now no Armenians are left to worship there. The chief member of the community at Madras was Petrus Uscan, a native of Julfa, the Armenian suburb of Ispahan. He was a very wealthy man, who rebuilt at his own cost the bridge which crosses the Adyar river on the way from Madras to the Mount. He also rebuilt the long flight of steps leading to the church on the top of the Mount. His religious sympathies were much more Roman Catholic than Armenian. His will, which was written in 1750, after an insufferably tedious account of his outstanding transactions, proceeds to give directions for his burial:

" I had a shroud brought me from Jerusalem, which shroud the French took away in the time of the war; my executors shall therefore purchase an habit of the Franciscan order, with which habit they shall dress my corpse and lay the same in a coffin."

His heart was to be buried at Julfa, and 100 pagodas was to be paid to the surgeon who opened his body and removed it. He then turns his attention to the Armenian Church:

" to which church I had a great desire to leave money, but as they did not keep up a good government among them, those that had the care of the church money consumed the same; and the present padrys and churchwardens are not clever men; and formerly from the time from which I can remember the said church even up to this day, which is now about 45 years since, the said church had a great deal of money from testators and living people which I know of; and for want of good government the said money was consumed and squandered away; and at present it is very well known how much money the said church is worth."

Such then were the motley elements of which society in the old factory days was composed. It must have been a queer world. Everybody would trade, no matter whether it was his legitimate business or not. In general there can have been but two subjects of conversation—the state of the markets and the conditions of salvation.

Almost certainly too the state of the market came first. You would meet the chaplain in his cassock, and the officer in his red coat, taking a part in the sales at the Sea Gate, among the professed merchants. Nor would you escape the prevailing passion even in the drawing-room. Women, Lockyer tells us, drove as large a trade as the men, and with no less judgment. "Nay," he adds, "some are so forward as to have invoyces, accounts current, etc., in their own names, though their husbands are in being." Mrs Nicks was a great trader, but she did not scandalise Madras nearly so much by her commerce as by her familiarities with Governor Yale, of which that little world thought the worst.

There was one other general feature. This little group of people was not only very small, but also very simple. You would meet there no specialists. Surgeon and soldier might be promoted into Council, but there they would have to share in sorting the Company's purchases of cotton cloth as well as in discussing political business. Sea captains were expected to be engineers as well as navigators, and were consulted about the laying out of the defences of the Fort as well as about the repair of their ships. Many laymen were as good theologians as their chaplain; and no member of Council would hesitate, at a pinch, to take command of a company of foot, to read a sermon, or administer a dose of physic.

CHAPTER III

THE COMPANY'S SERVANT

THE Company's servants had on the whole managed admirably down to the middle of the eighteenth century. They had had a simple job. The purchase of the Company's piece-goods, and the conduct of an administration which was really municipal in nature, had not made too heavy demands on either their heads or their morals. The fact is shown by the way in which Indians came to live under their government. None would have done so had it been corrupt or tyrannical; and indeed the idea which most closely fits the old councillors of Madras is that of industrious, sober merchants, living a highly domesticated life with their semi-asiatic spouses and broods of dusky children. The time of their trial came later, when they found themselves involved in political concerns, when great sums of money were to be had for the asking, when they had large armies in the field and a small difference on a military contract might amount to a handsome profit at the year's end. Added to this was the tradition of illicit gains in India. Even in the virtuous old days the governor had accepted yearly a commission from the merchants who had supplied goods to the Company, and when according to custom the arrack or the betel monopoly was farmed out, the farmer, also according to custom, would visit the governor with an acknowledgment of his gratitude. This was all strictly in keeping with the custom of the country. Had such gifts been refused, the giver would have returned next day with twice as much, in the firm belief that he had not offered enough. These were little sums and presented no temptation to the governor. But when you might be offered a lakh of pagodas in gold, or a large diamond, even honest men might become casuists and barter their virtue for a fortune.

At the same time the former methods of making money had decayed. The trade to Bengal and Manila, to Mocha and Gombroon, had fallen away owing to the wars and troubles of the times. But as one door shuts another opens. Instead of investing your money in a share of a cargo to Bombay or Bushire, you lent it to the Nawab of the Carnatic or to one of his renters, who were always having some instalment of debt or revenue to pay. Two per cent. a month was not a high rate to charge for such accommodation, though when the Company heard of what was going on, it forbade the exaction of more than 10 per cent. per annum. But this method of employing money was much more demoralising than the old one of open trade. It mixed up financial interests with politics; and the Company's servants became infected with the evils of high finance.

The evil was accentuated by the political position of the Nawab. He was wholly dependent on English forces, but the English Government had no right to interfere in the least act of his administration. There was always something that he wanted. Now it was their leave and help to conquer Tanjore; now it was an agreement to recognise his second son instead of his first as his successor. He was thus always ready to bribe, and unfortunately he was able to bribe high. A curious paper

among the records of his administration details the sums
which he alleged he had paid to the various governors of
Madras from 1761 to 1780.   Against Pigot is shown no
less than 30 lakhs of pagodas—say, £1,200,000; to Wynch
over 5 lakhs; to Rumbold 5¼ lakhs.   Even 5 lakhs would
make £200,000.   I cannot say to what extent this may be
taken as exact.   It is very conceivable that the paper was
prepared for some special purpose which we do not know.
The true history of the period probably will never be
written.   The possibility of such great gifts falsifies all
our calculations; and perhaps even the men who received
them could not have said to what degree they had influenced their conduct.

   With all these causes of demoralisation it would have
been odd if the Company's servants had not felt the change.
And yet I do not think in spite of it all that Madras
produced more than three persons who come up to the
contemporary idea of a nabob.   One of them was Paul
Benfield, who remains enshrined in the eloquence of
Burke.   He was a man with notable gifts for intrigue
and finance.   Bred an engineer, he soon got himself transferred to the list of covenanted servants; he was the
contractor who built a great part of the present walls of
Fort St George, the solidity of which shows that whatever
his other shortcomings he was capable of honesty.   His
financial doings were more open to question.   He became
to all intents the banker of the Carnatic.   At one time
every pagoda paid into the Nawab's treasury was paid
through him.   He was entrusted with the funds of many
inhabitants of Madras who were not a little dazzled by
his brilliancy of plan and execution.   In a few years he
made an enormous fortune.   But he was more than merely
the banker of the Carnatic.   He was besides an active
intriguer who tried to control the policy of both the Nawab
and the Council.   The governor who opposed his wishes

was sure of an uneasy time. He was, as befitted so eminent an advocate of private action, an ardent disciple of liberty. In his eyes the Government was always inclined to exaggerate its powers; and so he regarded it as a sacred duty to become the champion of the rights of Britons. Luckily the constitution of the Indian settlements did not afford many openings for activities of this sort, and in this direction Benfield was able to do little more than induce the Grand Jury on occasion to decline proceeding with its business. His career at Madras culminated in the seizure of the governor and the assumption of power by a clique the real heads of which were Benfield himself and the Nawab. He was, in short, the kind of person who contributed largely to give the nabobs their unsavoury reputation; and I know no good of him except that he built the walls of Fort St George and kept a French cook.

The deliberate, calculating falsehood of Benfield meets with a sharp contrast in the passionate vivacity of Black Jack. He was the uncle of Sterne's Eliza, and his real name John Whitehill. His niece dutifully puts his best side forward. " He's an extraordinary character," she writes, " unequal, but there's a great mixture of good, I might almost say of sublime in it—for he's generous, highly so, and literally despises money but as it serves to promote his happiness, which wholly centres in his friendships. Once attached, he is steady in these as the sun is regular in its course; but then he's passionate and jealous even to madness." Here we have, I think, something like the nabob of legend. His niece might acquit him of avarice; and with reason. But he was profuse; and profusion needs to be maintained; he was like the man in Tacitus, *alieni appetens, sui profusus.* He was for some time chief of the Company's factory of Masulipatam, and in that office was charged with the duty of collecting large amounts of revenue from the territories dependent on that place. This revenue was payable by native chiefs, always anxious to put off the evil day of payment and to avoid any increase in their assessment. " He now holds a most important post," says Eliza, " and his fortune will be immense if he's suffered to remain in it five years." When a committee of inquiry was appointed to examine the revenue administration at Masulipatam, Whitehill thought it prudent to quit his post. Nor was this the only instance of his misdoing. As the country trade declined, more than one servant of the Company began to wonder if he could not get a share in the trade to Europe—that strictly guarded privilege of his honourable masters. One group formed connections with the Danes at Tranquebar. Black Jack went into partnership with some Frenchmen. Such matters could not be kept entirely secret; and when, after war had broken out in 1778, the *Osterley* East Indiaman was taken by a French privateer and carried into Mauritius, people whispered that Whitehill had been and still was a part-owner of the *Elizabeth*. At last after a short and disastrous term as governor of Fort St George, he was suspended by the Bengal Government, dismissed by the Court of Directors, and at last disappears from view as an exile in Paris and protector of the famous Madame Grand before she blossomed out as the Princesse Talleyrand.

The third of this ignoble group was John Hollond. He was the son of an officer in the Company's service and Sophia Fowke, daughter of Randall Fowke and Ann May who had been married at St Mary's in 1713. He had been appointed writer in 1761, at the age of 17, and by virtue of seniority succeeded to the post of governor in 1789. His government was marked by an accumulation of scandals beside which the misdeeds of his predecessors sink into nothingness. He sold posts; he employed the

English troops on unauthorised expeditions for the behoof of the Nawab's creditors of whom he was one; when ordered to support the little state of Travancore, he tried to induce the raja to pay for the assistance which he had been ordered to give; finally he ran off with a sum of money which had been entrusted to him by the Nawab for the Company.

These were nabobs in the bad and popular sense of the word. But they should not be mistaken for fair samples of the Company's servants. They were extreme cases. The average was not very different from the rest of the generation at home, and achieved neither the enormities of Hollond nor the fortune of Benfield. Most men, then as now, have a natural propensity to believe the worst of their fellow-beings. There were always persons ready to accuse the nabobs of every kind of misconduct; there were always persons ready to give ear and repeat their stories; and always few disposed to ask what evidence could be brought to support them. The directors of the Company were not much better in this respect than other people.

" It is with great concern we must observe to you," they write to the Madras council, " that we have reason to believe the late unhappy situation of our affairs has afforded opportunities to many of our servants to enrich themselves at the Company's expense by unreasonable and unwarrantable profits in almost every office and branch of business; many practices have been hinted to us, such as extraordinary perquisites arising from the letting our farms, the contracting for investments, the supplying our forces with provisions and stores, and many others though not to so great an amount but equally unjustifiable; it has likewise been hinted to us that two of the Council attempted to commit a fraud by an overcharge in their accounts and that notwithstanding the person who charged them therewith offered to make oath to the truth of what he asserted yet no public notice or enquiry was made into the same."

The Council's reply was as follows:

" Before we close this paragraph in justice to ourselves we must beg leave to remark that if some fortunes have lately been acquired in India, they have been got out of the common road; if we are guilty of fraud dismiss us your service; but if it should happen, as sometimes it may, that anyone with a plausible show of regard for your interest and a flow of words, very probably unacquainted with facts, should address you on this subject, be pleased to enquire into the character of such person whilst abroad; and, if he afterwards should desire a superior post in your service, it may give some reason to conclude he was endeavouring only to serve his own purposes."

Both the letters from which these extracts are taken were written in 1754; but they fairly represent the case throughout the century. Those most eager to drag to light abuses often had dark secrets of their own; and what was common at Madras represented not the crimes of unbridled licence, but the perquisites and peccadilloes of a bad system.

The common career of the Company's servant was much as follows: he would arrive as a writer, on £5 a year, and be set to copy letters or accounts in one of the offices at Madras. His hours of work would be from 8 or 9 in the morning to midday, with perhaps another spell in the afternoon. He would be provided with quarters in the Fort, from which he would sometimes seek for obvious but discreditable reasons to escape; he would always be hard put to it for a little ready money; and the head of his office would watch him with a paternal eye. Here is a letter from Francis Jourdan, member of Council, to a young man employed under him:

" SIR,—I should not have declined your first request
had I had a favourable character of you; however, Sir,
I am notwithstanding willing to assist you, provided you
immediately take the room which formerly belonged to
Mr Cassey and which has been ordered by the Board for
yours; and provided that you immediately apply to your
business in a different manner than you have done, and that
you give up your acquaintances in the Black Town. On
these conditions I will lend you 50 pagodas; but I will
observe to you that, on the forfeiture of your word, I
shall apply to the Board to have you removed, from
my office at least."

The young man in question mended his ways, and did
not leave the service till 1803, having in the interval
filled several posts of consequence without disgrace.

After five years of routine the writer would become
a junior merchant, and, after a further period, senior
merchant, on each occasion entering into new covenants,
and providing the Company with sureties for a higher
amount. If he displayed due diligence he might receive
a gratuity of 50 or 100 pagodas from the Council, and
might reckon on being given some small independent employment. Francis Jourdan, for instance, less than two
years after his arrival was made coroner; he was then
favoured with a small post in the Manila Expedition, on
which everyone expected to make a fortune but did not.
As soon as he was out of his writership he went down to
Cuddalore in charge of the customs there with a seat on
the local council; then as Deputy Commissary General he
was responsible for the army accounts; and at last, after
two years' service at Masulipatam and in the fifteenth
year after his arrival in India, he took his seat in the
Council at Madras. He was much more characteristic
of the Company's servant than Benfield or Hollond. For
one thing he was very diligent in the discharge of his

THE FORT SQUARE FROM THE N.E.
After the aquatint of Thomas Daniell.

32]

duties. On one occasion the Council presented him with no less than 1,000 pagodas for unravelling a very tangled knot in the Company's accounts. In 1772 he was already beginning to look to a return to England, and was remitting money for the purchase of a small estate, somewhere " at a distance from the metropolis, where nabobs dwell not." He had no idea of ever trying to cut a figure in high life, where he would simply be laughed at. However, his schemes went awry. He was not able to get in his investments as he had hoped. Some of his money had been lent to the Nawab and could not be recovered; more of it was lost in unlucky voyages; and then he was caught up in that whirlwind of intrigue which Paul Benfield raised, and, though he had had nothing to do with its origin, he was involved in its consequences. He was dismissed along with the other members of the Council, and lingered on in India, hoping to recover his position and restore his fortune. In both he was unsuccessful.

" Had I," he writes at this time, " been what perhaps most are, I might this day have had more rupees than I have fanams, for there was a time in Wynch's government when I could, without doing anything equal to what others have done [he is referring to Benfield's operations] have filled my coffers; but I had a foolish virtue which is certainly out of fashion, for most conclude everyone received money from the Nabob; everyone, generally speaking, says if we did not we were the more to blame."

He had no influence in London to reach the directors; the Nawab turned sullen and would pay nobody; and Jourdan, after managing to pay his debts, was left with little or nothing for himself. He retired from Madras to a neighbouring village which had been granted to him some years before, and busied himself with trying to grow

spices that cannot be acclimatised in the Carnatic; and in
1784 he died without ever having returned to England
or realised his modest dream of quiet retirement. Yet
he was far from having been exceptionally unlucky. Very
few managed to carry home a fortune with them. Men
were much more likely to die than go home even with a
mere competence. Our experience in the eighteenth century corresponded nearly enough with the experience of
Ibn Batuta four centuries earlier. " Such," he wrote of
his own misfortunes, " is the customary end of wealth
acquired in India. Rarely does anyone leave the country
with the property he has amassed; and, if he succeeds
in doing that, God sends some misfortune to swallow
it up."

Some families, however, seem to have been dogged
by a peculiarly evil destiny. For instance, three successive generations of Charles Floyers served the Company
in the Presidency of Madras between 1730 and 1794;
and all three were specially unlucky. The first, who
came out in the year first named, married into a Madras
family, and finally rose to the chair of the presidency in
1747. Fordyce, the blackguard clergyman already mentioned, had informed the directors that gaming was prevalent among their servants; they therefore ordered an
inquiry. Floyer and his Council blandly replied that the
Company must be misinformed. But in this case Fordyce
had really been telling the truth, and early in the next
year Floyer and almost all the other members of the
Council were dismissed for that offence—no trust can be
put in a gambler, the Company observed—and for neglect
of public affairs. The second Charles Floyer, son of
the first, came out in 1754. After rising into Council, he
was suspended for the same reason that had led to
Jourdan's downfall in 1777. Luckier than Jourdan, he
succeeded in procuring his restoration to the service; but,

unluckier than he, he was afterwards prosecuted for malversation in the Mayor's Court at Madras, and cast in damages for 102,000 pagodas with costs. The third Charles Floyer was the son of this man and Catherine Carvalho, whom he had married at Madras in 1761. He joined the service in 1781. We catch a glimpse of him in 1785 ordering three dozen chairs as a present for his mother. He held various posts in the north of the presidency and finally was shot in a duel by Benjamin Roebuck on 1 May, 1794, occasioned by Roebuck's comments on his father's misfortunes. Four days later, as Quarter Sessions were sitting, Roebuck and the two seconds were indicted for murder. The crier of the court made proclamation for witnesses to stand forth; none appearing, as indeed all the witnesses had been indicted, the Petit Jury retired with the indictment and the inquisition returned by the coroner. Presently they came back into court with a verdict of Not Guilty. It was a good way of carrying out the law and yet not interfering with a well-established social custom.

Other families were well represented in the Madras Civil Service. One such was that of the Thackerays; but as they were rather later than the period with which I am concerned, and as they have been dealt with in a charming book of Sir William Hunter's, I need not pause over them here. But the Bourchiers should be mentioned. These were the two brothers, Charles and James, sons of Richard Bourchier, who after a long residence in each of the Indian presidencies, became Governor of Bombay in 1750. Charles, who had become a writer at Madras in 1741, when he was about 15, entered the Madras Council in 1754, and became governor in 1767. He became involved in the first of our unsuccessful wars with Hyder Ali, and went home as soon as it was over. He is described by Orme the historian as a man strong enough to follow his own judgment and anxious not to do the wrong thing, but with a good deal of warmth both in his temper and his expressions. He and his brother went home together in 1769, and settled in London, but not much to their satisfaction. Their father died penniless the year after they went home, and Charles soon found himself straightened for money. " Remember," he adds as a postscript to a letter of 1776, " I am much distressed for the money I have still in India, and that you can't render me a greater service than by remitting it as fast as you can." In a previous letter he had indicated what would, I think, have been accepted by most of the Company's servants of that time as a sound rule of conduct. " If you are wise, make yourself useful to the governor. By his means you may reap advantages abroad; from home you must not hope for any. By making yourself useful I do not mean you should do anything you can't reconcile to your own reason; but there are otherwise a number of occasions in which you may be of service, and [do] not enter into disputes and dissents on trivial circumstances." If the recipient of this letter had acted on the advice, he would have materially benefited.

With Charles and his brother the Bourchiers came to an end at Madras. Other families struck deeper roots. Such were the Wynches and the Turings, one of which had till recently and the other still has representatives in the Madras Civil List. The first Wynches at Madras seem to have been a chaplain who later was removed to Bengal and a military officer, both in the early part of the century. Then in 1738 appears Alexander, possibly the chaplain's nephew. He was at first employed as an unpaid assistant to the Secretary; and when he became a writer, and had to name his sureties, he could only name one person, having come from England " so young as to have no acquaintance there from whom to ask that favour." He possessed what was rare in those days—a knowledge of the country languages. He was a quick, passionate man, who, after becoming governor in 1773, found in the disputes reigning in the Council of his time sufficient reason to keep him always in a temper. He married twice at Madras, and brought up a numerous family, three sons entering the Civil Service and two the Madras Army. The Turings sprang from doctor's stock. The first one of the name was Robert, a surgeon's mate aboard the *Greenwich*, East Indiaman, and later a surgeon on the Madras establishment. John and William Turing were almost certainly relations of the surgeon, for in 1769 John was living in the same house as his widow, who in that year came into painful prominence, being indicted for causing the death of one of her slaves. Though acquitted, she withdrew from the settlement for some time.

Edward Croke, the last Madras civilian who need be particularised, arrived at Madras in 1708 at the age of 17. Nearly forty years later, being then arrived at the head of the list, he declined the post of governor when it fell vacant; and soon after received a pension of £200 a year from the Company as a special acknowledgment of his long and faithful, if undistinguished services. He was, it seems, the eldest son of George Croke and Lucy Field who were married at Madras in 1689; and he himself married in 1726 Isabella Beizor, probably of Portuguese descent. When war broke out with the French, Croke went to live at the neutral settlement of Tranquebar; and while there in 1757 he alarmed the Company's Madeira ship with news of the French squadron being off Madras (which was not the case), so that she made the best of her way to Calcutta without putting into Madras at all, thus depriving that place of its annual supplies of wine. One of his daughters, Sophia, married Alexander Wynch; another daughter, Frances, married first the nephew of the governor of Bengal in 1744; on his death, she married in 1748 another Calcutta gentleman, who died of smallpox a few days after his wedding; in the next year she married William Watts, of the Bengal Civil Service, and was imprisoned by Siraj-ud-daula at the time of his attack upon Calcutta; in 1760 she accompanied her husband to England, where she married their daughter to Charles Jenkinson, afterwards the first Earl of Liverpool; on Watts's death she returned to Calcutta, where she married a fourth husband, William Johnson, a chaplain, with whom she got on badly. The conclusion of the romance is narrated by Mr Justice Chambers, who was an intimate friend of this much-married lady and of her son-in-law. The embarkation of Johnson, who sailed for England by the last ship in 1788, is, he says,

"an event of which no friend of Mrs Johnson can be sorry who knows how very unkindly he has treated her for several years past.

"At the time of their marriage he made her believe that he was sincerely in love with her, and he has repeatedly declared to me that he was so in fact. The long continuance of that passion was not perhaps to be expected considering the great disparity of their ages, but she would have been content with civility and gratitude. . . ."

"He carries home with him a comfortable fortune, which he has made by the favour of those who thought themselves bound to confer benefits on the husband of Mrs Watts. . . ."

After this happy release, Begam Johnson, as she was usually called, lived on at Calcutta until 1812. One wonders in what unclerical manner her fourth husband can have made his comfortable fortune.

CHAPTER IV

THE COMPANY'S OFFICER—PART I

IN the old factory times the Company's servants had shown a clear superiority over the Company's officers. They had managed their job well, and, all things considered, with a reasonable degree of honesty. But after 1750 the balance inclined the other way. The officers rose to the level of their task, while the covenanted servants did not. The soldier's business in the second half of the eighteenth century was plain and straightforward compared with the politician's and the administrator's. The two bodies were composed of men of much the same type, origin, and standards; but they were placed in circumstances of very different degrees of difficulty. The Madras Army gradually shook itself free from the commercial ideas which quite naturally had dominated Madras in its earlier days; it developed an *esprit de corps* which had been impossible in four contemptible companies and a dozen despised officers; it acquired a pride of service, born amidst many victories and some disasters, inconceivable in times when duties were limited to guard-mounting and parade.

The first condition of this change was the expansion of the army. Within ten years of the capture of Madras the number of officers had risen to 87; by 1775 they were 412; and by 1800 they were 652. The change meant the removal of disadvantages which had weighed heavily on the earlier generation. Originally the only

promotion to which an ensign could look was the rank
of lieutenant-commandant. But shortly after the fall
of Madras the commandants became full captains; then
the grade of major reappeared, this time permanently;
lieutenant-colonels and colonels followed; and lastly
brigadiers, major-generals, and lieutenant-generals. By
that time the Company's army offered a fine career to
those fortunate enough to escape dying of a dysentery in
garrison or a bullet in the field. Promotion, through all
the lower ranks at all events, went by seniority, except
when, very rarely, an officer was promoted for special
gallantry in action. Indeed rewards assumed a military
appearance. The early officers, when Council was
specially pleased with their conduct, might get a present
of 20 pagodas or enough broadcloth, scarlet, to make
them a coat; their successors would expect to be mentioned in dispatches. Medals, which at first had been
individual matters, were employed to commemorate
collective bravery. The first distribution at Madras seems
to have passed hitherto without notice. After Lally's
siege of Madras in 1758–59 Governor Pigot not only
distributed a money reward amongst the garrison, but
also struck and distributed medals. As far as I can learn,
no example of them has survived, and indeed the only
reference I know of is the following, taken from a letter
of the Company:

" You certainly acted very right and consistent in publishing to the garrison that you would reward them if
they behaved gallantly; and accordingly we applaud the
measure; but here we must remark that our president's
taking upon him to order medals to be struck and distributed in his name was out of character. Honorary
rewards are surely our prerogative."

Accordingly the next distribution was by express order

of the Company, which in 1786 directed a special mark of distinction to be given " to such of the sepoys as resisted the many endeavours made to seduce them from the British service " by Hyder Ali and Tipu. On this the Council resolved to distribute a medal bearing the word *Fidelity*, struck in gold for the commissioned officers, in silver for the other ranks. The next general distribution of medals commemorated the capture of Seringapatam in 1799.

The recruitment of officers was also revolutionised. Most of the older officers had been rankers. But with the growth of the army and the development of its functions, this source of supply was more and more disused. Several such promotions were made in 1748; and when the sepoy corps were first organised in 1759–60, many sergeants were promoted to the rank of ensign and given the command of battalions. But such promotions became more and more exceptional. The later cases will generally be found not to be true examples. For instance William Farmer Cave Dickson went out as a private in 1767; but he had a cousin a captain in the Madras Army, who at once represented his case and he was appointed ensign in November. At least once the Company wrote out that a number of persons were said to have gone as private soldiers in the hope of becoming officers at Fort St George, and forbidding their promotion; and finally it resolved that no one should receive a commission without its previous approval. The great objection to these ranker officers was their unseasonable drunkenness. Clive refused to " roll " with Ensign Hyde Parker because he had met him reeling drunk in the streets of Cuddalore walking arm-in-arm with a sergeant or corporal; and Coote in 1760 gives pointed evidence of the same thing.

" I was obliged," he writes, " this morning to confine

Ensign Macquin of the Seapoys under a guard with fixed bayonets for his mutinous expressions to me when I took notice of his being so much in liquor as to be scarce able to walk. Indeed I can blame only myself for this, as I recommended him for a commission. I think it would be much better for the future to give such only brevets as officers, as there is so little dependence on these kind of men's behaviour who are raised from sergeants to rank with gentlemen."

Eighteenth-century manners lent these illiberal sentiments much truth.

The exclusion of persons on the score of mixed blood seems to have been more irregular. In the early days when it was more usual than not for councillors to have half-caste wives, and when a good proportion of *topasses*, as they were called, were to be found in the ranks of the Company's troops, colour could not have counted for very much. Persons like Clemente Poverijo could still receive a commission as captain in 1752, and, when he lost a leg in one of the actions before Trichinopoly, he not only received a pension of 15 pagodas a month from the Company and a village from the Nawab, but also was made Captain Provost to the troops in the field, an office which he was still exercising nearly thirty years later in Coote's campaigns against Hyder. But a different spirit was already beginning to show itself. In 1753 it was said of an applicant for a commission that his colour was so disagreeable to the men that he could never carry a proper command; and at a later time the Company required of cadets appointed in India a certificate that they were not the sons of " native Indians." The certificate regarding one such candidate runs as follows:

" Mr Patterson is the son of Lieutenant-Colonel Patterson lately deceased, born in wedlock, and in no way exceptionable. His mother was a Miss Pegu, and a lady of very good connections and character. . . . The eldest son is a lieutenant in the service, and a very diligent and good officer. . . ."

A commission in the army was indeed often given to the sons of an officer as an acknowledgment of their father's services, but this, appropriate as it was, often meant the introduction of much mixed blood. From the Company's regulations it would seem that (in West Indian phrase) anyone of the degree of terceron and upwards was admitted without question.

Neither were Frenchmen excluded from Company's commissions. The romantic story of the French officer who deserted to the English, revealed to them the weakness of Chandernagore, and then hanged himself, bequeathing a tarnished fortune to his family who indignantly refused to accept it, is familiar and apocryphal. M. Cossard de Terraneau bore the recollection of his treachery very well for at least eight years, rising to the rank of captain-lieutenant in the Company's artillery, and at last hanged himself owing to the misconduct of his wife; nor was his family able to mark their sense of his conduct by refusing his money, because he left them none of it. The founder, too, of the famous Martinière schools at Calcutta and Lucknow, was certainly a Frenchman, and perhaps a French deserter. At Madras, from its nearness to Pondicherry, such cases were even more numerous. There was Jean François de Vassaux, Seigneur de Vareille, a skilful officer and good engineer, to whom we gave a commission as captain in 1751. After consistently good service he was invalided, and died at Madras in 1793 at the age of 82. And there were several besides him. Coote formed a company of French deserters, whom he employed on desperate services in order to economise his Englishmen; and this body grew into what was grandiloquently called the Foreign Legion, under a body of French officers. This experiment, however, was not a success as a permanent establishment. Two of the officers had to be broke for misconduct in the field and a third deserted. Nor was it possible to trust them implicitly during a time of war with France. One of them, Captain Brulé, was confined at Vizagapatam in 1780, on suspicion of treasonable correspondence; when shortly after seven companies of a sepoy regiment mutinied, they released Brulé, who in fact behaved very well in a difficult situation, succeeding in preventing them from blowing up the magazine, as they had intended. Another foreigner, though this time not a deserter, was the engineer, Delavaux, who was sent out to St David's in 1748. He was a poor engineer, for his walls fell down as soon as they were built, and his main contribution to the defences of the Fort was popularly known as Delavaux's Folly. He was also unlucky. On his way from Cuddalore to the Fort, he encountered a party of drunken sailors; they upset his palanquin, and one of them seizing him by the throat struck him with a switch, on which he drew his sword, and ran the man through; this led to his retiring from the settlement. Before this he had served in the West Indies under the Dutch at St Eustatius. He had then gone to St Kitt's, where the lieutenant-governor employed him to plan new defences for the island, which provoked the jealousy of the governor of the Leeward Islands.

" The unhappy gentleman's designs for our defence," we read, " were hardly put upon paper when His Excellency, upon demand of the governor of St Eustatius, ordered him to be seized and delivered to the Dutch officer . . . and at St Eustatius he was thrown into the cistern, or dungeons for common criminals, and loaded with irons, as guilty of some heinous crime at Surinam,

but of what nature they did not know themselves. . . .
[He was then] transported to Surinam; I followed him
with two vessels to attempt his deliverance, but unsuccess-
fully.   The governor there gave him the reception and
treatment he had met with at Eustatius, and also attempted
his life, first by a trial for desertion, and afterwards by
poison; but providence and His Majesty's demand of him
upon my representation of his case saved him . . . to
return to Holland and clear his innocence to his
masters. . . ."

As commissions in the Company's service became more
beneficial, this branch of patronage became too valuable to
be wasted on foreigners without interest, and the directors
took an ever-growing share in its disposal.   First we
find them sending out volunteers, who served in the ranks,
on 5 pagodas a month, until vacancies occurred; and then
cadets took the place of volunteers.   Their choice was
almost altogether a matter of favour and interest.   They
were indeed interviewed by the chairman of the Company before their appointment, but that was a mere
matter of form.   Hickey, for example, was asked how
old he was, whether he had served, whether he knew the
manual exercise, and whether he agreed to the terms of
service.   From 1775 the cadets were distinguished by a
special uniform—a plain scarlet coat, lapelled, with white-
metal buttons, and shoulder-straps instead of epaulettes.
On arrival they were warned that they must not expect
commissions till they were familiar with an officer's
duties and could salute gracefully with fuzee and espon-
toon.   In the same year the Council resolved that even
those who came out with appointments as ensign or lieutenant-fireworker (the corresponding rank in the artillery)
should not receive commissions until they had served for
four months as cadets, and been reported as thoroughly
acquainted with their duties and qualified for commissioned

rank.   A little later, instead of being distributed among
the various regiments, they were grouped together in
specified garrisons, where they were ordered to attend the
garrison parades and take their turns in mounting guard.
Finally in 1800 a special cadet company was formed,
under its own commandant, with strict rules for its internal discipline.   This company was stationed at Chingleput, over 30 miles from the distractions of Madras.

" The cadets," so runs the general order, " shall rise
at daybreak, breakfast at 7 or 8, according to the season,
dine at 2, sup at 8, and retire to rest immediately after.
All lights shall be put out at 9 o'clock, and the officer of
the day shall be held responsible for an exact and punctual
observance of this order.   No cadets between 9 o'clock at
night and daybreak of the following morning shall go
out of the Fort. . . .
" Except on occasions of taking some manly exercise,
such as playing at cricket, fives, or other game, no cadet
shall appear out of his quarters otherwise than dressed
in the uniform established for the cadet company. . . .
The habit of lounging from quarter to quarter in a white
waistcoat is expressly forbid."

Thus a whole system of training was evolved for the
young gentlemen chosen by the Company to direct its
troops.

Another cause contributed greatly to improve the
Madras Army.   That was the appointment of King's
officers in considerable numbers to the service.   This may
be dated from 1746, when the Company appointed as
major commanding its troops on the Coromandel Coast
Captain Stringer Lawrence, of Clayton's regiment of
foot.   Under him the Madras companies first became an
efficient fighting force.   In this task he was assisted by
many others of the same service.   There was the gallant
Killpatrick; there was the brave but feather-headed

Dalton, late of the Marines, whose imagination, all the time he was in India, was running riot over what he would do on his return among the ladies of Covent Garden; there was the polite and skilful Caillaud, praised with justice as " by far the fittest person for the command of the war in this country of anyone now in it. His knowledge of the people [and] country, experience, generosity, happy turn of mind, . . . give him the superiority over any man whatsoever." Among the cadets you begin to find men like Laverock, who had been obliged to sell his commission in the Buffs. Then too after the Seven Years War, when many regiments had been disbanded and the country was full of distressed officers on half-pay, the Company sent out many more with the rank of captain or lieutenant. In 1770 13 captains and 19 lieutenants were thus sent out. The most notable of these was Captain Thomas Madge, who came out in 1768 with a commission antedated to 1763, and who died only five years later. He, as his epitaph tells us, " twined the scholar's with the soldier's bays "; and his inventory leaves the impression of a man of wide and cultured interests. He was a musician and played both flute and violin. He studied his profession in the works of Saxe and the regulations of the great Frederick; he had on his shelves the most highly regarded authors of his age—Shakespeare in Theobald's edition; Swift and Molière, Pope's works, Dodsley's Collections, Hume and Montesquieu, the essayists, Fielding and Smollett, Rousseau and Sterne, and many other writers once esteemed and now forgotten. Yet more worthy of note, he was interested in oriental things, and possessed a number of Persian manuscripts. In his will he leaves £100 to a friend's natural son; to his brother the sapphire ring set with diamonds given him by Colonel Monson on his quitting the King's service; and £1,000 each to his two " natural and adopted children," who were to be sent to England to the charge of his brothers-in-law.

These men brought with them new standards of efficiency and tactics, along with that army spirit which had been so conspicuously wanting in the old days. But their coming involved at first a good deal of supersession and discontent. " I cannot help complaining," wrote drunken Mr Hyde Parker, " of our hard fate that has been so many years in their honours' service, that this new major [that is, Lawrence who had once had to kick the writer out of his quarters] is providing for all those that came out with him over our heads though mostly never in service before." Hyde Parker was broke, and the service was well rid of him; others who would not submit to supersession were allowed to retire with certificates of conduct, such as the following:

" This is to certify that Arthur Nelson, gentleman, a lieutenant in the service of the United East India Company, as well since promoted to the rank of a commission officer as during the time he bore arms in the said service, has behaved to the satisfaction of his superiors, but, being judged by them unequal to a greater charge than that of a subaltern's command, some other his junior officers have been promoted above him; he resigns the service at his own request and has permission to proceed to England."

The reorganisation must have borne hardly on more than one; but it is not always possible to wait for a generation to die out before carrying reforms into execution.

A much more general cause of dissatisfaction was the position of superiority enjoyed by the King's officers employed as such upon the Coast. When Adlercron's regiment of foot—the 39th—landed in 1754, the Company had agreed that King's officers were to command all Company's officers of the same grade. This invidious measure was not annulled until 1788. It must have been very trying to an old and experienced captain of the Company's service to find himself under the command of a man who the day before had been only a lieutenant in a King's regiment. At first the matter provoked a great deal of comment, especially as the arrival of Colonel Adlercron took the command of all the troops on the Coast out of the hands of the Company's chief officer, Colonel Lawrence. " King's troops should not be accompanied by any officers of higher rank than that of captain," wrote Orme the historian, to his patron, Holdernesse. " It's men we want, not officers," he continued. " When His Majesty's commission to staff officers is produced in superiority to the character of the merchant and the Company's servant, our resolutions are perpetually obstructed." " Happy for me," wrote one of the Company's officers thus superseded, " that my service has been separated from that of the Royalists . . . They look down with such disdain upon the Company's corps that I could never have served with satisfaction." Nor even was the Council allowed without a struggle to promote Company's officers in order to obviate special disadvantages. The King's captains erected themselves into a tribunal to judge the validity of commissions of the rank of major which placed them under the newly promoted officer's command. Soon after the arrival of Draper's and Brereton's regiments in 1759, the validity of Caillaud's commission as major was called in question, on the ground of a rumour that the Company had reserved to itself the right of appointing to that rank. This point was yielded as a personal acknowledgment of Caillaud's individual merit and former standing in the King's service. But when, on his departure to Bengal, the Council resolved to promote two of their officers, neither of whom had ever borne the King's commission, to the rank of major, Coote wrote:

4

" The gentlemen you have been pleased to appoint as field-officers I myself have no personal objection to, nor do I believe any other officer in the army has, but as the gentlemen of the King's corps think that appointment a great injustice to them and an infringement of the rank given them by His Majesty, they therefore have protested against it and the captains have given me a memorial to that purpose . . . If this affair can be cleared up to the satisfaction of those gentlemen, I shall then with the greatest pleasure conform to your request by putting Captains Joseph Smith and Achilles Preston in orders according to the nomination you have been pleased to give them, till when I must beg leave to be excused."

The views of the royal officers are plainly stated in Coote's own diary at this time.

" If the gentlemen here," he says, meaning the Council, " are empowered to give what rank they please to their own officers, . . . no King's officer can serve in this country either with honour to His Majesty or credit to himself; for by this rule the different presidencies have it in their power to give the youngest ensign superior rank to any officer His Majesty may be pleased to send over, and consequently will command the army whenever they think proper. . . ."

After a good deal of dispute the King's captains were pleased to allow that the Governor and Council might temporarily nominate one major. The council finally resolved to send to Coote a copy of the order under which they were acting—

" and at the same time to intimate to him that being fully ascertained of the legality of our powers, we cannot on any account wave our right and must leave the consequences of the controversy, should it longer subsist, to those to whom they belong."

With the end of the Seven Years War and the consequent departure of the King's regiments, this particular
difficulty came to an end, only, however, to revive on
the occasion of the next war with the French and the
reappearance of the King's troops in India. And as
from this time onwards King's troops came to form a
considerable part of the forces in the Company's territories, a compromise was at last reached. The Company's
officers were given local rank according to the dates of
their commissions, and the King's officers were to waive
all local and temporary rank that might have been con-
ferred upon them.

But disagreeable as this long struggle must have been,
the Company's officers probably learnt as much from the
King's officers beside whom they served as from those who
actually joined the Company's service. In any case the
officers of the later generation, as characterised by their
inventories, showed a remarkable improvement over their
predecessors. Peter Eckman, for instance, left as outstanding items three-quarters of " a Goa physical stone "
and 12 old books. The principal articles in that of John
Crompton are a quantity of soldiers' shirts and stockings
—kept for sale to the men of his company under the
denomination of slops, and a considerable number of packs
of cards and escritoires inlaid with ivory, evidently for
purposes of trade. His books include *The Coasting Pilot*
and Harris's *Voyages,* but not a work connected even
remotely with the art of war. John de Morgan, *centurio
anglicanus quondam* as his epitaph in Pulicat cemetery
describes him, and ancestor, I believe, of the well-known
novelist of our own day, left an estate of 10,000 pagodas
—say £4,000—including two houses in the Fort and one
at Pulicat, but the only other item of interest in his inventory comprised two half-leaguers for bathing tubs—
interesting not because bathing was uncommon, but because

the usual method was to have a servant throw water over you as you sat on a chair. But with the disappearance of this generation comes a marked change for the better. There were no doubt many more skilful officers than poor Raillard, but surely few so sensitive of the disgrace of failure. Sent in 1759 to relieve a place attacked by the French, he was unable to prevent his men from breaking and flying.

" Lieutenant Raillard," says the letter reporting this misfortune, " being on horseback during the engagement escaped being made prisoner, but did not long survive the misfortune of his defeat, which made such an impression on his mind, as, we may suppose, produced his unfortunate end. His pistols being discharged and having no cartridges, he bruised himself so much with repeated strokes on the breast and head with his pistol, that he fell off his horse and expired about five miles from the scene of action, with no other marks of violence than what I have related."

I have no reason for supposing him to have been a student, but it is just about this time that technical works on military subjects make their first appearance in the inventories. At this time, according to Wolfe—and no authority could be better—our military education was the worst in Europe; and when he was making out a list of books to be studied by a young officer, he thought nothing in English (translations excepted) worth including. It is not surprising, then, that the earliest list worth mention should come from the inventory of a Swiss officer in the Company's service, the well-read but bilious Captain d'Illens. He possessed Puységur's *Art de la Guerre*, Vauban's *Mémoires* and *Attacque et Défense des Places*, and a number of other French books—*Mémoires d'Artillerie*, 3 volumes; *Art de la Guerre*, 2 volumes; *Histoire*

Militaire des Suisses, 5 volumes; *L'Art de Jeter les Bombes,* together with *The Perfect Ingenier et Bombardier,* 2 volumes, and *The Journal of the Last War in Flanders,* 5 volumes. When the engineer Captain Alexander Leigh was killed before Vellore, in 1761, he was found to have left his horse, sword, and books to his friend and fellow-engineer, John Call. Technical books become the rule rather than the exception among the effects of deceased officers. It would be tedious to enumerate them. The same works recur time after time; and the literature of the subject at this period was narrow and trivial. Humphrey Bland's *Treatise of Military Discipline* was still the standard work for English officers; and those who have explored that formal, unilluminating volume will agree that in comparison *Infantry Training* (1914) is a work of no small literary merit. The most valuable works which occur, or indeed existed at the time, are the Regulations of the Prussian infantry, Saxe's *Rêveries,* Vauban's works, together with a number of memoirs, those of Turenne, of Gustavus Adolphus, Charles the Twelfth, and Sully, and the classical accounts of the campaigns of Hannibal and Cæsar. All these were to be found in officers' bookcases at Madras, along with the compilations of Sime and Muller, and many anonymous publications. Moreover the increased number of books in general suggests a much higher level of general education than had been the case. Lieutenant James Minns, who died near Wandiwash in 1759, mentions in his will a bookcase containing 200 books. Captain James Cope bequeathed all his books and papers to Lieutenant Browne, who, I suppose, was responsible for the publication of that plagiaristic *New History of the East Indies with Brief Observations . . . by Captain Cope* (London, 1758, 8vo, pp. viii and 426), which is stolen word for word, for the most part, from Hamilton's *New Account of the East Indies,* with the addition of a few worthless remarks on the capture of Madras and the siege of Pondicherry. Captain William Lee reads Clarendon and Burnet, Locke and Shaftesbury, Cowley, Swift, and *The British Magazine.* Captain Timothy Bridge adds *Don Quixote,* Wycherly, and Milton.

Of course they had all come to India to make money. In that age no one but a lunatic would have gone there for any other purpose. But in many, many cases, where we can pierce below the surface, their motives appear anything but mercenary. John Call, for instance, writes: " Money I hope soon to have enough; the next thing I want is honour, and unless I can have it here with my right, I am determined to seek it in Europe." So he did go home, to become Sir John Call, Bart., M.P., and partner in the banking house of Pybus, Call & Company, an odd career for an officer of Engineers. Family motives were very common. Here is a letter from a Company's officer on the eve of battle:

". . . Never, I believe, were men in higher spirits than the Company's troops. I would not by this be thought to mean that they are superior to His Majesty's; but only that as I am oftener amongst them, I have more opportunity of hearing and seeing, and in short am more capable of judging of them than of the King's, with whom we don't mix so often, yet I dare say they are good lads too. Now I speak of the regiment, Colonel Draper's name is often mentioned, to-day, you may be sure, with much respect, and I cannot help saying with regret for his loss to the service. Yet we have a brave man to head us, and what can English soldiers wish for more? Refined manœuvres are certainly very clever, but where there is but a handful of men on each side, true courage must secure success, and it would be a sin to doubt that our honest hardy countrymen are braver than the French. Indeed I shall never doubt it till I find it otherwise.

" Our general friends desire to be remembered affectionately, and I myself, methinks, would say something very kind to you and other friends, but don't care to enter upon the tender strain. You won't, I'm certain, think the lightlier of my true friendship for you, nor have I so mean an opinion of my other India intimates, as to imagine they will be offended at my not leaving them legacies. My father had no great estate, and dying whilst his children were young, you may guess whether five of us did not find use for his small inheritance. I shared my own, and am now able to return it to my brothers with interest, thanks to my kind benefactor and yours. I assure you, my friend, that I have no inward hint that I am destined to fall to-morrow, but should it so please the Disposer of all things, I dye resigned and composed . . ."

George Bruce, the cadet whose diary supplies some details of the voyage to India, was appointed ensign in 1778, and killed in the storm of Chidambaram. He leaves his little savings of less than four years' service to his widowed mother and his three sisters. Or take the will of Captain George Jolland, " born in the parish of Louth in Lincolnshire, having imigrated into the East Indies with an intention of benefiting my family who have met with adverse fortune in this world, first think it necessary to render thanks to Almighty God for his great goodness in crowning my endeavours with success." In the first place his father's affairs are to be settled as quickly as possible; then provision is to be made for his father and mother; and lastly any residue should be employed in fitting out his nephew George Sheriman, probably his godson, for the East Indies.

In social origins the Coast Army at this time must have been extraordinarily mixed. At one end of the scale you would find those friends of Hickey's who had been compelled by their extravagance to sell out of the Guards; at the other the Company's captain who insisted on sending home his brother, the Company's cooper, " as he did not like to have a brother in that station so near him."(Then the Company's army afforded an ideal dumping-ground for persons whom their relations wanted to provide comfortably for somewhere outside England, wild nephews, out-at-elbows cousins, and natural or unnatural sons. As time passed, the sons of Madras officers appear in ever-increasing proportions. And at all times, from 1750 onwards, there was a strong influx from the children of the middle and professional class, brought up in the homes of country attorneys, like Clive, or of country parsons, like Madge. In a body of four or five hundred men thus recruited there was bound to be a goodly number of bad bargains; but many who might have been expected to turn out badly made good; and the surprising thing is not the number of failures, but their fewness.

CHAPTER V

THE COMPANY'S OFFICER—PART II

WITH the expansion in numbers went a great and necessary increase in the officers' pay. By 1788 this had risen to £456 a year for colonels, £364 16s. for lieutenant-colonels, £272 12s. for majors, down to £72 16s. for ensigns. Officers attached to Sepoy battalions drew extra allowances in recognition of their special responsibility. These rates compared very favourably with those paid in the King's service; but they were far from exhausting the remuneration of the Company's officers. Besides this pay, the field officers were entitled to a share in the fund known as the Gratuity, formed by a fixed percentage on the territorial revenues from, I think, the year 1783. This varied in amount; for the year 1783–84 and the two following a colonel received under this head about £1,000 a year; and even after that time, when the King's officers serving in the presidency were admitted to share, it more than doubled the colonel's pay and added £256 and £158 to the pay of the lieutenant-colonel and major respectively.

Besides this regular pay there was the allowance known as *batta*. This was payable when in the field or at certain distant stations where the cost of living was higher than at the presidency. The allowance makes its first appearance when the English sent troops into the field to support

the claims of Nawab Muhammad Ali to the rulership
of the Carnatic. For a time these troops were regarded
as being in his service, and he allowed 15 rupees a day
to the captains thus employed, and 10 rupees to the
subalterns. After a couple of years of this system, the
Nawab transferred territory to the Company to meet the
costs of such military assistance, and from that time the
officers had to look to the Company for their *batta*. It
was then fixed at 15 rupees for a commanding officer,
5 rupees for a captain, 3 for a lieutenant, and 2 for an
ensign. At this reduction there was a great deal of discontent; and, the captains protesting with such " positive
and mutinous terms as greatly surprised us," the Council
placed three of them in arrest; one died, another deserted
to Pondicherry, the third apologised and was forgiven.
However, it was not found possible to keep the rate so
low as this, and in 1755 it was raised by a rupee a day
for each grade of subaltern officers, and extra rates were
allowed for commanders. On this subject Caillaud in
1764 wrote an illuminating letter to the Company which
had asked him for information:

" I am very desirous of satisfying you in respect to the
questions you were pleased to put to me the other day
with regard to what I thought would be a sufficient allowance to the commanding officer of your army in the field.
I shall endeavour in this to do all the justice I can by
keeping in view the two great points which led you to this
enquiry; the desire of establishing a system of oeconomy
necessary for the interest and welfare of the Company,
and at the same time shewing some regard to your officers
whose services I hope will always merit your favour and
indulgence.

" The great article of expence to officers in the field
in India ariseth from the number of people they are
obliged to keep in constant pay both as servants and coolies
to carry their baggage. Nor have all our endeavours to

lessen this heavy charge been of any avail.   It is not in
our power to change the nature of the people; if you have
a horse, you must keep two servants to attend to it; and
the same proportion holds on for the number of servants
you may want about your person and at your table.

" Another very heavy article of expence is that of wine
—I mean not to include in this wines such as claret etc.
These are articles of luxury, and for which we have no
right to claim any indulgence; I confine myself to Madeira,
which is given to your servants as cheap as the Company
can afford it, yet by the time that it comes to your table in
the field, the expence of carriage adds at least a third,
often a half, to its original price.   Every article necessary
to your living (meat and salt excepted) you must carry
with you or must be sent after you from the settlement,
from which we are commonly at a great distance, no sutlers
following the army in India as in Europe, with wines and
other necessaries, and no towns passed through from
whence the officers can be supplied with such things—
therefore all comparisons drawn between pay and allowances made to officers in Europe and America with those
in India are unfair and unjust, as the inevitable expences
of the one and of the other in the field bear no proportion.

" The last campaign I made on the Coast, the Governor
and Council were pleased to allow me 10 pagodas a day;
I had besides my yearly salary as a field officer, the profits
on the clothing of my company, and an allowance as a
member of the council, which altogether nearly amounted
to what the Company have been pleased to fix my yearly
allowances now in India; and yet I can assure you with all
the care and attention I could give, I was considerably out
of pocket . . ."

I do not doubt that Caillaud was telling the truth about
his expenses; but I do not think that officers in general
found that they lost money by taking the field.   It all
depended on their standard of comfort.

It will have been noticed that Caillaud refers among

other sources of profit to the clothing of his company.
Odd as it seems, these tailor's profits were a much-prized
perquisite not only of the commercialised Company's
officers, but also of the King's service. Did not Hanbury
Williams write of a noble colonel?—

> " Now Bolton comes with beat of drums
>   Tho' fighting be his loathing;
> He much dislikes both guns and pikes,
>   But relishes the clothing."

This source of income was wrested out of the hands of
the Company's servants in 1748. As at that time there
were no colonels in the Company's pay, the captains enjoyed the clothing of their companies. These profits were
known as the Off-reckonings, and at an early period the
individual captains were relieved of the duty of separately
providing for the clothing of their companies; an agent was
appointed who provided the whole, but each captain still
kept the difference between the cost of provision and the
stoppages which he made from his men. As against this
he had to pay for burying those who died out of his company. This simple system broke down with the increase in
the size of the army, and especially with the appearance
of numerous field-officers each of whom claimed his share
in the Off-reckonings. When the Sepoy corps were established, a separate fund was formed, in which the captains
commanding battalions and the subalterns employed under
them all shared. When in 1786 the army was remodelled,
the Off-reckonings also were reorganised. The European
and Sepoy funds were amalgamated, and were distributed
among the officers at the rate of 600 pagodas or £250
per man as far down the list as the fund would allow.

Other sources of profit were more irregular in origin.
Such were the bazaar and arrack duties, one of which was
at last sanctioned by authority, while the other was pro-

hibited. The first of these seems to have originated in the levy of a small tax intended to pay the men employed in inspecting the bazaars. Colonel Heron, a King's officer who joined the Company with an indecent devotion to his material advantages, claimed to levy it as a grant to him personally from the Indian prince to whom he was attached. The Council firmly rejected such claims, and Heron was dismissed for this and other offences. But in the First Mysore War (1767–69) the matter cropped up again in connection with the supplies of troops in the field. Colonel Wood was accused of seizing for himself supplies of provisions captured in the enemy country, and then having them retailed to his troops in the field-bazaars accompanying his detachment. He was court-martialled on this and other charges; and the court found " that Colonel Wood acted no otherwise with regard to the buzar than what has been the constant practice with other commanding officers in the service, and that the service does not appear to have suffered from the concern which Colonel Wood had in the buzar." The comment of a civilian on this finding was as follows:

" The court . . . could not condemn Wood for many things which most of themselves had probably been guilty of, nor disapprove of his proceedings without acknowledging those perquisites to be illegal which they would fain establish as their right. The privileges of a commander-in-chief appeared therefore in a great measure to depend on the issue of this affair."

Wood was dismissed from the service as soon as the finding of the court was known, so that the question was fairly settled. The arrack profits, however, were secured. Under no circumstances could the sale of arrack in camps and cantonments be allowed without regulation, for the men would always have been incapacitated by the quanti-

ties of bad liquor they would have bought and consumed.
So in 1771 orders were issued that in future no arrack
should be sold to the troops but by the Company's agent,
instead of by the commandants of the cantonments as
heretofore, but that the profit on the sale at each cantonment should be paid to the commandant. With the
growth of the army this became more and more valuable;
and in 1789 the arrack profits produced to General Horne
at Trichinopoly no less than 1,614 pagodas, or over £645,
while the profits on an average station amounted to £250
or thereabouts.

A source of profit, not formally prohibited until 1826,
but regarded with an ever-growing disfavour, was the
once-universal private trade. The growth of an army
spirit and the influx of King's officers must have tended
to limit the practice; but it is certain that it died out very
gradually, and that it was not necessarily inconsistent,
whatever we may think nowadays, with military skill or
dignity of character. At the same time it is true that the
average person could not combine successfully the profession of arms and the occupations of commerce. Clive
was one of the earliest men to perceive this in India.
" Trade is a study," he says, " very foreign from an
officer "; but at the time few agreed with him. Almost
all those who had served with him in the Madras Army
were concerned in commercial speculations; and he himself
had laid the foundations of his great fortune by the
management of a victualling contract. At that time it
was a thing of course. When Captain Rudolf de Gingens
came out in 1744 with a near relative of his, the pair
entered into joint engagements with English merchants
for wine and other goods which they brought out with
them. In 1747 we find Ensign Wardlaw selling arrack
in Cuddalore and Ensign Turnbull doing the same in
Fort St David. Lieutenant John Harrison, whose exer-

tions and *sang-froid* saved the fortress of Trichinopoly when the French besiegers had actually effected an entrance by a night escalade, was found at his death to have a stock of looking-glasses, pistols, and fuzees, presumably for sale.   William Pye, who was killed fighting against Siraj-ud-daula in Bengal, made a trading voyage to Manila the year before he received his commission as captain in the Company's service.   Captain John Hume sends up oil-seeds from Fort St David to Madras consigned to the engineer, John Call, who in return supplied him with wax candles, tea, and ginghams.   Captain Edmund Pascall deals in salt.   Lieutenant Weston Greenwollers acts as agent at Trichinopoly for a Company's servant, and retailed such small articles as buttons, quills, paper, and boot-straps.

The officers take part too in what the covenanted servants regard as a good substitute for trade—i.e. advancing money to revenue officials.   Pascall did so, and was recalled from his station to the presidency.   Another officer, Captain John Bowman, was found to have claims on a raja of the Chicacole country; and the Company directs the Council to assist his executors in getting in the debt.   But these practices were found to lead to many abuses and were finally prohibited in 1786.   It appearing from the proceedings of a court martial that Ensign Butler had disobeyed this order, the Council declare " their marked displeasure and disapprobation of his conduct.   In this first instance they are pleased to remit the punishment he has incurred of dismission from the service, but, while they announce this act of lenity, they repeat to the army that it is expected the strictest attention shall be paid to the above order."

Meanwhile the custom of trade lingered on.   *The Trader's Pocket Companion* can still find a place in 1778 on a major's book-shelf.   Captain Mathias Calvert is sued before the Mayor's Court over a parcel of red wood supplied to him, and succeeds in casting his adversary. Lieutenant Beatson, on his way from Masulipatam to Madras, loses an immense quantity of longcloth, northward chints, and other goods, by the wreck of the vessel on which he had laded them. Major George Browne enters into a trading partnership with an Indian and goes to law about it. Lieutenant Alexander Read accompanies the escort of a Company's servant, sent as envoy to the Nizam at Hyderabad, and Read hopes to turn his expedition to profit.

" I had a letter from him at the beginning of last month," writes one of his correspondents, " but he knows nothing how long their stay may be or what they stay for. He does not seem to like the trip so much as he at first did, nor has he gained anything by it as yet; he was in hopes it would have proved very advantageous to him, and carried a great many things with him to sell, besides his painting materials, neither of which has answered his expectations."

Read's case is of particular interest, because he was a noteworthy man in himself. He was an excellent officer who obtained the special thanks of Cornwallis and of the Court of Directors for his conduct in the Third Mysore War. He was then selected to administer part of the territories ceded by Tipu after that war; these duties he discharged so honestly and well that he was presented with a sword of honour as a mark of the Company's sense of his services; what is more conclusive than this is that he earned the affectionate respect of Thomas Munro, who served under him as his assistant and who learnt from him his first lessons in revenue management; and when he retired in the last year of the century, both Governor and Governor-General bore joint witness to his untiring and honourable exertions for the public good.

Prize, though better warranted by custom, is in itself as ugly a topic as trade, in connection with the life military. Nothing produced so many quarrels between the Council and its officers, nothing produced so many quarrels between the officers themselves. The matter was complicated in India by the habit of our allies of making a special donation in lieu of plunder—an arrangement which usually left both sides discontented, the ally at having to give his auxiliaries so much and the troops at receiving so little compared with their excited estimates of the plunder. Nothing was more difficult to define. Wellington, who had witnessed sacks in both Europe and India, defined plunder as " What you could lay your bloody hand upon and keep." The Company obtained letters patent reserving to the King the disposal of booty taken where his naval or military forces were present, but granting to the Company the disposal of all plunder taken by its forces acting alone; and on the strength of this it decided to allow to its military servants half of any plunder so taken, exclusive of all cannon, powder, and military stores. But the provisions of the patent excited great discontent in either case. Where King's troops were present, and it was necessary to await the King's pleasure, there were great delays in the distribution; where they were not, the Company's claim to a half was regarded as a grievous wrong. Forde, marching against the French in Masulipatam in 1759, was confronted by a demand of the troops that the whole of the prize should be divided among them or else they would not march. Before the troops for Manila went on board, long discussions took place about the disposal of the expected prize-money, the royal officers refusing to agree that half should be reserved in case the Crown should be pleased to grant it to the Company. The division of the £140,000 arising from the capture of the *Santissima Trinidad* on that occasion affords a good illus-

tration of the way in which prize was divided on a joint
naval and military expedition. The admiral and general
divided one-eighth between them; the naval captains and
field officers shared two-eighths; an eighth each was
allotted to the naval lieutenants and military captains, to
the warrant officers and subalterns, and to the non-commissioned officers; and two-eighths to the able seamen and
private soldiers. The individual shares ranged from
£8,750 received by both the admiral and general, and
£2,187 10s. received by each naval captain and field officer,
down to £128 received by each warrant officer and subaltern, and £9 7s. 10d. received by the able seaman or
private. The delays in the distribution were often
enormous. The *Santissima Trinidad* had been taken in
1762; but the distribution just described was only notified
in Army orders in 1768; the prize-money for the capture
of Pondicherry in 1778 was still unpaid ten years later;
and only one instalment of the Negapatam prize-money
had been paid in 1789, though the place had been captured in 1781. The latter also affords an example of
the difficulties that would arise about sharing. At the
opening of the Second Mysore War, Coote and the whole
body of officers had agreed that all prize should go into
a common fund, to be divided among everyone irrespec-
tive of presence at a particular siege. The navy had not
of course been included in this agreement; but the navy
contributed a good many of the men who took part in
the siege of Negapatam. These refused to share the
prize with the army at large, which would have reduced
individual shares to trifling sums, and the body of officers
present finally decided that the distribution should be
limited, according to immemorial custom, to those present
at the capture. This apparently was the chief reason
why Coote, thus excluded from any share, felt and wrote
so bitterly about this particular part of the war. In the

time of Cornwallis attempts were made to bring under strict rule this matter in itself essentially irregular. At the beginning of the Third Mysore War, four prize-agents were chosen, two by the King's, two by the Company's officers, to account to the army for such part of the prize-money as Government might be pleased to allow it; and now for the first time we find the distribution of prize regulated in proportion to the *batta* which officers and men were entitled to receive, save that sergeants, who drew the same *batta* as privates, were to be allowed a double share of prize-money. This war did not raise the prize question in an acute form; but the last war with Mysore, culminating in the capture of Seringapatam by storm, revived much of the old eagerness. " The army conceive," wrote the Governor-General, " that as the place was taken by storm, they are of right entitled to what was found in it." Much that was found was never brought into the prize-fund. A soldier of the 74th was related to have found Tipu's armlets, set with great diamonds; he passed them on to a Company's surgeon for 1,500 rupees; and the surgeon, after carrying them about round his waist for two years, sold them for a sum that brought him in £2,000 a year, of which he not ungenerously allowed £200 to the private. The prize-fund itself was reckoned at 5,000,000 pagodas or £2,000,000; and such was the difficulty of disposing of the jewels at a fair price that many officers received their share in jewels. Probably in this way General John Pater, whom we shall meet again, obtained the Elephant Pearl advertised in the sale of his effects in 1817.

The troubles connected with prize were new, because in the old days there had been no prize for officers to quarrel about, either with the Council or among themselves. But old abuses persisted too, and were specially prevalent in the Sepoy corps. When a field officer was first appointed to command the whole body of Sepoys, he was informed that "we [the Council] have too much reason to suspect that money is lent to the sepoys by officers and others, and that considerations are given for the recommendation of sepoy officers for promotion." In 1756 Captain James Spears, who had gone out in 1747 as a midshipman with Boscawen, on taking the command at the station to which he had been posted, accepted 600 rupees from the Sepoy subadars on the footing of a present, but Council thought it more likely to be a reward for improper promotions or enlistments. Being dismissed and appealing to the Company for reinstatement, he was sent out again, this time to Bengal, apparently on the ground that "many, if not most of the captains in the service who have had Sepoys under their command, have done the same thing." But he profited so little by his lesson that he was soon after broke by court martial. In 1761 we find the commandant at Wandiwash refusing to allow the agents of the paymaster to take account of the casualties there. More curious still is an extraordinary letter, addressed by Lieutenant Edward Hudson to the famous missionary, Swartz, and which was accepted by the Mayor's Court as a valid will. It was dated at Trichinopoly, 13 April, 1768:

"Oh dear Swartz, after all my boasted honesty and my sometime persevering therein, I at last most assuredly have suffered myself to be led away by the devil, his many emissaries, my own vile and wicked nature, and the constant example of others. I have accepted presents. I have taken from naigues, havildars, and jemmidars, for their promotion. Oh these dubashes, these sepoy officers, they are devils.

"Pray, my dear, dear friend, as you value the happiness of souls in a future state, do what you can for me to make my peace with God. Let what I am possessed of at my death be given to the sepoys of the 11th Battalion from whom I have taken it. The orderly jemmidar knows these people, as does that vilain of a dubash of mine, the commandant, and many of the sepoy officers. I will endeavour to leave behind me a more particular account both of the names of these people and of the sums taken from them.

"The first cause of my apostacy was owing to an information that a subedar had taken this money from the officers I had made in his company, and that my not taking it was saving them nothing . . ."

The "particular account" to which he alludes is dated 4 May, 1768, and headed "Devil's Money." It is a list running from 26 August to 14 December of the previous year, of small sums, none exceeding 20 pagodas or £8, and amounting altogether to 111 pagodas. Few of the Company's officers, however, were afflicted with so tender a conscience. In 1771 Lieutenant Edward Collins was sentenced by court martial to be reprimanded for making unauthorised stoppages from his battalion, which the Council thought so inadequate that they suspended his promotion for a year. Leniency was indeed the order of the day. When in the next year Lieutenant Samuel Baker Evance was dismissed for taking money from Sepoys for passports, enlistments, and so on, the Company ordered him to be restored to his rank. So they did with Captain Mathias Calvert, who had been broke for bearing non-existent Sepoys on his rolls. It was even laid down by an exceedingly incompetent commander-in-chief in 1787 that in order to maintain battalions at a real strength of 400 men it was necessary to have 800 on the rolls; but by then the Government had thoroughly awakened to the importance of the question, and orders were issued regarding musters and inspections which went a long way to check these abuses.

It is clear that the discipline reigning at Madras had

at times been very relaxed. In fact it varied with the character of the commanders-in-chief. Stringer Lawrence had exacted a strict obedience; Caillaud, excellent as a leader in the field, was too easy-going and polite; Coote was too fond of popularity to attack widespread evils; and Dalling's ideas in 1787 I have just criticised. Even the most elementary duties might be neglected. The governor in Army orders complains that he has found the officer of the main-guard absent from his post; garrison orders declare that subalterns must not sleep at their quarters when on night-duty; a regiment of Europeans might parade with only one officer present; and leave was so easy to obtain that some officers were absent from their corps for years together. If then the Company was sure to get some bad bargains among their officers, the bad bargains were sure to make the most of the opportunities offered to them. Some of the crimes which appear in the proceedings of the courts martial provoke curious reflections. One subaltern is broke for using oaths and imprecations inconsistent with the character of a gentleman; Ensign William Price West was first reprimanded for sitting down to table with a publican, and then, being brought to trial for desertion, defended himself on the ground that his creditors were pressing, that he feared imprisonment for debt, owed in great part to the publican in question, and that he had hoped to come to an arrangement with his creditors from the safe distance of Pondicherry. He was sentenced to be cashiered in the most ignominious manner, his sword broken and his sash cut to pieces at the head of the troops. A brother-officer was broke for asking the same publican to forgive him the 55 pagodas which he owed him. Even so late as 1787 an ensign was broke "for associating with persons of mean professions and discreditable characters, and for drinking, rioting, and quarrelling with them on several occasions." Hardly less surprising is the extraordinary fact that in 1775 the Commander-in-Chief had to issue an order in which he " positively forbids officers appearing in fancy uniforms or in any but that of the corps to which they belong."

In spite of all this, however, I do not think that the number of positive incompetents was large. There were a few. From time to time men prefer to resign rather than stand a court martial. A nephew of Madge offers a case in point. He had been kept by an ill-judging father too close to his books, and appeared to his uncle no better than a learned block-head, who in his first action " discovered such uncommon tokens of cowardice as I am ashamed to mention." He begged to be allowed to resign before he was put to any further trial; and crowned this scandalous act by running away from Madras. I do not know what became of him. Of the same type was that Ensign Moody with whom his fellow-subalterns refused to rank, or that Mr Mitchell who could hardly be induced to join his regiment, and, when he did, spent all his time muddling himself with brandy and water.

Unrestrained addiction to liquor was naturally at the bottom of many of these failures. Of one, accused of being drunk on duty, a friendly witness deposed that he was " a little disguised, but not so much but that I think he might have marched the guard off." A son of Robertson, the historian, appears getting drunk, and beating a man to the effusion of blood, a few hours after reporting sick. Another officer is suspended for being always drunk; and the proceedings on a third for drunkenness display the mess etiquette of the time:

" The court find the prisoner guilty of the first charge exhibited against him, viz., ' for gross ungentlemanlike behaviour on the night of the 6th instant in the presence of the greater part of the garrison in the following instances:—(1) For being extremely intoxicated before the victuals were removed from the table and conducting himself in a most shameful and scandalous manner, unbecoming the character of an officer and a gentleman. (2) For quitting his seat and coming to me, his immediate commanding officer, with an apparent intention of insulting me for having recommended through the medium of the adjutant of the corps his retiring, as his situation rendered him unfit to sit in company. (3) For drawing his sword and laying it across the shoulder of an officer, thereby menacing and disturbing the harmony of the company.' "

He was therefore sentenced to be cashiered.

Finally just as a certain number of Frenchmen ran away and joined our ranks, so also a few of the Company's officers, who had no doubt made the place too hot to hold them, ran away to the enemy. One of these, being recaptured and sent home to England, took to writing books and set up a coffee-house at Cambridge, where he died in 1767 at the age of 88. A private letter, dated in March, 1768, tells the story of another:

" I believe you may remember one Hitchcock, an officer in the service . . .   His behaviour, I believe before you left us, was far from being correspondent with his station. He was sent down here [Masulipatam] a lieutenant of grenadiers about two months after my arrival, and shortly after joined the army in the circars, where his conduct was such as rendered him disgustful to all his brother-officers. The beginning of last year he marched with Colonel Smith through the Deccan and continued with him until a few nights before the first action, when he mounted his horse and deserted to Hyder Ally's camp. He was first taken for a spy and closely confined, but we have since heard he is still among them as an officer, but in great distress."

By this time such pranks were looked on as too serious

to be punished merely by sending the culprit home to England. About the same time as Hitchcock deserted, a Bengal cadet, who happened to be serving at Madras, tried to run away in company with another, and, on being recaptured, was sentenced to be drummed through the ranks with a halter round his neck, and to be confined till he could be sent to England. The latter part of the sentence seems to have been relaxed, for he reappears serving in the ranks and again deserting, with the same ill-fortune as before. This repetition of his crime was too much. He was sentenced to be shot to death, and his companion received 1,000 lashes.

CHAPTER VI

THE SOLDIER

IN the nature of things the soldier has left few records of himself save those of the battle-field and the court martial. We know him at his best and bloodiest, ready to march through hell to revenge a favourite officer; and we know him in his worst and most dismal mood, betrayed by tedium into drink, and by drink into crime. But it is much more difficult to form any idea of his normal life. No one of course would expect the barracks of the Madras Europeans to be a school of civic virtue. Indeed anyone watching a squad of the Company's recruits being marched on board for their voyage eastwards would wonder what good use could be made of those poor creatures, driven from their country by want of food or fear of the hangman; but he would be surprised to see the change wrought by regular food and constant discipline in those who were stout enough to survive the voyage and their first year or two of India. I suppose on the whole that their lives were nasty, short, and brutish; but I do not think that the philosophers of their age could have found a better use for them.

Normally these men were picked up by recruiting agents whom the Company employed at so much a head. It was a bad system. At times the Council complains that the men must have been picked up in Bedlam and Newgate.

74

Lockyer wishes " for the honour of the English nation they would decline sending such diminutive, dwarfish, crooked recruits as of late have gone." At another time we read, " They are for the most part the refuse of ships, such whom neither good example, instruction, nor correction can reduce to civil conformity." The contractors naturally got not the fittest men, but the cheapest; and were themselves not of the best characters. In time of war, matters were worse, for the Company was in greater need of men and less inclined to reject any, while the national requirements made recruiting more difficult. This led to another method.

" I find," runs a memorandum of 1752, " the Company is under great difficulties, as they say themselves, in getting both officers and men, and are ready to give commissions to any persons skilled in the art of war, provided they can give good security to raise the men that they agree with them for."

Where the recruiting officer was a man of local influence, this system was better calculated to produce good recruits than that of agents. Such was probably the case with the company raised by Captain Robert Delaval, and afterwards commanded by his brother Henry; in 1763, when the most pressing need was over, and plenty of men were available from the disbanded regiments, the Company received numerous proposals of this sort; and one officer engaged in raising an independent company fell into a dispute at a tavern, ending in the death of a waiter. On the outbreak of the American War, the inspector was authorised to accept lads under 20 provided they were at least 5 feet 3 inches in height; and in 1781 the Company was authorised to establish a recruiting depot in England. That relieved it from the obvious inconveniences of having to get its recruits together about the time of the dispatch of the shipping.   At last the War Office undertook to recruit for it.

Sometimes, in despair of getting Englishmen, the Company raised bodies of foreigners. In 1752 a body of 60 Protestant Germans was sent out for the artillery company at Madras; and in 1756 agents were sent to raise 200 men in the neighbourhood of Hamburg, Lubeck, and Bremen. But the principal experiment of this nature was the enlistment of companies of Swiss raised in the Protestant cantons. Of these upwards of 500 men were sent to India between 1751 and 1754. But the experiment was a failure, partly because the men would desert to the French, partly because the officers claimed special privileges, such as that of holding separate courts martial of their own and administering their own martial law. The Company accordingly resolved that, as soon as the Swiss capitulations expired, all those who chose to re-enlist should do so on the ordinary terms (excepting the special bounty to which they were entitled by agreement) and be distributed among the English companies. Nor was any large body of foreign troops again raised by the Company, though in 1771 the people of Gravesend were astonished to see in their midst 120 men in green waistcoats with arms, supposed to be Swiss troops for the Indian service, and though Colonel Erskine complained that the Company had authorised him to raise a company in Switzerland, and then denied having done so. At a later time the King sent out two regiments of Hanoverians to serve for a short time at Madras; and on the conquest of Ceylon, the Company entertained the Swiss regiment de Meuron, which then passed from the Dutch service to ours.

Desertion being a common practice in all the European forces in every tropical settlement, lack of men always made the Governments eager to turn deserters to some

military use. In the early peaceful days, they were just
entertained as ordinary members of the garrison; but in
the later more troubled times, their disposal was a matter
of more difficulty. We find them sent, for instance, on
board the Company's ships as foremast men, or dispatched
to the distant island of Sumatra, where the French had no
settlements. Bounties would be offered to encourage
desertion among the enemy varying from 10 rupees to as
many pagodas; and Coote formed the best who came
in into a company " who are always to be ready upon any
particular attack where I may expect to lose men." When
the Seven Years War was over, the numerous deserters
from the French, and the numerous prisoners who fell
into our hands on the capture of Pondicherry, provided so
many accessions to our ranks that they were formed into
the body called the " Foreign Legion," comprising both
horse and foot. Their officers were Frenchmen, and
naturally not the best sort of Frenchman; their discipline
was poor, so that they were always doubtful auxiliaries
and were broken up about twelve years later. The Bengal
Government had done much the same, calling their corps
the " Foreign Rangers," but with no better success; and
in 1786 desired no more deserters to be enlisted at Madras
for service in Bengal.

The only other sources of supply were re-enlistment
of time-expired men, very rare local recruitment, and
sometimes the accession of a body of men out of a King's
regiment, disbanded or recalled to Europe. The Company's troops were enlisted for a period of five years;
and for a long time were re-enlisted for the same term.
For this they received a bounty of 25 pagodas, or £10.
Most time-expired men accepted these terms. They had
no object to carry them home; and nothing but a lucky
occasion of plunder could give them money enough to live
on when they got there. So that, though a discharged

soldier could always work his passage home on board one of the Company's returning ships, they mostly preferred to remain where liquor was cheap though women might be black.   In order to disguise a little the fact of their permanent exile, the term of enlistment and re-enlistment was in 1788 reduced from five years to three, and then they only received a bounty of 15, instead of 25 pagodas.   As for local recruitment, in times of great necessity, a few men might be raised from the Company's shipping; but vessels on reaching the East Indies were always short of men, and captains were seldom willing to surrender any.   Nor were attempts to raise men out of royal forces returning from India without their difficulties.   When the troops with Boscawen were recalled, they were permitted to enter the Company's service; but Lawrence could only induce 80 of them to join until he agreed to receive such officers as would bring their men with them.   When the 39th was recalled in 1757, all subalterns and other ranks were allowed to quit the service if they pleased; and 350 out of 500 accepted the council's offer of 10 pagodas for three years' enlistment. In 1764 five lieutenants received Company's commissions as captains for bringing in fifty men apiece out of the four royal regiments about to sail for England.

Of the barracks in which these men were lodged we know little.   But at a much later date they remained dark, low, and stuffy; nor can they have been otherwise in the eighteenth century.   Except in the monsoon, the men preferred sleeping in the street outside to stifling within.   The barracks too were certainly infested with vermin.   One item of expense was the constant repair of the beds—light frames on which were stretched interlacing tapes—which broke when the men beat them on the floor to fetch the insects out of them.   No doubt they were periodically whitewashed; but that served only to cover up for a while the pests teeming in the walls. No mosquito-curtains were served out; and the men must have been perpetual victims of malaria.

Their diet was under some degree of supervision. In 1748 the Company had ordered that the men were to be obliged " to regularity in their diet, by messing or such other methods as the nature of the country and service will admit of." This, like many other orders of the Company, was not carried into immediate effect; but in 1755 the directors wrote:

" It having been represented to us that the method of dieting His Majesty's troops in messes, and which is likewise followed by the Swiss, is of great advantage to the men, we can but recommend to you the ordering the same to be observed by all the military in our service."

Lawrence and the Governor now took the matter up, and the messing system was definitely introduced. In 1762 the meat to be served out to the garrison was beef on Sundays and Wednesdays, mutton on Mondays and Thursdays, and pork on Tuesdays and Fridays, Saturday being left blank. Each corps informed the Town-major the evening before how much meat it wanted, and a sergeant was directed to see that the men took what they had asked for; a market was set up in the Fort for the sale of rice, salt, etc., at least as early as 1766, in order to discourage the soldiers' going into the Black Town for supplies. This plan, however, was not entirely successful. As nothing, we read in an order of 1770, contributes more to the health of soldiers than messing regularly, which is in a great measure prevented by giving them passes to go into the Black Town in the morning and remain until the evening roll-call, as the men are unwilling to pay their contribution to the mess when they can go out and spend their money on spirits, company officers are recommended to let

their men go early in the morning but to require their
return by noon. A few years later the routine of beef,
mutton, pork, had given way to an unchanging fare of
mutton, 29 sheep being supplied for the daily consumption of the troops at the rate of four sheep to the pagoda,
or 2s. apiece. Later on the price of sheep had risen considerably, and at the end of the century you only got two
good or three ordinary sheep for a pagoda.

Though the men had to pay for their own provisions
in garrison, in the field they were of course supplied with
them at the Company's expense. This should have led to
all that apparatus of sutlers and commissariat that followed
armies in Europe. But in fact it did not. Our early campaigns with the French were fought without that vast
quantity of baggage that so embarrassed later generals.

" It will be impossible," wrote the Council to a King's
officer, new to the country, and anxious to take the field
with the equipment he would have had in Europe, " when
you march, to carry with you a store for more than ten
or twelve days, and we have no reason to doubt your being
constantly supplied with more from the different countries
you pass. Our armies have hitherto followed this method
and never been at any loss for provisions."

This field-diet, or *batta*, consisted of daily rations—a pound
and a half of beef or mutton, a pound of biscuit or a
pound and a half of rice, and two drams of Batavia arrack
at 40 to the gallon. Clive was for some years allowed
6 fanams—say, 1s. 6d.—daily for each man victualled.
It was a very profitable contract. Orme, and he was in
a position to know, says that Clive made £40,000 out of
it. With his usual generosity he did not keep all his good
fortune for himself. For instance, he gave the garrison
of Fort St David to Charles Saunders; he allowed his

friend, Lieutenant Repington, to provide coolies and bullocks, which were also included in his contract; and he allowed his friend, Captain Dalton, the *batta* on Dalton's own command at Trichinopoly.

" I have put my own command separate," writes the latter, " as you were so good as to allow me the advantages arising from their batta; and the remainder, sick, weak, French prisoners, and French hospital men, I have paid 4 fanams per day, for all of which you must draw the 6 fanams at Fort St David's on your own account. You'll please to draw at the same time for my 205 men, and pay what you were so generous as to give me to Vansittart monthly. It is undoubtedly a very great advantage to me, and I am extremely sensible of your generosity in giving it to me. . . . The men are much better satisfied with the 4 fanams than provisions; the sergeants and corporals only grumble, as they used to have 1 rupee per day. I think if you approve of it to give it 'em and place it to the Nabob's account as extraordinary charges. When I came here the French [prisoners] were all victualled by a Portuguese and almost starved; so I took the whole on your account and gave 'em four fanams. The Nabob desired I would. It is much better for him as it takes off a charge here. . . . I pay your rupees at 12 fanams by which you have a considerable advantage . . ."

In another document Dalton computes the profit on 212 men for 31 days at 909 rupees. The whole business throws a curious light on the customs of the time. One is of course tempted to condemn Clive and his associates off-hand as bad, unprincipled men; but that naïve conclusion means that we are applying to the eighteenth century the ideals of our own time. It is probable that the Nawab was consulted and agreed to the extraordinary charge that Dalton mentions; and apart from that the affair offers no greater example of irregularity than

6

Calcraft's employment of War Office balances. Clive's profits were an open secret. Governor Saunders (no relation, I think, of the Charles Saunders to whom Clive allowed a share) certainly knew all about them; and he acquiesced because he considered that Clive's services merited a considerable reward. The men either got their victuals or an amount which satisfied them; and when, after Clive's departure, the contract rate was reduced from 6 fanams a day to 4, they were, I suspect, no better supplied than they had been, although the contract was held henceforward by a civilian, whose conduct would be subject to a more jealous examination by the officers in the field than Clive's had been.

The matter of the field commissariat offered an unsolved problem until the time of Cornwallis. He established a system of camp bazaars. Three grand bazaars were established in his camp, one behind each wing and one behind head-quarters, with regimental bazaars for each native regiment; and severe regulations were made to ensure the safety of the native merchants supplying them. Any irregularity committed against them, or any attempt to impose upon or plunder those useful people, was punished with severity. Nor were these empty words. A European soldier, for plundering a quantity of ghee, received 200 lashes in front of the right wing, another 200 in front of the left, and then 250 in front of the centre.

The soldier in the field was entitled to two drams of arrack a day; and I gather from the order-books that he drew this not only on campaign, but also in all garrisons which were entitled to half-*batta*. In Madras itself, the men frequented the local arrack-shops, where they could buy liquor cheap but bad. By an order issued in 1765, alluding to recent fatal accidents due to excessive drinking, an officer was required to attend the evening roll-call of each company, and absentees were to be confined and refused fort-liberty for a month or more. According to ideas universally prevalent at that time, a certain amount of alcohol was thought necessary to counteract the ill effects of the bad water that the men drank. But its value as encouraging the spirits of the men was also recognised. Before going into action, they would receive an extra dram and a biscuit; on St George's, St Patrick's, or St Andrew's days, a free allowance of arrack and provisions would be issued; and an extra dram after a satisfactory review. But efforts were also needed to prevent men from saving up their arrack in order to have a grand drunk. Once there was a proposal that the men should either swallow their liquor as issued in the presence of a commissioned officer or that he should see it mixed with at least a pint of water to each dram. A little later they were warned that if they did not drink their drams on the day of issue, the allowance would be stopped altogether. An order of 1790 runs as follows:

" The abominable drunkenness which prevails amongst the European soldiers and of which complaint has been frequently made to the commanding officer, is supposed partly to arise from a traffic carried on amongst themselves of exchanging and selling their drams amongst one another, which is hereby positively prohibited; and commanding officers of European corps are directed to take care that each man shall make use of his own regulated allowance or that it shall not be drawn at all. . . ."

On campaign, when at a distance from the Coast, it was not always possible to maintain the supply of arrack. On such occasions the Commander-in-Chief became absolutely apologetic. " The general," we read in an army order, " wishes he could give the soldiers four drams a day instead of two; but in the present situation of the army he is determined to secure one per day for them as long as possible." And of course, as soon as supplies were replenished, extra drams were issued every third day until the deficiency had been made good.

Training in those days of complicated drill and elaborate manual exercise was a long business. Lawrence and Clive saw to it that their men were well broken to the demands of manœuvre and musketry; but after their time, the discipline of the Madras army certainly fell away, as is shown by the following army order of 1769:

" The non-commissioned officers, both sergeants and corporals, doing the duty of the garrison, having been remarked to go through it in a most slovenly manner, carelessly marching to their post and other small guards, and permitting their men to have their hats on in different ways, particularly in relieving the centinels when scarcely any two men dress together and each has his hat on as he likes and in constant talk with the next to him, all of which is so contrary to orders and discipline; it is the commanding officer of the troops' orders that an officer of each company do acquaint their non-commissioned officers at roll-call this evening that the first of them who relieves guard or centinel otherwise than in a steady and soldier-like manner shall be confined and tryed by a court martial.

" The sergeants and corporals are also to be attentive to place none but the best-looking centinels at the Governour's and Commander-in-chief's. It is expected that any officer, seeing a non-commissioned officer behaving contrary to these orders will immediately confine him."

Matters improved much later on, especially under the government of Sir Archibald Campbell, under whom was introduced a new fire-lock and exercise. In order to secure uniformity of movements in the different units, he established a general drill, attended by select non-commissioned officers and privates from every regiment, so that they could instruct the remainder of their battalions.

THE PARADE AND WEST FACE OF THE FORT SQUARE IN FORT ST GEORGE, 1785.

After F. S. Ward.

84]

But however we look at it, the life of the private soldier must have been a wretched business. His only rational amusement was to get drunk. The only women he could find to live with or marry were sluttish half-castes. His sole exercise and recreation the unending exercise of the parade-ground. The ferocious punishments of the time grew naturally out of its conditions. We do not indeed hear of the gyves, manacles, shackles, bolts, chains, bilboes, whips, etc., of which the provost-marshal was set in charge in 1678; but for the slightest offences the private would be confined to the Conjee House. In the previous century this had been known as the Cock House. It was a military prison in which defaulters were confined on rice and water. It corresponded with the Black Hole of the contemporary English army, and like that was inflicted without sentence of court martial. English writers of the time describe the Black Hole as a place made as dark and dismal as possible, and advise that the straw on which the men lay should be changed twice a week " to prevent the encrease of vermin." The Conjee House was probably no better. But, as it did not cure the soldier of drunkenness, it was decided to make it more rigorous in 1772. A man's pay was stopped during confinement, and the sergeant-major was to provide each man with " weak conjee seasoned with salt "—a quart of this at 9 in the morning, and another at 5 in the afternoon; and men confined there were to attend all recruits' parades.

The commonest crime, after drunkenness, was desertion, as was also the case in the English army. In the early days of the factories, this had been so common and so little regarded that at one time cartels had existed as a matter of course between the Europeans' factories on the Coast for their return without punishment. But what had thus been treated as a venial offence became in the altered conditions of a later time one that encountered the sharpest penalties. Coote thus addresses his army in 1782:

" The commander-in-chief is sorry to have to address the men on the subject of desertion. Their spirit, obedience, and perseverance has been so uniform . . . that he is happy to learn, under the very disagreeable reports of the late desertion in camp, that none but men of worthless, abandoned, and unsoldierly principles have quitted their companions on the day of danger. . . . The commander-in-chief has not the smallest doubt but that officers and men are convinced not only of his readiness but also of his particular desire to attend to and to rectify every real grievance, and that nothing can give him more hearty satisfaction than an opportunity of testifying in the most ample manner to their advantage the very high opinion he has of their merits and gallant services."

And the penalty of desertion was no longer a mere return to the boredom of a familiar garrison, but at least the cat, and often the firing party or the gallows. In 1755 an attempt was made to produce a moral effect by going through all the preliminary ceremonial; but the attempt failed because the secret had leaked out. Care was taken that the next case was more impressive.

" The prisoner, Scott," writes the governor, in the January of the next year, " suffered this morning. He died in a very becoming manner, representing to his brother-soldiers how justly he deserved the punishment he was going to receive, how dreadful the consequences might some time or other be to the nation should this habit of desertion still continue amongst them, and recommended them not to trust to mercy for their first offence as it was for his first desertion he was going to suffer. . . ."

We find ceremonial hangings of deserters taken in arms
—such as the drummer taken at Porto Novo, hanged at
troop-beating the next day but one after the battle in front
of the European corps of infantry; or that other deserter,
found in the fort of Palghaut, who was hanged in the
breach he had helped to defend. Even when death was
not inflicted, few prisoners for this offence were let off
lightly. On two typical occasions, one in 1787 and the
other in 1789, sentences running from 500 to 1,500 lashes
were given; and though on the first occasion a considerable number of these were remitted, on the second the
sentences were carried out in full. Where more than one
prisoner was sentenced to death for desertion, it was not
unusual, by a practice borrowed from England, to allow
the prisoners to throw dice for their lives. On the first
time this was put in practice at Madras, all three prisoners
threw the dice on coming out of morning church, and the
one securing the highest throw was spared. But in such
cases it was more common to execute only the one who
threw lowest. For instance the sentence delivered on
four men in 1773 was " that one of them shall be shott
to death in the usual manner, that they shall throw dice
at the place of execution on a drum-head, and he that
throws the least number at one cast shall be the man to
die." Accordingly three days later all the troops in garrison were ordered to parade on the following morning
at 6 o'clock to witness the execution of the sentence; a
sergeant's party of six men, three from the artillery, and
three from the infantry, parading at the same time for the
execution duty.

Mutiny was not a common crime. Cases occurred; and
then they were encountered either by concessions or by
a drum-head court martial followed by immediate execution. But it is hard to say why they were not common.
There were always a considerable number of men in a state

of sullen discontent. In the records of the Quarter Sessions at Madras may be found within two years three cases of men who committed murder out of boredom. In one case, William Beck deposed that the prisoner said to him that " he was tired of the regiment, and would rob some man or kill some black fellow to be rid of it." That night he and the prisoner went out; passing by some huts, they saw an Indian, who began to shout; on which the prisoner killed him with his bayonet. Another, released from the Conjee House to attend the evening parade, suddenly presented his musket and shot a lascar who was passing by the parade ground; he said he would rather do that than starve in a Conjee House. The third shot two palanquin-boys while on sentry-duty; he was alleged to have said that he would shoot himself or someone else before he came off guard; this was denied at his trial, but he offered no reason why he had fired. All three seem to have been executed.

After this gloomy series of events, it must seem strange that any of the Company's Europeans came to good. Yet in 1787 were resident at Madras no less than nine men who had come out privates in the Company's service. One was engaged in trade; another kept a punch-house; a third kept livery-stables; two more were employed in the arsenal; two had held commissions in the Nawab's service; and two were supporting themselves by keeping schools. Of one of these we know a good deal, because a good deal of his correspondence has survived among the records of the Mayor's Court. He belonged to a family of small farmers settled near Dundee. After two or three whaling voyages, he decided for unknown reasons to join the Company's military service, and he reached Madras sometime before 1760. In 1768 he left the army, and settled down as an agent for supplying officers up country with the articles they needed from the presidency. His position was in many respects unusual. He was well known to many gentlefolks residing in or near Dundee. He corresponded with them on terms, not indeed of equality, but certainly of familiarity. When their relatives or friends came to Madras, they were always recommended to David Young, who would sometimes receive them into his house until they had found suitable quarters for themselves. Nor was this the case only with penniless cadets; well-connected and prosperous folks did not disdain his assistance in such ways; and a retired surgeon of the Company's service undertook to supervise the education of his child. All these and their friends entrusted to him their commissions at Madras.

Another group of his friends consisted of seafaring people—captains of country ships, or mates and pursers of Europe vessels. He conducted the sale of their investments; he kept an eye over their dubious ladies and reputed children; he acted as their universal agent during their lives, and as their executor afterwards; and had correspondents at most places from Calcutta to Canton. Having thus amassed a certain sum of money, he launched in an unlucky moment into a wider trade. He bought a small ship with which to traffic up the coast. She was wrecked, and he bought another; but this second venture was captured by the French. At the same time he lost money in a Madras house which suddenly failed; and these repeated losses devoured the little fortune which he had so industriously accumulated. He had to reopen his shop, to which he added the business of a baker; but I fear he never regained his old prosperity.

But though it ended in failure, this was surely a remarkable career for an ex-soldier of the Company's service. Some who enlisted evidently turned out shrewd, honest, and respectable men. Young, moreover, was inspired by a truly Scotch solicitude for education. He not only urged his relatives at home to send their children to school, but also sent them money to enable them to do so. He writes to the daughter of an old friend, when nearly of an age to return to Madras:

"MADAM, . . . I am happy to see how well you have improved in your writing, and, as I hear, in other branches of learning necessary to compleat a young lady's education; and although it has been attended with a great deal of expence, you will find it better bestowed on that account than in any other way you could have spent it; but by this time I hope you are compleated in any education you can have any use for, and if you do not come out next year, I think you cannot employ your time better than to go into a good family for a few months and give your attention as much as possible to the business of a house-wife. . . . It's not below the character of a fine lady to make any kind of victuals . . .; and, if you come out, bring a book of cookery with you as an assistant, of the best you can get. . . ."

He treated his own child in a similar manner. He paid 300 pagodas for her passage home, and committed her to the care of his surgeon-friend; she was to be as well educated as if she had been his lawful daughter. It throws an interesting light on the position of such children at this time to find that on the voyage home Mrs Mathias Calvert, wife of a captain in the Company's service, " acted the part of a mother by her," and that on her arrival she spent three months in the house of a captain of the Royal Navy, one of Young's many friends.

In himself Young certainly was no extraordinary individual; but he was a douce, respectable body, who attests the existence in the ranks of the Company's military of a merit and intelligence that we could not have taken for granted, and who illustrates the harmonious relations that could exist in the eighteenth century between very different classes of society. This " little light man," as he somewhere describes himself, successively whaler, soldier, and trader, owing much more to character than to brains, belongs to the very type that more than any other has contributed to the building of the empire.

CHAPTER VII

THE CHAPLAIN

THE general character of the English clergy did not run high in the eighteenth century. Fielding has given us living sketches of them at their best and worst; probably for every Parson Adams there was a Parson Trulliber; and the average no doubt was, as we should think nowadays, overmuch concerned with his tithes and glebe. Nor indeed did the character of the chief statesmen who had the disposal of ecclesiastical patronage encourage the better type among them. When Sir Robert gave to Parson Keene a living worth £700 a year to marry his natural daughter, it was small wonder that, the parson being safely inducted and Sir Robert dead, the former should grant himself a dispensation from the wife; nor yet is it surprising that he rose to be a bishop. More than one prebendary would go into residence for " the better part of the year," that is for audit week. And if, as is said to have been the custom, the parson was expected to retire from the table with the ladies, in many cases it would not have been for fear of shocking his ears. There were many worldly priests, and worse, in England; I think they were fewer than might have been expected at Madras.

There were on the Coast two groups of Protestant clergy. One was composed of the Company's chaplains;

the other, of the Danish missionaries. The latter, though
not under the jurisdiction of the Company, had a good
deal to do with the English. Their principal activities
centred at Trichinopoly and Tanjore, where English
troops were regularly in garrison; and for them the missionaries performed marriages, baptisms, and funerals,
which otherwise would have been conducted by an officer,
or dispensed with altogether. They were also eager
educationalists, nursing that perennial fallacy that instruction in Western learning was a sure method for the
destruction of heathendom. At Tranquebar, the head-
quarters of the Danish East India Company, the inhabitants had been required ever since 1725 to send their
children to school to learn to read, write, and cipher; and
there the Danish Mission controlled seventeen schools, at
which the children were made to read the New Testament,
and to learn Christian texts and the catechism by heart.
They set up a press at Tranquebar, where they printed
vernacular tracts and school-books; and gradually their
educational activities spread into the country surrounding
their settlement. Swartz, the most famous of them all,
secured the favour of the Raja of Tanjore, who allowed
him to build churches and schools in his little dominions.
The English East India Company also favoured them
when it could be done without expense to themselves,
allowing their founts of type to be sent out freight-free,
and permitting the Council at Madras to encash the
missionaries' bills of exchange. After the restoration of
Madras by the French, the relations between the English
and the Danish missionaries became still closer. The
Capuchins ever since the foundation of the place had had
a church in the Fort itself; but they were thought—indeed
unjustly—to have given information to the enemy; and
when the English returned to Madras they pulled down
the Capuchins' church, and obliged all Roman Catholics

who had houses in the Fort to sell them. The Danish missionaries seem to have been quick to perceive the advantage that might be made out of the position. When it was known that Madras was to be restored, but before the rendition had actually taken place, two of them had addressed a petition to the Council, lamenting the way in which the Capuchins had perverted children at Madras from the Protestant faith, declaring that the capture of Madras had been a judgment of heaven for favouring the Roman Catholics, and asking that St Andrew's Church should be taken from the Capuchins and given to them. By way of demonstrating how sectarianism blunts the moral senses, they concluded by urging that if the priests made large offers to procure the restoration of their church, the best way would be to accept their money and then turn them out. The names of the true Christians who signed this letter were Fabricius and Breithaupt. St Andrew's was pulled down; but the Danish missionaries were given another church which the Roman Catholics had in the suburb of Vepery; and from that time onwards we find them permanently established at Madras. Indeed one of them, Fabricius, solemnised Clive's marriage, probably in the house of the bride's brother, Captain Maskelyne, near the Vepery church. Another of these Danish missionaries was Kiernander, well known on the Coast at Fort St David and Madras. On occasion he served as interpreter to the English forces in the field; and at one time he owned a large house in Cuddalore. At a later time he went up to Calcutta, where, on his wife's death, he obliterated his sorrows " in the silken embraces of opulent beauty."

Swartz was undoubtedly the best of the bunch. He devoted himself principally to the cause of education, opening and superintending numerous schools in the Tanjore country and Ramnad. The Madras Council

made him a small allowance for ministering to the garrison at Trichinopoly, and Hudson's letter which I have
already quoted suggests that over some at least he exer-
cised a considerable influence. He was employed more
than once on political missions. Sir Thomas Rumbold
sent him to Hyder; and Lord Macartney wished to employ
him as interpreter with the envoys whom he sent to Tipu
Sultan. He had a wide knowledge of the languages of
southern India and an intimate acquaintance with the
people themselves. Eminent in another way was the
physican Koenig, who came out to the Tranquebar mission
in 1768, and founded the Society of United Brothers
for the Study of Indian Botany. Another of them is
described in Bruce's diary:

" Came on board . . . a German missionary who was
going out to India to convert the infidels. . . . Mr
Lindsay and I soon became a little acquainted with this
foreigner, as we could talk Latin, a language he well
understood, but could not speak English with any sort
of propriety, nay, not even intelligibly. He seemed to
possess a large stock of good nature and commonsense,
but no uncommon one of erudition. He is good enough,
however, and learned enough too, I think, for the glorious
ends he has in view . . ."

A little later in the voyage he attempted to read prayers
one Sunday on the quarter-deck, but " with an accent not
altogether agreeable even to a Scottish ear."

The Company's chaplains continued on the same footing
as earlier in the century. Like the officer, they tend to
reflect the changed spirit of the age; that is, they incline
to seek wealth rather by professional means than by the
old universal way of trade. But that change was only
gradual. The Rev Mr Palk, for instance, went out to
India chaplain on the *Namur* with Boscawen; he then

secured appointment as one of the Company's chaplains; he took part in Clive's victualling contract; he was employed as paymaster and commissary of the troops; he was sent on political missions to Tanjore, Sadras, and Pondicherry; and at last was ordered by the Company to revert to his post as chaplain. Two years later, he went home, with a reasonable fortune, obtained by trade and presents, and in 1760 was announced as the next governor of Madras—a post which he filled from 1763 to 1767; and during that time he cast over the place something of the shadow of his black gown. That, however, signified dullness rather than virtue. Finally he bought a baronetcy and a mansion in Devonshire.

This secular-minded cleric seems to have set the model in all but opportunities for his successors. As the Council said, it was not easy to find good men on a salary which barely allowed a chaplain to live; and I do not think anyone accepted the Company's £100 a year for love of apostolic poverty. In that age it was out of fashion. Instead we have Parson Salmon, a namesake and perhaps a relative of the runaway officer. He was encouraged in his duties by receiving the appointment of secretary to a new board—the Board of Police, set up in 1770—to supplement his salary; but this was not enough for him. He resigned, went to Bengal, got Warren Hastings to introduce him to the Nawab of the Carnatic, and last appears in Madras as manager of a gun-factory for the Nawab at Tanjore. By him may be set the Rev St John Browne, who shortly after his arrival was punishing his servants for some misdemeanour when one of them fell, in trying to escape his blows, from a terrace some twenty feet high. The wretched man was left lying there all night, and died two days later. The most charitable supposition is that the chaplain was drunk.

Another ecclesiastical oddity was Dr Christopher Wells,

who describes himself in his will as rector of Leigh in Worcestershire, chaplain to Earl Harcourt, one of His Majesty's chaplains in the Royal Navy, and chaplain of the army in the service of the Honourable the East India Company. He died in 1792, and among other bequests he left £200 to Caroline, daughter of Margaret Rosser, otherwise called Morton, born at Hampstead on 2 May, 1788—by an odd coincidence the year in which he left England. The girl was to take the name of Wellville, and the interest was to be laid out on her until she was 21, when she was to receive the principal. All this may have been perfectly innocent, but it plainly opens a wide door for speculation.

As the Company refused to listen to the Council's requests for the sanction of higher pay, the Council set itself to find other devices to secure the same effect. It took to appointing the chaplains to charges at one of the out-stations or to one of the Company's regiments, without expecting them to discharge these additional duties. It also transferred the duties (and profits) of the undertaker, till 1784 performed by a civil servant, to the junior chaplain. With their efforts the chaplains heartily co-operated by applying their ingenuity to the matter of fees, and these had finally to be regulated by the vestry, lest the poorer sort of people be unable to afford to be married, christened, or buried. The chaplains then thought of another expedient. They suggested separate fees should be charged for registering baptisms, marriages, and burials; and these too were regulated by the vestry.

The fee for burials was fixed at 10 pagodas for the better sort, and 5 for others; with another fee of twice as much if a monument was erected over the grave. " In burials," the vestry resolved, " the rule shall be governed by this distinction: those who use the best pall shall be considered in the first class, those who do not use the best pall shall be allotted to the second class." But the church kept not only a best and second-best pall for these uses, but also a mourning palanquin, for which a fee was charged. In the account of the estate of Charles and Eliza Bromley, the following items appear, relating, I think, to the latter's funeral:

To one coffin covered with Europe black cloth . .	22 pagodas	
To 19 scarves and hat-bands .	19 „	
To the use of the mourning palankeen and boys . .	3 „	12 fanams

The most singular of the funeral customs prevalent at Madras was that described and abolished in the following general order of 26 June, 1803:

" The commander-in-chief has recently learnt with much surprise that the sword and sash of a deceased officer, which by military usage are carried in the funeral procession, have been claimed as a perquisite by the staff officer of a garrison, and that this claim has been asserted as a right derived from ancient custom long practised in all, and still continued in some of the garrisons and military stations under the presidency of Fort St George.

" That the arms of an officer, the symbols of his honour, the most flattering memorial of affectionate esteem which a dying soldier can bequeath to a surviving friend, should be thus indecently claimed, cannot but excite a sentiment of indignation in the minds of military men.

" Without investigating the origins of this pretended right, or tracing the antiquity of a custom which no extent of precedent can stamp with the character of propriety, the commander-in-chief forbids the continuance of this disgraceful practice in any garrison, cantonment, or military station under the presidency of Fort St George. He publishes to the army that no claim of right exists in any officer or soldier officiating at a military funeral to the arms of the deceased, and directs this order to be inserted in the standing orders of every garrison, cantonment, and military station, under the presidency of Fort St George."

Most of the funerals at Madras were military; and in some few years these were very numerous, averaging two a day. The difficulty of a military funeral was to ensure a sober funeral party. A garrison-order of 17 August, 1770, enjoins the sergeant-major of the Madras Europeans to inspect every funeral party on parade and carefully to exclude any man at all disguised in liquor, " as the soldiers have frequently been guilty not only of drunkenness but swearing and other shameful indecencies," such as a failure of due respect to the reverend clergyman (this would be Padre Salmon) who officiates. Three notable funerals took place, in each of which the corpse was buried within the walls of St Mary's church in the Fort, in spite of such a practice having been expressly forbidden in the documents authorising its consecration. The first of these was that of Lord Pigot, who, having been imprisoned by a section of the Council, died while still in custody on 10 May, 1777, and was buried on the evening of the following day. The account quoted below was written by David Young, who followed the coffin from the Governor's garden-house. The procession set out at 6 o'clock in the evening, and though it had scarcely a mile to go it did not reach the church till 8.

" The procession was far from splendid, but very decent; he was carried by soldiers in a pallanqueen till we came near the gate [i.e. of the Fort], and then he was carried to the church on their heads. There was the greatest concourse of black people at the Garden House, and from that to the fort, as ever I seed, but a party of soldiers without the gate prevented them from giving us any . . . trouble; it was impossible for us to march in any order from the Garden House to the Fort, and made it so very disagreeable that most of the gentlemen got into their pallaqueens and went over the river to the southward of the bridge; so that by the time we got to the Fort, we was very thin. . . . I was told that Mr Stratton offered to order two battalions of Seapoys to attend the funeral, but that Mr Monckton refused any assistance, which I think was very imprudent, as the procession would have been very splendid had they accepted of them, and the whole of the council would have attended, and all the officers present, as well as ladies. The invitation chit [letter] was so worded that none attended who could be supposed to give the least disgust. Only ten ladies met the corpse at Mr Stone's and came to church, including the two daughters. The corpse is interred in the church before the alter. . . . The Commodore began to fire minute guns at one and continued till about half-past 3, and the Fort fired minute-guns for every year of his age, and began when the corpse was taken out of the Garden House."

The next burial in the Fort church was that of Sir Eyre Coote. The old general had been unable to endure the anxiety of watching a French cruiser chasing the *Resolution*, armed vessel of the East India Company, Captain Wemyss commander, on which he was returning to Madras. He was seized with an apoplexy, and was brought ashore only to die. On 28 April, 1783, he was carried with all military honours from his house in the Fort to the church; but I think no detailed description of his funeral survives. Men were perhaps too busy with greater things to count the minute-guns or enumerate the pall-bearers; moreover Coote was not to lie permanently in Fort St George. On 6 February following sailed from Madras the *Belmont*, Captain Gamage, with Lady Coote on board and also the body of her late husband which had been dug up and placed in a lead coffin. On arrival in England, it was reburied at Rockbourne, near the estate of West Park, which Coote had bought in 1762, out of the profits of the Seven Years War.

The next interment in the church was that of Major-General Sir John Burgoyne, baronet, colonel of His Majesty's 23rd Regiment of Light Dragoons, who, like Coote, died worn out by disputes with the civil Government. Over him one need not linger, but there is another monument on which, in the abominable funerary taste of the age, Britannia, seated on a lion, crowns with laurel a Company's officer of humble origin and great desert. This was Joseph Moorhouse. Born of yeoman stock from Cumberland about 1744, he joined the Company's artillery, it is said as a matross; he received his first commission in 1768, and in the year of his death rose to the rank of lieutenant-colonel. On 7 March, 1791, he was killed at the siege of Bangalore. For twenty-four years he had served with such spirit, zeal, and ability that the Council sought the permission of the ministers and churchwardens to bury his remains in St Mary's. Some six months later, when the body had been brought down in safety to Madras, the actual ceremony took place. Moorhouse had been a Mason; and on arrival his body was deposited in the Freemasons' Hall, on the site of the present Scotch church. There all the settlement assembled. The chief mourners were the governor, his councillors, and the Commander-in-Chief; and six field-officers carried the pall. The escort consisted of 300 men; and, as the procession entered on the glacis of the Fort, the slow ceremonial march was accompanied by the minute-guns from the saluting battery. I suppose that to anyone who had witnessed a public funeral in London, the thing would have seemed rather a poor imitation; but I have paused over it for the sake of its significance. Our empire east and west was brought into existence by extraordinary men, by men possessed of an instinctive insight approaching

genius.   But their success depended upon being backed
by men like Moorhouse on whom they could rely.   Had
our people at Madras been like Benfield or Whitehill,
greedy schemers, had even many of them been so, not
the genius of Clive or Hastings or Wellesley could have
set up or maintained a stable dominion.   Because a man
went out to India to make a fortune, and because he
employed methods which we regard as improper, that does
not mean that he would resort to any kind of robbery
and peculation.   Most of the Nabobs of Madras more
nearly resembled Moorhouse than Benfield.   And again
Moorhouse seems to illustrate the great value of our
overseas possessions in affording a wider scope than could
be found at home for men of humble rank.   Moorhouse,
had he remained in England, would no more have commanded a regiment of artillery than Clive in like case
would have died a lord.

The trite symbolism of his monument does him less than
justice.   Indeed nabobs' taste, ill in many things, was at
its worst in tombstones.   They were usually pretentious,
unenduring, brick-and-plaster affairs.   Few things are
more lamentable than the older English cemeteries in
India.   You are surrounded on every side by fantastic
obelisks and eccentric masses of masonry, crowded together
in a little space, and deeply seamed by the short century
or so that has passed over them.   A tombstone should be
either very unpretentious or so durable that time at last
may invest its vanity with pathos; but our Indian tombs
were seldom one or the other.   In this we contrast to
our own great disadvantage with the Dutch, whose mas-
sive stones, with their deep-carved coats of arms and
finely wrought lettering, are still as fresh and clean as
when they were first laid down in that swift-rotting Indian
soil.   Compared with them, our monuments are poor.
Yet we desired to commemorate ourselves—witness John

Douglas, " formerly of London citizen and fishmonger, but now by a train of unfortunate incidents of Fort St George in the East Indies free merchant," who desired that a strong arch should be turned over his grave, and " thereon laid one of the best and largest tombstones procurable." Or again take this passage from the will of John Powney:

" I will that my body be interred in the burying ground of St Mary's church, near my three children that lye buried there, and that a vault be built, and their coffins be put in with mine; let the vault be made large, and a large tombstone be put over me, and a monument of iron-stone be put over the vault 30 foot high, which I reckon will cost about 700 pagodas . . ."

Powney's intention, not to spare money, was respected, for his monument still stands on the glacis of Fort St George, marking the region where the first inhabitants were laid to rest. But most heirs, executors, and assigns were more economical of the estate and careless of the memory of the departed.

The congregation of St Mary's was organised like an English parish, with a vestry which annually chose the people's churchwarden and sidesmen, and received the accounts of the year. This vestry seems to have constituted itself automatically, very much as we find representative institutions and trial by jury establishing themselves wherever possible in the early colonial world. The early emigrants were as tenacious of their ecclesiastical as of their political birthrights. For a good deal more than a century the Madras vestry met and transacted business, controlled considerable funds, and conducted schools, although at last, when the matter was brought to the test of law, the vestry proved to have no legal existence. But that did not happen until 1805, and all through the eighteenth century it was acting vigorously and well. The funds which it controlled were derived in the usual way from collections, fines, and bequests. Monuments still survive to at least two persons who bequeathed their estates to the church of St Mary's; and many more must have given legacies. Others appointed the ministers and churchwardens guardians of their children, and large amounts were normally in custody under the head of the Orphans' Stock. This practice fell into disuse in the later part of the century, when testators seemed to prefer confiding their children to private hands; but the activity of the vestry in other directions continued unchanged. Under the impulsion of particularly zealous chaplains, Lewis and Stevenson, a charity school was opened in 1715. This, however, was not the first school at Madras. In the previous century the Company had appointed a schoolmaster, on a salary of £50 a year, " now that you have so many married families and children increase." This first schoolmaster was mainly occupied with the management of the land-customs, and presently applied for relief from his educational duties, " inasmuch as he says he has a large family, lives out of town, and teaching the children is much prejudicial to his health." After him the post seems to have been filled by time-expired soldiers on a reduced salary; and at last the vestry resolved to establish a charity school, at which provision should be made at first to receive thirty poor Protestant children, diet and education gratis. The Council approved of the scheme, and persuaded the Company to bestow a site and building for its accommodation. To manage this new institution was appointed John Mitchel, who had come out a private on the last year's ships with the story that he was a priest in Holy Orders and had served as chaplain aboard a man-of-war, but had been obliged to leave England for debt contracted by being bound for his brother. He had the impudence to solemnise his own marriage with the daughter of the commandant, Captain William How. He had also in that brief space been " guilty of many irregularities and scandalous actions, altogether unbecoming the profession he pretends to." But " as he has appeared under the notion of a clergyman, and been entertained as school-master, it will not be proper to expose him to public punishment in the eyes of the natives "; it was decided to require him to find sureties for his future good behaviour, or in default to be kept in confinement till he could be sent home.

Mitchel's successors were more reputable than he; but the place itself outgrew the means of the St Mary's stock; and in 1787 emerged a new scheme on a wider basis. Lady Campbell, wife of the governor, Sir Archibald, was much moved by the wretched condition of the soldiers' orphans, and set on foot a project for establishing an asylum for their reception. A private subscription was raised; 30,000 pagodas were thus provided, and the Nawab of Arcot presented a large house and compound. With this it was determined to open a home at which 50 girls could be received and educated; and, as this would relieve the church stock of the girls in the charity school, it was suggested that the vestry might open a similar home for boys. The Company was induced to declare its sympathy with and approval of the scheme; and, later on, when additional funds were manifestly required, it sanctioned an annual subvention from its funds, protesting the while that the scheme it had approved was one which promised to be maintained by voluntary contributions. Thus came into existence the Male and Female Orphan Asylums, which with many changes have survived to our own times.

The eighteenth century thus both began and ended with considerable charitable enterprises. Indeed I think the

nabobs of Madras were as charitable as their simpler
predecessors. But in the general religious outlook, in
the size of congregations, in love of sermons, there was
a great alteration. The earlier inhabitants had been exclusively merchants, but very religious merchants. It was
shown even in their mercantile transactions. Take a bill
of lading, which preserved in its traditional formulas the
ancient unity of religion and the daily life. It would
begin, " Shipped by the grace of God in good order and
well-conditioned by Nicholas Morse in and upon the good
ship called the *Morning Star* whereof is master under God
for this present voyage Captain George Heron, now riding
at anchor in the roads of Madras, and of God's grace
bound for Mocha and the Red Sea . . ." They would
attend the daily reading of prayers in the factory chapel,
in which would hang the printed directions of the Company
for the Christian and sober deportment of all its servants.
Swearing, drunkenness, and duelling were punishable by
fine for the use of the poor. On Sundays the Council
would attend the governor and accompany him solemnly
to church. In all this great relaxation took place as the
size of the settlement increased. In 1754 the Company
could still order the governor and Council and all their
servants, civil and military, to attend church every
Sunday, unless they were sick; and enjoin the governor
and Council to attend to the morals and way of life of all
under them; but it was no longer possible to enforce these
provisions. The authorities tended more and more to
overlook a young man's getting drunk overnight, but to
reprove him for neglecting his work next morning.
Government was becoming increasingly secular. So far
as actual vice went, there was probably small change. In
the old days and in the new, chaplains would inveigh
against the enormities of their flock; in 1676 Mr Patrick
Warner would write to the Company of the swearing

and profanation of the name of God, of writers so sinful in their drunkenness as to play at cards or dice for wine, and of the party that drank 36 bottles at one sitting; just as in 1807 Dr Richard Kerr could draw the most dismal picture of the morals of the age. But we must beware of such professional diatribes. The governor and Council thought there was but little luxury and that even moderate play constituted but a small part of the amusements of the place. No doubt a smaller number of people went to church. Instead of that they took to spending their week-ends at their garden-houses, and just at the close of the century a small settlement was springing up on the banks of the Red Hills Lake, some 10 miles out of Madras. Here many used to spend their sabbaths boating, feasting, and card-playing. Charles Darke had a house there in 1787; and Benjamin Roebuck, who had an indigo farm there, may have built a house in that neighbourhood. A cadet, brought up in an Evangelical household, was horrified at this profanation of the sabbath. What had really happened was that Madras had felt the influence of the indifferentism which had sprung up in the eighteenth century, but had not yet come within the sweep of the Evangelical movement. That was to come in due time; and in the early nineteenth century was to produce wonderful schisms in society. But in those days you could hardly live on the other side of the world and keep yourself quite abreast of contemporary fashions in thought and religion.

CHAPTER VIII

THE SURGEON

IN view of the crowded graveyards of Madras, the reputation of the place for healthiness seems almost inexplicable. " Asiaticus " describes it as " the Montpellier of the East." " The inhabitants," says Lockyer, " enjoy as perfect health as they could do in England, which is plainly discovered in their ruddy complexions." Francis Jourdan writes in 1767 to a bereaved father:

" After having been thus unfortunate in the loss of two most amiable youths, I scarcely know in what terms to recommend your permitting another to try his fortune with us. The country is as healthy as most parts of England, our settlements in particular, and the prospects of acquiring a fortune by industry much greater than there . . ."

An officer reassures a friend at home that he keeps perfectly good health, that people monstrously exaggerate the dangers of the Indian climate, that the heat of course is great, " but refrain from excess of drinking and you'll weather it very well." Robert Orme complains that " my constitution . . . is now loaded with infirmities even in this, the best of climates." There are two explanations which may go some way towards accounting for these astonishing statements. Just as savages so seldom witness

any but a violent death that they are said to regard man
as naturally immortal, so in India obvious imprudence
or accident cut short so many lives that the toll exacted
by the climate passed unnoticed; and further, Madras
was certainly much less unhealthy than most places frequented by Englishmen in the East, so that it appeared
healthy by force of contrast. Thus Masulipatam, set in
the midst of its swamps, was notoriously pestilential.
" This is so sickly a place," we read, " that it is very rare
to have all of us well at a time." Or again, " The
council taking into consideration the unhealthfulness of
the place and the uncertainty of man's frale life and duration in this world, doe order that those . . . who are in
perfect health doe negotiate and carry on the business for
those that are indisposed." Calcutta, particularly in the
damp, hot season, was as mortal a place as a man could
choose to live in. Of Bombay, it should be called the
unfortunate island; wounds will not heal there; not one
English child in twenty lives; " I reckon they walk but in
charnel houses, the climate being extremely unhealthy."
Worse still were the settlements to the eastward. It never
was easy to recruit men for the Company's factories on
Sumatra; and as for Batavia, the phlegmatic Dutch on
learning of a neighbour's death, would merely say, " Well,
he owed me nothing," or " I must get my money from his
executors."

Compared with these, Madras possessed a healthy
climate. But it was only by comparison. Middle-aged
arrivals were almost certain to die within the year. " Experience," wrote the Fort William Council, " teaches us
to verify this general observation, that men's lives, advanced to or nigh the age of 40, are very precarious in
such a change of climate." Benjamin Robins, a distinguished engineer, was sent out to remodel the Company's fortresses in India, and died a year after his

arrival; Colonel Caroline Scott was then appointed for the same purpose, and died within nine months; William Cockell, appointed Deputy Governor of Fort St David, enjoyed his office for three months; Miss Katherine Read, a painter of sufficient eminence to have received an inaccurate notice in the *Dictionary of National Biography*, came out to Madras to practise her art and died within the twelvemonth, on her way to the Cape where she had hoped to recover her health; Major Kinneer, appointed second in command under Stringer Lawrence, died in the same year as he arrived; and "the old cock" himself, as his subordinates affectionately called Lawrence, almost alone among those who reached India in middle life, survived to a green old age.

Nor was it only the middle-aged whom the climate threatened. All new arrivals were likely to suffer from it. No newly arrived regiment could be reckoned at its full strength. The men of the 39th a few weeks after landing "daily sicken and die." "The Europeans in our garrison," writes the commandant of Arcot, "being chiefly the last year's recruit, suffer greatly this sickly season by fevers and fluxes; above one-third part of them being in the hospital. . . ." Unfortunately no exact figures are available except for very small bodies of men, so that it is not possible to estimate the average mortality of Madras. But I find that of the 30 ensigns who received their commissions in 1775, only 16 survived to become lieutenants in 1780, although their only campaign was the siege of Pondicherry which fell without assault; but of those 16 no less than 12 survived the severe Mysore War to become captains in 1786. The inference suggested by these figures is strengthened by the muster-rolls of the two companies serving at St David's in 1742. Of the 136 Europeans contained in them, 34 had served for 5 years or less, 51 from 5 to 10 years, 23 from 15 to 20, and 28,

or over one-fifth of the whole, for upwards of 20 years.
I fancy, then, that if you could live long enough to get
acclimatised, " salted " as the local phrase went, you had
a good chance, short of an epidemic or an unlucky duel,
of ripening into one of those red-faced, hard-bitten old
fellows who seemed to thrive on arrack and malaria, and
who welcomed ashore and helped to bury generation after
generation of new-comers.

We may take it, then, that of a hundred men arriving
in Madras in any one year, half would probably be dead
in five years' time—at Batavia they reckoned half would
die within the year—but that some twenty would still be
living many years afterwards. The reasons of a mortality
so much greater than what is experienced at Madras to-day
are many. In the eighteenth century there was no easy
escape into a cooler, healthier climate. The hills had
not yet been discovered; and, when the Nilghiris were
first explored, in the 'twenties of the last century, men
could hardly credit the existence of their " sweet half-
English air " so close to the torrid atmosphere of the
surrounding plains. The only escape from the climate
of Madras, in the older days, short of going home, was
to take a voyage to China on the east or to the Cape
on the west. And worse than this, people consistently
overate and overdrank. Nor was medical science suffi-
ciently advanced to detect the evils of so doing, or to
cope with the resultant sickness. The principal memorial
of most of the Madras surgeons must be the monuments
of their patients.

In those days the social position of the surgeon was still
insecure. He had hardly shaken off his former association with the barber, and at the beginning of the century
could still advertise his tariff for visits and medicine. In
India were to be found many exercising the profession
without even the knowledge that prevailed in Europe.

The Venetian Manucci is the classical example; and so late as 1719 he was still to be found at Madras, suing a "Moorman" for medicines supplied and winnings at backgammon. But he was far from being alone. There was, for example, the French private, Voulton, who ran away from Pondicherry, reached Golconda, then Delhi; and took service as physician first with the wazir and then with the Great Moghul himself. Nearer home was "Raphey the doctor," who was accused of absconding with his employer's pearls. In 1787 was still living in Madras Charles Loyd, a Hanoverian Jew, who deserted to us the last war with Hyder, who had employed him as a doctor. The Madras Council itself recruited persons of most doubtful antecedents. In 1688 they discharge a private on condition of his paying the cost of bringing him out, as he has had several successes with his practice and there is great occasion for surgeons in these sickly times. Half a century and more later a recruit is released on similar terms and sent aboard the *Bombay Castle* as surgeon's mate. Another private soldier is reported to have made several cures, and later appears in Bengal undergoing an examination of his medical knowledge. Even those who had studied medicine without success were welcome. In 1772 Surgeon Pasley picks out a cadet who had been bred to surgery, and packs him off with a detachment to Trichinopoly. Ensign Ferrier, with a detachment of Madras troops in Sumatra, takes medical charge of them as well, and, on his return to the presidency, turns surgeon.

The reverse process was equally easy to the men of that age. Surgeon Edward Bulkeley becomes justice of the peace, then land customer, and lastly paymaster. Mr Kellett, surgeon to the King's regiment at Cuddalore in 1756, deals in arrack. But like the officer, the surgeon improved out of all knowledge in the second half of the

century; and when he is guilty of misconduct, it was professional misconduct rather than the picturesque mistreatment of the earlier age. In 1693 a councillor died under
the treatment of Mr Samuel Browne, because the latter's
servant " negligently powdered pearl in a stone mortar
wherein arsenic had been before beaten, the mixture
whereof with the pearl is supposed to be the occasion of
his death "; and in 1748 the English doctor, sent to attend
on a local chief, " clapped a kind of poultice to my legs;
this was so hot that the gold ring on my finger turned
white, and it . . . made my tongue sore; it was great
difficulty to me to drink water." Instead of such things,
nineteen covenanted servants complain of the conduct of
Dr Andrew Munro, and particularly, when one of them
wanted a powder to cure him of scurvy in the teeth, of
his writing to his mate, " Sir, pray give that impudence
what he wants and let me not be plagued with his nonsense." In the following year the same surgeon sued
a covenanted servant in the Mayor's Court, setting forth
in his bill of complaint that he had attended the man's
wife for ten or twelve months, had expended on her £30
worth of medicines, and had frequently visited her at
the defendant's request, but when the latter departed to
Fort St David he forgot entirely " to gratify or consider
your Orator for his trouble." He therefore prayed for
a decree of 55 pagodas for his attendance and 45 for
his medicines. The defendant's rejoinder averred that
his wife had not had more than three doses and six or
seven visits. The court desired three surgeons to assess
the value of the medicines, which were described as six
or seven phials of " Hysterick drafts, two boxes of ditto
pills, and three phials of ditto mixture," alleged to contain " cordial waters and juleps, tincture of castor, spirit
of lavender, hartshorne, etc." The assessors put the medicines at 20 pagodas, and attendance for a month at 30

8

pagodas, and Munro got a decree for 51 pagodas and costs. So far as I know, this is the only case which throws any light on the cost of medical attendance at Madras. As Munro's plaint shows, there were no established fees, but each " gratified or considered " the doctor for his trouble according to his means; but of course the Company's civil and military officers were entitled to free medical attention.

The later generation of Madras surgeons was largely recruited from ships' surgeons arriving on the coast or from those attached to royal regiments, and normally were full-trained men, sporting the professional cane with as much dignity as in London. Dr John Sprat, who died at Madras about 1780, left four of these emblems of his quality, three gold-headed, one silver-gilt, for which his four nephews were to draw lots, " on account of the one that is silver-gilt." James Wilson had served for upwards of fourteen years on the Company's ships before he was appointed to the Coast establishment. Mr Gilbert Pasley came out surgeon's assistant with Adlercron's; he then passed on to the *Chesterfield* as surgeon there; in 1756 employment was found for him ashore, and in 1761 he was appointed surgeon at Madras. He was, I think, the best doctor of his time; certainly no other is mentioned with so much affection and respect. He occupied a house in the Fort belonging to the Nawab. If he could do nothing for you, all you could do was to try a change of air. The inscription on his tomb calls him " the common friend of mankind," and this description is corroborated by the many testimonies from all sorts of men in the Madras will-books. James Chambers, mariner, leaves him a silver bowl and a Patna hookah, " which is all I have worthy his acceptance." Samuel Ardley, covenanted servant and member of Council, leaves him a silver cup and epergne, along with the silver washing-basin and its ewer which were brought along instead of the modern finger-bowl at meal-times. John Ross, free merchant, leaves him a diamond ring worth 350 pagodas. James Cam, lieutenant in the Honourable Company's service, appoints him his sole executor. James Richardson of Vizagapatam describes him as his patron and bequeaths to him 50 pagodas. Lord Pigot acknowledges his services in a legacy of £500. And William Richardson leaves him the diamond ring left to the testator by a common friend. One of David Young's letters throws a clear light on the relations between the doctor and his patients. Young had suggested that the executors of a dead friend should give some memento to Pasley, who had attended him in his last illness; they were Calcutta people, and had inquired the reason for so doing. Young replies, "All I meant was that as Mr Pasley had taken a great deal of pains with Mr Hearn, I thought his executors could not do less than acknowledge it, which I knew would please him, as he never accepts anything for his trouble unless it is a trifling acknowledgment" such as a few potatoes from Bengal. In 1780 Pasley's services were recognised by being made the Surgeon-General of the presidency. But his work was done. Only three months later he wrote:

"I was called in the year 1761 from the army to reside at the presidency. Since that time I have not had a single day I chose to call my own. My hands have never been otherwise than full of business, but my health kept uniformly good, and no employment was a trouble to me. In the month of August last by means of fatigue, anxiety of mind, and other professional circumstances, my health became so much impaired that ever since it has been with the greatest difficulty that I have been able to attend the duties of my station. . . . I wish, with the permission of the Honourable Board, for the sake of leisure and change of situation, to avail myself of the cruize one of His

Majesty's ships is to make in the course of two or three days to the southward. . . ."

But he thus secured short respite. He died on 23 September of the next year, at the age of 48. David Young writes just afterwards: " We have all lost a most worthy and useful gentleman in Mr Pasley. Perhaps this settlement will never be able to boast of such another of his profession, nor need his memory be afraid of being outdone by any other."

Pasley's friend and successor, James Anderson, benefited by that reorganisation of the medical department which Pasley just missed. In 1786 he became Physician-General, Director of the Hospital, and member of the Hospital Board, on a pay of £2,500 a year. He was one of those numerous doctors by whom the natural sciences have been greatly advanced. His botanical garden is still remembered at Madras, and was maintained by his son-in-law, Dr Berry. About this time the doctors were almost the only persons of any scientific knowledge, and were much employed in what was so close to the heart of the directors, the economic development of the country. William Roxborough and Benjamin Heyne, employed as Company's botanists, were both surgeons by profession; and so was Patrick Russell, who, after some twenty years spent as physician to the English factory at Aleppo, came out to Madras in 1781 and devoted his leisure to zoology, publishing an *Account of Indian Serpents collected on the Coast of Coromandel*.

Another Madras surgeon worth mention is the singularly named Tysoe Saul Hancock. After serving for some years on the Coast, he was brought down to the presidency as surgeon in 1758, and in the next year at Clive's special request sent to Bengal. There he became the subject of a correspondence between Clive and Warren

Hastings, which illustrates the way in which surgeons were chosen for the subordinate factories in early days. Hastings informs Clive that he means to appoint Dr Alves, "by unanimous agreement of the gentlemen here," as surgeon at the Kasimbazar factory; and, when Clive indignantly condemns this proposal as an attempt to usurp the rights of the Council at Calcutta, and proposes Hancock, Hastings replies:

"You certainly have been misinformed with respect to the custom always practised in the appointment of the surgeon in this factory, which office has ever been the sole gift of the chief and council here, and I cannot but think it reasonable that every community should have the disposal of a trust in which their lives are so nearly concerned. This, I do assure you, has ever been the custom, and, though the board has an undoubted right to break through it, yet it will afford a precedent that may some time or other prove of very cruel consequence to the subordinate factories, though not in this instance, as I am not unacquainted with Mr Hancock's character and have heard him spoken of as one of the most capable of his profession in India . . ."

Not until the end of the eighteenth century did regimental doctors in the King's service receive military rank, as captains; but they were given commissions at a much earlier date; and though some time elapsed before they secured it, an equal privilege was the natural ambition of the Company's surgeons. The sort of reason which gave urgency to their demands is illustrated by the proceedings of the court martial in 1772 on Lieutenant-Colonel Ross Lang of the Company's service. He was found to have treated Mr James Potters, surgeon, with disrespect, in threatening to bamboo and horsewhip him, calling him besides a dirty lying rascal. Such language might of course be used of anybody; but had surgeons borne military rank, Mr Potters could not have been refused the pleasure of trying to shoot the colonel, whereas the only satisfaction he received was the lukewarm censure passed by the court on the latter's conduct.

This incident took place at Trichinopoly; and was not unconnected with a letter which Surgeon Thomas Davis addressed from that place to the Governor and council on 25 May, 1773:

". . . My character, both in readiness to oblige and to obey as well as in a strict attention to the many hospitals which have been put under my care, I flatter myself, will on enquiry be found rather favourable; and, if so, I am led to believe the Honourable Board will adopt some method of relieving me from the terrors of a court martial in future upon any private disagreement with a commanding officer. May I beg leave to observe that all His Majesty's surgeons have commissions which put them beyond the reach of private resentment. For want of such commissions it is generally said here that the Honourable Company's surgeons may be brought to a court martial, nay, to the halberts, the same as a private sentinel or follower of the army. . . . I hope that you will coincide with me in opinion that the bare idea of such a disgrace is rather affecting, and inconsistent with the character of a physician; and if so, I flatter myself, the honourable President and council will take into consideration the case of the surgeons as they stand at present in the eyes of their military . . ."

In spite of this representation, however, surgeons did not obtain military rank until the reorganisation of 1786, when a much wider range of promotion was opened to them, the Physician-General receiving £2,500 a year, the Chief Surgeon £2,000, and head surgeons of hospitals £1,500 or £1,000, while regimental surgeons ranked and drew pay as captains, hospital mates as lieutenants, and regimental mates as ensigns. Moreover it was specially ordered that whenever a surgeon was put in arrest, his case should be reported at once to the Hospital Board, to which was entrusted the general management of the department.

The number of surgeons had necessarily expanded with the size of the army. At one time the men had been scandalously short of medical attention. After the battle of Wandiwash Coote had written:

"Such a multitude of poor objects, and not in my power to give them the least assistance, for want of every one necessary requisite for a hospital. . . . If it is possible to send surgeons, . . . you may by that means save the lives of many gallant men, several of whom have not been dressed since the day of action. As I shall be obliged to carry away some surgeons out of the few, numbers must lose their lives."

On the day after the battle of Porto Novo, the chief surgeon, Thomas Davis, reports to Coote:

"Almost ever since the commencement of the action of yesterday, my hands have been imbrued in blood, and the number of the amputations have made the dressing of the wounds tedious, insomuch that I have not yet done, or I should have done myself the honour to have waited upon you in person to represent the expediency of the gentlemen giving up their pallenquins, when the army moves, for the carriage of the unfortunate wounded, who for the most part (far more than we have doolies for) are too desperately wounded to admit of any carriage but that of a dooly or pallenquin. Such lacerated gun-shot wounds I have seldom met with; and, unless an easy carriage can be found for them, few will recover. I have been as sparing of limbs as possible, but great numbers have been taken off, and many are without a dooly, and, should we have an action before these poor objects can be lodged in an hospital or put on board a ship to be sent to Madras, I dread the consequences . . ."

It was left to Cornwallis to organise a regular system of field-hospitals and to allot adequate supplies of money for their maintenance.

The first sign of the professional rise of the surgeon, like the first sign of the professional rise of the officer, consisted in wresting a professional profit out of the hands of the covenanted servants. Just as the officers secured for themselves the profits of clothing their men, so the surgeons obtained the profits of dieting their hospitals. Whereas the steward had once drawn the pay of the soldiers in hospital on condition of providing them with such victuals as the surgeon prescribed, at a later time the surgeons drew the pay of the inmates of the hospital, apparently doing this month and month about. In 1749 the one-legged surgeon, Belsches, in charge of the separate hospital for the King's troops, was allowed 8 fanams a day for each patient, nothing exorbitant (we read) if rent, diet, and attendance be considered. Then, just as the clothing was put out to contract, so too was the diet in hospital, the earliest being, I think, that accepted for 4 fanams a day in 1759. In 1760 it was decided no longer to withhold the full pay of the inmates, but only 2 pagodas or 84 fanams a month, the Company bearing the additional cost. In field hospitals, however, so late as 1791, the surgeon in charge still provided the victuals, though he was allowed certain quantities of wine and spirits per man.

The first hospital at Madras was built by public subscription, but in the course of time became an institution wholly supported by the Company, and inspected for some time at least by a member of Council every week. The hospital servants were either ordinary coolies or " coffree " slaves. In 1758 it was divided into wards for fevers, fluxes, venereal complaints, and malignant fevers and smallpox, together with one for invalids and incurable cases, an operating-room, a dispensary, and a bathroom. The wards were furnished with cots 6 feet by 3; and on admission a patient received a suit of hospital clothes, a gown, cap, shirt, and drawers, the last three items being changed twice a week; and the hospital diet in most cases consisted of rice-water and milk, white bread, mutton broth and greens, with a glass of Madeira when the fever was abating.

The principal difficulty was the maintenance of discipline. Thus we find orders that no privates were to be admitted unless sent there sick; and that no women or Pariah boys should be allowed in. To prevent the sick from selling or otherwise making away with their daily provisions, a man was appointed to see that they either declined or ate them. In 1768 the riots in the hospital had become so frequent, and the conduct of the sick so disgraceful, that, the Governor being resolved upon making an example, Domenick McGuire, pensioner, guilty of causing a disturbance there, was flogged in the presence of all the sick. In 1772 a code of rules appears. The hospital servants are not to be beaten or abused; the patients may not play cards or bring in women; patients will be put under stoppages if they burn or lose their clothes or break their cots; they may walk in the verandas, but may not loaf about near the gates; soldiers pretending sickness, or bringing in arrack, or climbing the walls, will be severely punished; visiting is allowed only between 5 and 8 a.m. when the surgeon is there; non-commissioned officers are to be answerable for the general conduct so far as their sickness permits; and the sergeant of the Hospital Guard is to attend the distribution of rations, and confine the riotous and disorderly.

For the moment these orders seem to have been effective; but irregularities reappeared as soon as supervision was relaxed. In 1794, when poor Surgeon Raine, who

had behaved so well in Hyder's prison, was in charge,
the following dreadful indictment of the hospital discipline appears:

". . . I never heard of such irregularities as at present
exist in the presidency hospital.   I have frequently, during
my short attendance, found in visiting the sick two or
three of them lying in a state of intoxication, and I have
heard of others who were not under my charge being in
a similar condition.   It is not an uncommon practice of
the patients to form parties, often with the sergeant of
the guard, to go into the Black Town, where they generally
remain during the greater part of the night, committing
every act of enormity.   The hospital in consequence
becomes a scene of riot and confusion during the night,
and the shade and other unoccupied parts of the hospital
are places of resort for gaming and boxing during the
day."

As a result Raine was placed in arrest and brought to
trial for neglect of duty.   Perhaps at an earlier time
such irregularities would have been overlooked.   But now
the standard had risen.   Only recently a surgeon, for
neglect of wounded soldiers under his care, had been
suspended till the pleasure of the Company might be
known and deprived of his share of the gratuity granted
to the army.   " It is incumbent upon Lord Cornwallis,"
he wrote, " to show that he sets a higher value on the lives
and limbs of the soldiers than to expose them to the hazard
of falling under the charge of a man who has been guilty
of such gross neglect."

The common diseases were malaria, enteric (generally
described as a putrid fever, as indeed it is), and dysentery,
together with periodic visitations of smallpox and cholera.
Inoculation was known and practised in Bengal, but not
elsewhere in India, Ives tells us; this assertion seems con-

firmed by a report of the Hospital Board of 1793. It states that smallpox has broken out in the Male Orphan Asylum, and recommends that such of the soldiers as have not had it should be inoculated; if inoculation could be introduced among the Sepoys, the report adds, it would be most beneficial. The diet during inoculation should be: for breakfast, conjee and rice; for dinner, mutton broth with greens or mutton with bread and rice; and for supper, conjee with sugar. The practice of inoculation had already been warmly recommended in 1787; and at the beginning of the nineteenth century vaccination was being advocated and advertised, and a subscription was opened for Dr Jenner in 1806.

Another disease which afflicted Europeans in India with cruel horror, and continued so to do until Pasteur released them from their fear, was hydrophobia. Periodically an order would go out for the slaughter of the dogs that infest every Indian town and village—mangy, unkempt brutes, whose pointed ears and strident bark furtively announce their kinship with the jackal. On 10 March, 1770, for instance, we find in garrison orders a reward of 2 fanams offered for every dead dog brought to the Governor's garden-house. A couple of years later a similar order appears, but this time, as though warned by experience, carts were ordered to attend at the Fort to carry the corpses out to a pit at Chintadripet, where the reward would be paid to the camp-colourmen of each company. Such campaigns were usually prefaced by a caution to officers to keep their dogs up till it was over. In 1788 a letter announces the existence of a man at Tanjore who had a medicine for hydrophobia said to have been successfully used by both Europeans and Indians. The same man also claimed to have a specific against the bite of venomous snakes. This announcement seemed of importance enough for Council to desire the man to be sent

up to Madras. The matter was referred to the Hospital
Board, which resolved as follows:

" The Hospital Board, being assured by Mr Duffin, one
of their members, that he has repeatedly exhibited the
snake pill, as it is called, as an antidote in cases where
persons were bit by serpents supposed to be venomous, as
well as in cases where persons were bit by dogs of which
there was very satisfactory proof of madness, without
perceiving any deleterious effects from the use of this
medicine, yet, some of the component parts of these medicines being such as they are unacquainted with, and in a
state which it may be difficult to analyse, they can only recommend to Government to leave every practitioner to
administer remedies as his own judgment may direct, as
heretofore, in cases of venomous bites."

The Council on this decided to publish in the *Madras
Courier* the composition and manner of using the medicines " in cases where persons have had the misfortune
of meeting with those accidents."

CHAPTER IX

THE MERCHANT

THE free merchants of Madras grew in numbers nearly as quickly as the other classes of society. The Madras Almanack for 1800 shows 213 European inhabitants of the better sort, apart from the Company's servants and the officers of the army. At that time there were altogether in the presidency between twelve and thirteen hundred Europeans, besides the troops; but many of them must have normally resided at up-country stations; I do not suppose that you would have found more than four or five hundred in Madras at any one time; and of the Madras residents about a third would have been free merchants. But under this name were included many whose occupations were not mercantile. The attorneys of the Mayor's Court, the Nawab of Arcot's employés, professional musicians and hairdressers, and others, all came under this comprehensive title. Such persons may more conveniently be described in other chapters; and in this I wish to limit attention to the merchants properly so called. Yet here at once another difficulty arises. It is impossible to describe the trade of the free merchants without at the same time bringing in the covenanted servants, for, as the century passes, the jealousy which once separated them disappears and the closest alliance between individuals from both sections is established.

Indeed the century transformed the merchant along with every other class. In the old days the principal merchant had been the governor, and the next largest the members of the Council. But at the end of the century none of these had anything at all to do with trade, and, although trade was still not forbidden to the covenanted servants in general, " the Wise Ones at home " had just decided no longer to allow servants in responsible positions to engage in houses of business. So that the control of trade had really been transferred from the covenanted servant to the free merchant. Along with this had gone a great change in the methods of conducting business. It came to be organised on a more definite and permanent basis, just as happened to the administration of the place or the conduct of war. In the case of trade firms took the place of loosely associated individuals. At the same time the free merchants ceased to be a group of mingled English and Portuguese colonists, settled at Madras and not seriously looking forward to any change of domicile, and became a group of temporary inhabitants almost entirely English in stock and character, and looking forward to an ultimate return to their native country.

The gradual extinction of the old families is one of the outstanding features, and especially of those Portuguese families which had provided a dusky and passionate background to the sober English merchants. For instance, in 1782 died at Negapatam Francisco Carvalho. He had been one of the wealthiest men in Madras; his daughters, one of whom had been reckoned among the many " most beautiful women in India," had all married prominent persons, French or English. One had married Dupleix's nephew, de Kerjean, and had comforted him for the infidelities of his former wife; another had married Jacques Law, who had commanded the French troops till he was defeated and disgraced; another daughter had married the second Charles Floyer, and the son of a fourth, Charles Smith, for a few months occupied the presidential chair of Madras. Such a multiplicity of daughters naturally spelt the ruin of a family. Each son-in-law expected a handsome dowry with his bride. Then too the unending struggle with the French made things difficult for the Portuguese; they were suspected of sympathising with their co-religionists; they were deprived of their houses in Fort St George; and lost such profitable posts as that of captain and supercargo of the English ship that went annually to Manila, long held by Geronimo de Yta y Salazar. No Portuguese firms arose to compete with the English firms that sprang up; they failed to adapt themselves to the new conditions; and gradually fell into a position of marked inferiority, providing mistresses where they had formerly given wives, and serving as clerks where they had acted as principals. Along with them disappeared the old English families. Captain John Powney, who had established himself at Madras about 1700, died there forty years later, having accumulated a fortune of some 80,000 pagodas—upwards of £30,000 —and begotten sixteen legitimate children. Several of the daughters married into the covenanted service, and, under the names of Savage, Lucas, and Casamajor, their descendants continued to serve the Company; the eldest surviving son joined the same service and finally established himself in England; and the sons who remained at Madras disappear into obscurity. The family ceased as a family of free merchants. Other individuals, less prolific, make a fortune and die. Such a one was Samuel Troutback, who came on shore, " naked and shipwrecked, in 1719; after which it pleased God to cloath me and prosper my honest endeavours, and to raise me in the East Indies." He married, and had a son; but both wife and child died before their father; and he lived on alone till 1785. Many persons were willing to call cousins with the lonely old man and to comfort his declining years; but he firmly made up his mind that all they wanted was his money. No doubt he was right; but he would probably have done well to buy a little family affection.

" I waited on the old man, Mr Troutback," writes David Young to Robert Wedderburn in 1781, " agreeable to your desire, although I knew it was to no purpose, as there is nothing so offensive to his ear, as the notion of his having any relation on earth; you or all mankind cannot persuade him that there is a single person on earth in any manner related to him from Adam down to this day, and I doubt whether he believes he ever had a father or mother, such an unaccountable being is he. . . . He is a man worth above £40,000, but incapable of doing any man a disinterested or good office with it all, or having any enjoyment of it himself, but as desirous of augmenting his fortune as if he was in hopes of purchasing eternal happiness with it . . ."

When at last he died, it was found that he had left all his fortune to the charity school in Wapping where he had been brought up; but the will was so drawn that the estate went into Chancery, and finally lapsed to the Crown, only £5,000 reaching the school he had wished to benefit.

With his generation went the old system of individual traders. The joint-stock method of trade had of course always been in vogue. But in its early form it was a mere temporary alliance. Two or three persons would resolve upon a voyage to Manila or Canton, and then induce their friends to make up the capital required for the venture.

" To almost every ship and stock," says Lockyer, " there

are several owners, each having a part suitable to his in-
clinations, or estate, which is again divided in proportion
amongst them on her return from a voyage, when the ship
and cargo are sold by out-cry, or auction, at the Sea-gate."

Another way of spreading the risk was by taking up
money *on respondentia,* as the phrase went. This was
similar to, if not identical with the loans at bottomry in
Europe. The lender advanced his money for the duration of the voyage, and, in the event of the ship's being
cast away, he was entitled to a proportion of any salvage
that might be recovered. The rate of interest paid ran
high. Twenty-five to thirty per cent. were often thus
paid on the twelvemonth, except when merchants were
anxious to remit money to a certain port, when of course
the shippers were able to get lower rates. Thus I find
one bond for a voyage to any port or place in India at
30 per cent. per annum; and another to any port within
the Company's limits at 24 per cent. A time limit was
often set; thus a bond for the Manila voyage carried 30
per cent., but if the voyage exceeded a year principal and
interest were to run at 10 per cent. per annum. Ten per
cent. may be taken as the rate at which a merchant of
good credit could borrow money on his personal security.

About the middle of the century these haphazard and
short-lived associations for a single voyage begin to give
place to more permanent partnerships. In this connection
I find some curious evidence regarding the Manila trade.
This was a branch of trade in which Madras had taken a
great deal of interest, and it was the custom to send at
least one English ship there year by year. Its cargo
would be composed of the piece-goods made on the
Coast, and the returns would principally consist of silver
that overflowed into Manila from Spanish America. The
profits of this trade at one time ran high; but they de-

9

clined in the middle of the century. An account filed in the Mayor's Court shows that a parcel of piece-goods sent thither on freight produced net $4\frac{1}{2}$ per cent. profit after paying 14 per cent. freight and $7\frac{1}{2}$ per cent. commission; and that was regarded as exceedingly bad. After peace had been made with Spain in 1763, the English attempted to reopen the trade; the country ship, *Sultan-un-nissa*, was sent under the Nawab's colours, with an English supercargo; but the supercargo was imprisoned and not allowed to sell his goods. The next voyage, under Armenian conduct, turned out better; and the concerned cleared 14 per cent. About this time we find a more definite organisation.

" We had a meeting of the association the other day," writes Jourdan to Crawford, in 1771, " wherein it was determined to send a ship to Manilla, whether there be war or peace, as the vessel is to go under the Nabob's flag. . . . I think this may be done without much risk, insomuch that I shall lend some money on my own account. There are relations here of Infinale and Blaneca [Manila merchants] who have letters of credit; to these money at all events may be lent. If you think this not prudent, you will acquaint me in time, as it was a condition on which we got the Manilla trade that we should borrow of the gentlemen in council the sum of 25 or 30,000 pagodas at respondentia, which Mr Chamier had offered to take up of these. We are now calling for the money . . ."

Ten days later he writes that the *Crescent* will sail in June, with 20,000 pagodas on account of the association and 35,000 respondentia of the Council's. I do not know how the voyage turned out; but Jourdan retained the management of the Manila trade until he left Madras for Masulipatam.

Jourdan's letters afford yet another illustration of the

more permanent form which trading partnerships were assuming and which were clearly an intermediate stage between the casual unions with which we begin and the houses of agency with which we close. In the 'sixties Jourdan and John Sulivan had, among other ventures, projected a voyage down the Straits with opium from Bengal and blue cotton cloth from Porto Novo, for their vessel the *Indian Trader*, 350 tons burden, Gowan Harrop supercargo. They aimed particularly at re-establishing the English trade at Achin, a small kingdom at the northern end of Sumatra. In the seventeenth century the Company had had a factory there; but this had not been very profitable, and had been withdrawn. But private English adventurers continued to visit the place. Bowrey describes it as pleasant and healthy; it had an excellent harbour, which was safe at all seasons of the year; the king was, as usual in those petty kingdoms, the chief merchant of his capital; Captain John Powney and Captain Alexander Hamilton knew the place well; but it was subject to periodic rebellions, when no trade could be done; and, when a few vessels had been seized, and their crews massacred, the country traders forsook the place. One of the last of these permanently connected with the place must have been Daniel Willeboorts, whose will was proved at Madras in 1737. It is dated at Achin, 27 June, 1736. He directs his ship to be sold, with all his goods, " and the ground Betty lived upon, the said ground begins from the washers' town and ends near the river "; he leaves one slave to his son Daniel, and another to his son Matthew, but " all the slave-wenches and girls who ... attend on Maria are her own "; Leonor, to whom he owes 15 buncals, is free, and never was his slave; her chest is not to be opened or examined; and all that is in it, except a Malay dagger, is her own.

The place was entirely deserted by Europeans when

Jourdan and his associates thought of reopening the trade. But the place was still troubled by internal commotions; and their first venture fared badly. The cargo could not be sold, and Harrop had to land a Muhammadan agent to take charge of it, while he continued his voyage down the straits. Presently the agent was obliged to transport the goods under his charge on board a ship belonging to the King; and while there, they were seized by a French ship sent to settle a long-standing dispute which that nation had with the Achinese. The Madras adventurers, however, soon had an offer which promised to make good their initial losses. On Harrop's return to Achin, the King offered him ground on which to build a dwelling and warehouses, and engaged to give the English merchants

" half of the advantages of the retail trade of his country, which from custom belonged to him, on the condition that we would advance money for the purchase of goods, and keep on shore a number of our people armed, that, in case of his being attacked, we might give him the assistance of a few men with fire-locks, of which the Malays are still very apprehensive."

The offer was accepted. Some 75 men were engaged and shipped at Nagore, on the Tanjore coast; and other assistance was given also. " I am by no means for supplying the Malays with arms," Jourdan wrote in 1768, " could we carry on our trade without; but others will ever supply them, and, unless we do the same, we shall have no encouragement at their ports." " I intend," he says a fortnight later, " to supply the king of Achin with some sixpounder guns I have, as they will be a good assistance to him. As he has the character of being as good as any of them, I could wish him formally settled; it was once a place of considerable trade."

These measures reaped a large harvest of success. Not only did the trade of the adventurers increase, but also many other ships, English and native, began once more to frequent the port,

" as Mr Harrop frequently assisted them in the sales of their goods, sometimes taking off whole cargoes on account of the king for bills on me [Jourdan], by which vessels, that would have been obliged to wait many months to collect the goods of the inhabitants in payment of the goods by them sold, were enabled to proceed further into the Streights and to take advantage of other markets."

At the same time, it was stated by a Company's servant, not concerned in Jourdan's venture, that were Harrop and his people to depart, the old troubles would break out again at once. Thus the Company's servants in their private capacity were doing on a small scale in 1770 what the Company itself was destined to do on the continent of India.

Achin was not the only scene of Jourdan's activity. On the western shore of the Malay Peninsula, on almost the same latitude as Achin, was the little state of Kedah, from which considerable quantities of tin could be procured. Thither also the association traded, and there also it had a permanent agent, who in 1771 wrote:

" The king of Quedah has granted to you the dualla or sea-port of Quedah, with a fort lying near it, to be kept by you in consideration that you will promise to assist him against the people of Selangore; the force it will be necessary to maintain for this service, and the expense of the factory the king proposes, should be equally divided between you and him, and that the trade should be carried on on your joint accounts. . . ."

A later report shows that the agent removed into the

Fort, which commanded the entrance to the river, and had built a redoubt—I suppose a very trifling work—" to prevent surprises." The Danes from Tranquebar had also sent proposals to aid the king with 300 sepoys. Nevertheless, the agent writes:

" If you will but send seapoys and a few Europeans, with leave to assist the king against Selangore, I will engage not a slab of tin, a grain of pepper, a beetlenut or dammer, shall go out of my hands."

Such an opening was as promising as that at Achin. But just as affairs reached this point, a dispatch arrived which brought the whole enterprise to a sudden end. The directors of the Company had been astonished to learn that a factory had been established at Achin, supported, as they had been told, " by a naval force and some hundreds of sepoys from your coast "; and they ordered the factory and all the privileges which its private owners had secured to be taken over on the Company's behalf at a fair valuation. But the trade was too small to be profitable to the Company. Covenanted servants and Company's Sepoys were both sent to Achin and Kedah; but both factories were speedily withdrawn. Perhaps it was as well that Jourdan's adventure was brought to this sudden end; his local agents were not under close enough control. But as it stands, the story is an apt enough illustration of the conditions which thrust political power into the hands of European traders. Rival chiefs anxious to dispossess one another of their ancestral territory; consequent wars which interrupted trade; invitations for an alliance, readily accepted by the merchant as the speediest means of re-establishing tranquillity—such were the conditions which for a moment gave Jourdan and his friends a half-share in the royal trade of a Malay state on condition of military support, just as the same conditions led the Dutch Company through island after island of the archipelago and the English Company over most of the expanse of India.

This curious but significant episode has led me some distance from the free merchant, who was only represented among Jourdan's associates by the supercargo of the *Indian Trader*, Gowan Harrop. But it shows how groups of individuals were forming for long-continued rather than for occasional enterprises. This was probably the consequence of that decline in the profits of the country-trade lamented by every contemporary writer. Greater resources and more sustained efforts were needed to make a fortune than had been the case; and so partnerships begin to appear. But just at this time the trade of Madras was overwhelmed by a succession of misfortunes. The first of these was the expansion of the Nawab of Arcot's debt. That had begun on a small scale when there was still a good deal of money in the country, and when the stock was being constantly replenished by large imports from Bengal. But even when the war with the French had ended with complete victory, the Nawab's demands still continued, and he was willing to promise almost any rate of interest. Then the province was desolated by the unsuccessful war with Hyder in 1767–9. The result was an acute depression, heightened to a catastrophe by the Nawab's failure to honour his promises. A large part of the liquid capital of the place was thus destroyed; and almost every merchant had large amounts locked up in bonds which he could neither raise money on nor sell except at a heavy discount. The position is again illustrated by Jourdan's correspondence. "There is such scarcity of money here at present," he writes in November, 1777, "that I have at this time ... 87,000 pagodas, and cannot get in a pagoda to answer clamorous people." Even Benfield was distressed. Jourdan writes to him five months later:

" If I have an expectation of averting the ruin which now threatens me, I must have the money. You told me of your distress; I know it; but consider in how different a light I stand. You are a man of fortune, and, although it is known you do not pay the demands made upon you, it is as well known that you are a man of fortune. . . . My fortune is small, a part is at stake, and from . . . my backwardness in payment, men are led to remember all the losses I have met with. . . . The governor on the part of the Company has demands on me, and on his own account he has demands on me. What must he think? He knows me not. What right have I to expect he will let bills for 7,700 pagodas continue longer unpaid than two months? How must a protest at this time affect me? . . . I request you to let me have the money I desired of you, and, if you cannot do without it, you shall have it again out of the money that I have reason to expect; but if I fail in that, the arch-usurer shall be applied to and you supplied at any rate . . ."

Less than a fortnight later he answers an appeal from Andrew Ross begging him to stop a suit he has begun against him. He cannot stop the suit unless the money is paid.

" Even while I was writing this letter, and since, the servants of Buccanjee the sowcar [money-lender] have been not only dunning me for money, but making in my house a most indecent noise, which, from my situation relative to that sowcar, to whom I owe money, I cannot resent as it deserves . . ."

Jourdan just managed to escape ruin; but many others did not. Charles Darke, for instance, who came out a cadet but afterwards resigned his ensigncy and was allowed to reside at Madras as a merchant, writes in 1787, " I now reside with my family at the Red Hills from my having unfortunately so many years ago been involved with H.H. the Nawab, so much so as not to permit me to transact business in the mercantile line." Darke's failure, which took place in 1777, made no little stir in Madras. " Our great merchant," writes David Young, " is failed, and has shut himself up in an apartment at the Nabob's to keep himself out of jail; all his effects will be publicly sold if he does not get his money from the Nabob in time." " There's no news in this place worth notice at present," he writes in another letter, " but the greatest scarcity of cash there ever was, which has put an entire stop to trade, and makes everyone afraid to trust another; and no one is so great gainers as our lawyers."

On the top of this, in 1780, broke out the Second Mysore War, which lasted for four years, while Hyder laid waste the Carnatic with systematic thoroughness, and the French secured a superiority at sea such as they never had established before. Jourdan no longer comments on affairs, but his place is taken by Young. " This promises to be a very hungry monsoon for us," he writes in September, 1781. " It is astonishing how dear every article for the table is, or rather how we get anything at all to eat; drink is as dear, and no money to be had; nor is there any appearance or even hopes of better times." Early in the next year we read: " Money is so scarce that it is impossible to borrow or get in money . . . You will perhaps not believe me, but there is not a merchant to buy rice or any one kind of grain, and, if it was sold at ever so low a price, ready money could not be got . . ." This was followed by the loss of many ships, some of which were taken by the French and others destroyed by a great storm that burst upon the coast while many vessels were lying at Madras waiting to be unladed.

" It's impossible," Young writes on 16 October, " to

describe the dreadful sight that this morning has presented to our view.   From the Sea-gate as far as Chepauk the whole beach is covered with wrecks. . . .   I went to the sea-side this morning with a piece of paper and pencil to take an account of what was lost, but the sight appeared to me so shocking that I did not attempt it. . . .   The fleet either cutt or slipped about 4 o'clock and got all safe to sea.   General Munro and Mr Davidson was on board the Admiral's ship and carried to sea . . ."

And this storm was followed by a great famine, during which the streets of the Black Town were cumbered with corpses both of the starving inhabitants and of the poor wretches who had hoped in vain to find food and shelter in the city.

Amid these destructive circumstances appears the final form in which the merchants of Madras organised themselves.   This was the house of agency.   It was a definite partnership.   No single person possessed the means to encounter such risks alone.   We have Chase, Sewell, and Chinnery, or Tulloh, Connell, and Brodie, or Roebuck, Abbot, and Maitland.   These, by origin, were generally mixed firms, consisting of both covenanted servants and free merchants, just as the older forms of association had been.   These houses of agency transacted business of every kind.   They advanced money, they bought and sold on commission, they conducted business on their own account.   The best known perhaps was that of Lautour & Co.   This was founded by Francis Lautour who came out to Madras with Admiral Harland in 1770, after serving many years aboard King's ships in various parts of the world.   He acted as agent for some of the King's regiments that came out to Madras; and the firm early in the nineteenth century became known as Arbuthnot & Co., under which title it survived until 1907.   Another house, Roebuck, Abbot, and Maitland, is represented by a

number of letter-books in the Mayor's Court Papers.
Their correspondence, which begins about 1792, traces
the course of business at Madras during the last ten years
of the century; and they were particular to report by
every ship the prices of the Nawab's bonds and of the
Company's paper in the settlement. It is clear that the
victory of Cornwallis over Tipu in 1792 did much to
revive trade, but that another depression set in which
was only dissipated by the influx of funds after the fall
of Seringapatam in 1799. Thus the Company's 12 per
cent. bonds were paid off and replaced first by 8 and then
by 6 per cent. paper. But then in 1796 a new stringency
had developed, and Government was once more offering
12 per cent. and not getting all they wanted. Once more
the Madras ships were at the mercy of French privateers
fitted out at Mauritius, which in less than a year captured
prizes valued at £300,000. By 1798 "the scarcity has
got to that pitch that money is not to be procured on any
terms" and paper was unsaleable. The Nawab's bonds,
which had now been taken over by the Company, followed
a similar course. Roebuck & Co. seem to have had orders
from Benfield to buy at 50 or 60 discount and sell at 20
discount. In 1792 they were rising fast to the upper
limit, which they attained at the close of the year; and
by the middle of 1794 they had reached the extraordinary
price of 3 discount. But then they began to fall again,
and by 1798 were back at 25 discount once more.

In this period too we find the first mention of banking
houses at Madras. The earliest was the Carnatic Bank,
founded in 1788; in 1795 followed a rival, the British
Bank, in which Francis Lautour had a share. These were
of course private banks with unlimited liability. But
beyond that little is known about them. However, they
evidently illustrate the general tendency to a closer
organisation, which is also shown by the history of marine

insurance at Madras. The practice was one well known
in India. Mention is made of it in the seventeenth century; and in a suit brought in the Mayor's Court in 1744
the owner demands payment of a policy on a ship that
put into harbour for repairs and was burnt; against which
the insurers reply that according to the custom of the
country, the risk ceases whenever a ship drops anchor.
Other insurances by groups of Indians appear in cases
heard in 1764 and 1767. A case heard in 1781 mentions a policy for 2,500 pagodas on a ship for her homeward voyage from Tavoy, in which 21 insurers took part.
The first group of English merchants formed to undertake this kind of business was probably founded by
Warren Hastings during his short term of office at
Madras. In the Pleadings for 1772 is a policy on a
voyage from Madras to the Nicobars and Pegu limited
to three months' duration, and signed " For Warren
Hastings, Esq., and company Madras Insurers " by
Jourdan and two other Company's servants. The first
reference to it I have met with was in 1769. For voyages
up and down the coast from 2 to 4 per cent. seems to have
been charged; but for the voyage to Bengal, including
the dangerous entrance into the Hugli, a policy is mentioned at 11 per cent. for 12 months with 1 per cent.
extra for every time the vessel entered the river after
the first. The *Four Friends,* when sailing eastwards in
1769, with a considerable quantity of gunpowder on
board, could only be insured at 17 per cent., which permitted her to go to all ports and places for the period of
one year. The troubles of 1778 broke the company; and
indeed losses under this head contributed to Jourdan's
downfall. But new companies sprang up afterwards. The
first was, I think, the Madras Insurance Company, secretary James Daly, first mentioned in 1791, when two shares
belonging to a covenanted servant were sold, and, being

much below par, the seller seems to have had to pay the buyers to take up his shares. I infer that little or nothing was paid up on them. In 1794 other insurance companies appear, though of course they may have come into existence earlier. These are the Exchange Insurance Company, the New Madras Insurance Company, and the Commercial Society. But I know nothing of them beyond their names, and Roebuck's opinion, that "the premium that insurance offices in this country require for covering one's property is so very extravagant that upon certain occasions it becomes more expedient for the proprietor to bear the risk."

Mr Abbot, of the house of Roebuck, Abbot & Maitland, was a friend and correspondent of Paul Benfield; and, as might be expected from the connection, a hanger-on of the Nawab's. He hoped to secure the entire management of the Nawab's debt, and on 31 July, 1792, he writes to Benfield:

". . . Mr Richard Sulivan arrived on the *Melville Castle* and returns by this conveyance. He has effected the object that, it seems, brought him out, which was to get the Nabob to put his debt to him (about 1½ lacks of pagodas) in a train of future payment from the deposited bonds. . . . The Nabob appoints R. Sulivan his agent irrevocable in the room of Binny and Storey, and, as Sulivan has appointed us his attorneys, . . . we shall not only be the sole trustees, but agents by attorney on the part of the Nabob . . ."

Abbot hoped to succeed Charles Binny as secretary to the Nawab; but Binny was evidently reluctant to give up his post.

"Binny is still here," we read on 7 February of the next year, "and no one knows for certain when he means to quit this country; I have no reason to doubt but that I shall succeed him; the only person who has opposed me, though without success, is now on the point of proceeding to Egypt to carry a plan into execution, which is to form a settlement somewhere in the Red Sea that is to be attended with political and commercial benefits to the nation.   You can easily guess that I mean Major Macdonald.   I do not know exactly what his schemes are, but, knowing him to be a bold man that does not stand at trifles to carry his point, I am apt to think he has promised Lord Cornwallis more than he can perform, for he has been at Calcutta for that purpose, in order to serve his private ends, which is to get money from the Durbar by persuading them that he has his Lordship's support in the expedition that he is going to undertake . . ."

A year later, however, he is still waiting for the post. On 19 February, 1794, he writes:

" Binny has at last taken his passage on the *Rodney*, and though he has done everything in his power to prevent my succeeding him, yet I have not the smallest doubt but that they will keep their promise with me.   The moment, therefore, that his back is turned, I shall lay in my claim, and, if I meet with any difficulty, I shall make use of the interest that I am promised, which, I think, cannot fail; having once got firm footing in B's situation, I hope we shall find no difficulty in putting the Ameer's debt into some train . . ."

In the middle of that year he was still being put off with promises; but a little later he apparently secured the appointment.

Besides that, however, he was made Deputy Master Attendant—Deputy Port Officer, as we should say nowadays.   He clearly expected some pretty pickings out of this, apart from the advantage to a house of business of such intimate connection with the shipping.   In this, however, he was disappointed.   On 17 February, 1796, he informs his correspondent:

" The recovery of my health . . . as well as the shameful treatment I have met with from Lord Hobart [the governor] and Mr Adderley [the Master Attendant] has made me anxious to visit England. . . . Meanwhile, in order that you may be acquainted as early as possible with the cause that has led to my dismission from my situation of Deputy Master Attendant, I have desired Mr Richard Lee, junior, to wait upon you with a set of papers that have passed on the occasion. . . . In the course of a few days, when I shall know the determination of Government on the papers I have laid before them, or know that they do not intend to determine upon them, for his Lordship has not as yet thought proper to bring them before the board, I shall call upon Mr Adderley to retract the assertions contained in the paragraph of his letter which he sent me the 2nd inst. . . ."

The next letter, of 24 June, announces that he " went out with Mr Adderley and . . . got wounded through the lungs," but is now recovering to the astonishment of the doctors.

The governor, Lord Hobart, a well-meaning but brusque and hasty man, was bent on bringing to an end all the abuses with which the Nawab's administration was encrusted, and which were in great part the result of the interference of the creditors. On 14 July, 1796,

" I received a letter from Mr Secretary Webbe . . . informing me that the President in council having seen cause why I should leave India, has ordered me to prepare to transport myself to Great Britain according to the terms of my covenants [as free merchant]. The reasons assigned you will perceive are for having appealed to the Court of Directors through the Bengal Government. . . . The object of this tirant has been to injure me in the eyes of the people here [i.e. the Nawab] who, you know, are much influenced by the hand of power. This unwarrantable conduct of his, added to a letter which he has written to Roebuck [a covenanted servant] tending also to injure my prospects in the mercantile line by attempting to intimidate him from longer continuing his name joined to mine, gives me I conceive sufficient grounds for an action for heavy damages against the proud lord . . ."

Moreover Hobart had to all intents suspended Abbot from his post as secretary to the Nawab.

" In order to secure the success of his plans," we read in a letter of 18 September, 1796, " Lord Hobart ordered, three days after the present Nabob took the musned [i.e. succeeded to the throne], the Europeans, and me among the rest, no longer to attend the durbar, and consequently I have not been there since. Had the Nabob been manly enough to have demanded me, the Supreme Government would no doubt have sent orders round to allow me to attend His Highness, . . . but I have in vain attempted to get him to do himself and me that justice; but I hope the face of affairs will soon change, as it is generally understood that Lord Hobart is about taking his departure, and General Harris coming round will again strengthen my interest at the Durbar, as it was by his influence that I was first placed there . . ."

But Hobart's departure only marked a respite in the Nawab's affairs. Generosity may have pleaded for the maintenance of a princely family which had long been in alliance with the Company; but when, instead of attempting to manage his own affairs, he confided whole districts to the administration of his creditors, it was high time that a system for which Abbot and his friend stood should be swept away. So when in 1800 it appeared that the Arcot family had not always been so constant to their allies as had been thought, advantage was taken on the next vacancy, which occurred in 1801, to abolish it as a ruling family and to assume in the name of the Company the direct government of the Carnatic.

Benfield's extinction had already taken place. He had given up politics and returned to banking, for which he certainly had a real talent.

"We had heard," writes Abbot in 1792, "of your having left Parliament previous to the receipt of your letters. I am satisfied that you have some object in view that is of more consequence to you than representing Malmsbury, and I sincerely hope it will succeed . . . I could wish you could turn your attention to the Government of Bengal or Madras. There is no one so capable of filling those situations with credit to himself and honour to his nation and employers."

These amazing sentiments were perhaps less amazing with that inveterate jobber Dundas at the Board of Control than they sound to-day. But anyhow Benfield's restless mind was turned to other objects.

" I am happy to find," Abbot continues on 30 December, 1793, " you have engaged in a house of business so much to your satisfaction, and can easily conceive that, from the command of capital and the connection with the first houses in Europe, that your concerns must be immense and adapted to occupy the abilities that you possess, and also to carry into effect the proposed plan of a general remittance to and from this country. It is a thousand pities that it was not established two years ago, for the late blow that commercial credit has felt in England has created a great demand for remittance from this country without the means of obtaining any, even on very dis-advantageous terms . . ."

At first the venture prospered. Benfield bought Wood-hall Park; " I recollect passing it once, and was struck with the beauty of the situation," says Abbot on learning

10

the news. Then follow congratulations on Benfield's marriage with Miss Swinburne of Hamsterly, county Durham. But a time of war was ill-suited for such experiments as Benfield's. His Madras correspondents became alarmed.

" We must confess," Abbot writes on 17 February, 1796, " the sudden and large draft you have given upon us at unusual short sight and the want of letters from you informing us whether you intend to follow them up by others, have made a serious impression on our minds, and in order therefore to prevent inconvenience to ourselves and injury to your credit or property which might be occasioned by your drawing further bills upon us which might be presented at a time when we might have no funds of yours in our hands to answer them, we have come to the determination not to remit to you for the present the balance we have of yours in our hands . . ."

In the following year matters were still worse. The Madras house cannot sell bills on Boyd, Benfield & Co., because every house is trying to sell bills; the next two letters complain of the bills which Benfield has drawn, and especially of their being at only 30 days' sight; at last, in the middle of 1798 bills drawn by Boyd, Benfield & Co. were presented for acceptance for a sum of 161,725 pagodas; Roebuck and Abbot had no funds belonging to the firm, and Benfield's private bonds would hardly realise that amount; the bills were therefore protested; and by the time the protested bills could reach England, the house itself had been obliged to close its doors. The last glimpse which the Roebuck and Abbot papers afford us of the unfortunate Paul occurs in a letter to Roebuck from Sir John Call, engineer and member of Council at Madras thirty years earlier.

" When I was in town," he writes, on 30 July, 1799, " I saw our friend Benfield only twice. He was very low, and burst into tears on seeing me. I have felt much for him from the beginning of his misfortunes, and sincerely pity him, notwithstanding he may be accused of too inordinate a desire to augment a fortune which was more than sufficient for any private man before he entered on his new schemes . . ."

CHAPTER X

THE LAWYER

"LAWYERS are plenty, and as knowing as can be expected from broken-linnen-drapers and other cracked tradesmen, who seek their fortunes here by their wits,"—so says Lockyer, at the beginning of the century. And perhaps he was not far out. In 1704 there was no one in the place who knew how to draw an indictment; and so criminal justice was like to come to a standstill. In fact not Madras only, but all our early colonies suffered much from the complicated nature of our English law. All the letters patent lay it down that their laws shall conform as near as may be with the laws of England; and the colonists themselves seem to have felt that they carried with them that vast, inchoate mass of law, statute, and common, that was supposed to guarantee the liberties of Englishmen. A system that could hardly be mastered by the study of a lifetime had thus to be put into force by persons scarcely acquainted with its elements; there was therefore a fine opening for those who could persuade others that they had any legal knowledge. You had to put up with makeshift justice, even as you had to put up with makeshift defences and makeshift divinity. The Mayor who heard your bill of complaint, or the magistrate who tried you, might (as an indignant suitor once wrote) be better read in Hoyle's *History of the Four Kings* than in the law-books sent out by the Company for the guidance of its courts.

Even the early courts themselves were of doubtful powers. They were only set up by the authority of the Company on the authority of its royal charters; and were they to put a man to death for murder, would not those responsible lay themselves open to a præmunire? In 1712 four murderers were lying in confinement at Madras, but the Council did not consider they had power to bring them to trial; and notorious offenders daily bragged that they could not be put to death. When Hamilton and Lockyer wrote, there was only one crime which could be tried at Madras without legal uncertainty. That was piracy. By an act at the close of the seventeenth century the king was empowered to set up courts of admiralty in the colonies for the trial of pirates, and so in 1700 a commission was issued to the President and Council of Madras enabling them to constitute a court for the determination of cases of piracy, felony, and robbery on the high seas or in any haven-side, creek, or place where Admiralty jurisdiction ran, and to give sentence and judgment of death, and to execute the same upon offenders convicted of those crimes. After so long a period of immunity from punishment, this grant of powers was most unpopular with the captains of country ships. Hamilton, for instance, says that if anyone who was injured by a governor's tricks talked of revenge, " he is infallibly declared a pirate."

Despite such mutterings, the establishment of an admiralty court was a good thing; and in 1726 came the letters patent establishing regular civil and criminal courts at Madras. The civil court was called the Mayor's Court, after the court which had already been set up by the Company. The patent established a corporation consisting of a mayor and nine aldermen, of whom seven were to be natural-born British subjects; the mayor was annually elected by the aldermen; and the aldermen, named in the patent for life, were to fill future vacancies by co-option.   They formed a court of record to hear, try, and determine all civil actions; and from their decision an appeal lay to the governor and Council, or, where the subject of dispute exceeded 1,000 pagodas in value, to the King in council.   A criminal court was constituted at the same time by appointing the governor and the five senior members of Council justices of the peace, and directing them to hold quarter-sessions for the trial of all crimes, treason excepted, as much as possible after the manner in which crimes were heard and punished in England.   Accordingly all indictments were in the first instance referred to a grand jury, and only those on which they had found a true bill were tried by the justices before a petty jury. As in England the trial was opened by the traditional dialogue between the prisoner at the bar and the clerk of the peace.   " How say you," asks the clerk, " are you guilty or not guilty? "   " Not guilty," says the prisoner.   " How will you be tried? " is the next question, to which the consecrated answer must be returned, " By God and my country."   " God send you a good deliverance," concludes the clerk, and forthwith the petty jury is summoned and sworn.   And when the prisoner stood obstinately mute and refused to plead, so that the trial could not legally go forward, then the justices were instructed to pronounce, as the assize judge would in England, the dreadful formula of the *peine forte et dure*:

" You shall go to the prison from whence you came, and shall be laid there in your dark and low house, where you shall lie naked on the bare earth; . . . and one of your arms shall be drawn to one corner of the house, with a cord, and your other arm to another corner of the house, and in the same manner shall be done with your legs, and

there shall be laid upon your body iron and stone, so
much as you may bare, and more; and the next day
following you shall have three morsels of barley-bread
without any drink; and the second day you shall have
drink thrice of the water next unto the prison excepting
running water; and this shall be your diet until you be
dead."

But before this was inflicted, the jury was to decide whether
the prisoner was mute " fraudulently, wilfully, and
obstinately, or by the providence and act of God." This
terrible relic of another age was actually observed in the
eighteenth century in England; but so far as I know no
occasion for its use ever arose at Madras.

Indeed the whole tendency of the age was to mitigate
the ferocious code which it had inherited. At Madras as
in England juries would assess the value of stolen property
at 10*d*. in order to bring the crime outside the limits of
felony and permit a milder sentence than death. So too
when a man found guilty of manslaughter pleaded benefit
of clergy, he would be declared possessed of no goods,
lands, or chattels, so as to avoid the confiscation of his
property to the Crown. A further relaxation probably
consisted in branding with a cold iron. But here I
think the practice varied. Levere, a French prisoner, who
killed another man in a duel which he had deliberately
provoked, was ordered to be burnt F with a hot iron in the
right hand; a private found guilty of manslaughter was
branded M in the left hand; but two others also found
guilty of manslaughter were brought in, sentence delivered
on them, " and the punishment is immediately inflicted."
I doubt if the iron was hot in the last case; I think it
probably was in the other two. Murders judged
peculiarly atrocious are punished with hanging in chains
near the scene of the crime, and thieves are whipped at
the cart's tail through the Fort, and sometimes this

punishment is extended to the two principal streets of the
Black Town.   A sailor, who got drunk and stabbed a
woman, was transported for fourteen years to Sumatra.
Indeed most of the crimes were committed in liquor.
Sergeant Thomas Walker, of the 2nd Battalion of Artillery, gets excessive drunk and shoots Lieutenant-fireworker
Matthew Daly; to be executed next day and his body
hung in chains.   Pat Cunningham, of the 72nd Foot, gets
mad drunk and shoots Jim Murray of the same regiment
without a word; to be hanged.   Or Thomas Short, of the
Company's infantry, at Ellore, drives his bayonet into a
comrade's belly as he lay upon his cot, and the sergeant
and others present carry off the wounded man with the
worst forebodings because they had not been able to suck
any blood from his wound; to be hanged.

As a rule there seems to have been considerable inclination to take Indian customs and sentiments into
account in the jury's verdicts.   It was a long-standing
practice to empanel a jury half Englishmen and half Indians when an Indian was on trial for his life, though
in one case a Muhammadan accused of murder chose to be
tried by twelve Englishmen.   Abd-un-nabi, a Muhammadan of Vizagapatam, was acquitted of murder although
he had strangled his daughter, because she had prostituted
herself to several and was three months with child.   But
two cases which raised the question of what might be done
to a slave were occasions of long debates among the jury-
men.   One was a peculiarly brutal and disgusting murder;
another was a painful but more ordinary case of excessive
punishment.   In both cases the jury was composed of
six Indians and six Englishmen, and in both cases the
Indians were for acquittal, the Englishmen for a verdict
of guilty.   On both occasions they had to be shut up for
the night, and the Englishmen were given a loaf of
bread and a couple of bottles of wine, while the Indians

were given an allowance of pan. At last verdicts of Guilty were found.

The Grand Jury imitated its English counterpart by making presentations of matters which they thought needing amendment. Thus they constantly presented the state of the town jail, which must have been full as bad as any English prison of the time. There was no means of separating the imprisoned debtors from the criminals; the water-supply was unspeakably polluted; a lunatic confined there killed one of the prisoners; and two murderers escaped. Other regular presentments were the high price of provisions, the need of fixing prices and wages, the neglects of the scavenger of the town. The Grand Jury claimed that these and their other presentments should be read out and answered in open court; and when on one occasion the justices refused to do so, the Grand Jury attempted to hold up the course of justice by refusing to examine the bills of indictment. The first time this happened, a new jury was empanelled; but that also stood upon its rights, and twice came into court announcing that it wished to proceed with other business before examining the bills. At last the court summoned the jury, took the evidence of one of the witnesses in its presence, and then ordered it to find a verdict. Three of the members said that they considered the present jury disqualified and incapable of acting. They were required to enter into recognisances to appear and stand their trial at Westminster for contempt of court and obstinate obstruction of justice. They replied that their objections were matters of conscience, not of contumacy, and refused to enter into recognisances. At last the court ordered them to be committed to the common jail and resolved to move the Council to send them to England by the next ship. This unexpected vigour brought the matter to an end. After a half-hearted application for bail, which of course was refused, the three defenders of liberty made their submission and entered into the recognisances. The leader of the three was Paul Benfield.

The proceedings of the court show us many queer things. A coroner's jury finds that Samuel Garside perished by the visitation of God and excess of liquor. The favourite grog-shop for sailors in the Black Town was Black Joe's tavern. A private, accused of murdering a comrade, had, it appears, given him a vomit that worked hard, and brought about his death. Mr George Moubray, driving in his chaise across the island towards the governor's garden, saw a European and an Indian woman struggling in the road. Stopping as soon as he could, he shouted at the man and got down from his chaise, on which the man ran away. Several people had been passing by, but, Moubray says, they did not seem in the least concerned until he stopped, and then they helped to catch the man, who was duly tried for attempted robbery. One witness tells us, what we should expect from other sources, that of an evening the hospital would be almost empty; and, when parties of soldiers and sailors met, there was sure to be a brawl, unless one side or the other was too drunk to fight, and then the drunken party would probably arrive home without its purses.

All this of course presents Madras from its least favourable angle. Madras cannot be judged by it any more than our own society can be judged by the contents of the Sunday papers. But this queer underworld exists and must be taken into account, although it must not be exaggerated either. We must set the woman screaming for the necklace that has been torn from her neck, and the man bound to the cart's tail parading his bloody back through the street, beside the trim civilian stopping his chaise to interfere, and the justices assembled to inflict punishment.

The Mayor's Court naturally does not offer the same police-news relish as the court of Quarter Sessions. But even this has its scandals. Its early constitution invested it with full independence of the Council save in so far as the latter formed a court of appeal with power to review its proceedings. Actually the situation bred a good deal of jealousy and dispute. The court assumed a power of collecting fines which Council held to exceed its charter; it imposed penalties on persons who refused to serve as aldermen; it re-elected a mayor, to whom the governor refused to administer the oath because the charter made no provision for re-elections. To the Council it seemed that these quarrels were undermining the very basis of their authority, and that all government would be dissolved if the court continued on its early footing. The Company agreed that it had exceeded its powers and had been " wanting in a due respect and deference to you their superiors, in awe and reverence for the Company, and concern for the welfare of the settlement." If its members did not mend their ways, the Company promised that they should no longer be allowed " to trade within our limits." One great cause of difference was finance. Six small duties had been assigned for the maintenance of the court; but it had long been notorious that they did not suffice to meet the expenditure. There was only one other source from which the court could possibly find the money, and that was the money deposited in court by the suitors. Dark rumours concerning this breach of trust were confirmed in 1744 by a letter addressed to the Council by the register of the court, stating " that the revenues appropriated for the ordinary and necessary expences of this court have not been sufficient of late years to defray the same, and that the court are in arrears the sum of 357 pagodas, which they have been obliged to take out of the deposited estates." The Council, however, believed that the real deficit was much larger than that. They reckoned it at 2,375 pagodas, and thought the difference had been made good by the proceeds of lending deposited estates at interest. The other great source of contention was the vexed question of oaths administered to respectable natives. This was a practice which the more respectable native merchants had striven constantly to avoid, and the Mayor's Court to enforce. When enforced, it usually consisted in visiting a temple, bathing in the temple tank, solemnly declaring the truth of the matter in question, and finally in confirmation " putting out the lamps according to custom." In 1735 the principal native banker of the place, a Gujarati, was fined for refusing to take an oath, on which the Council resolved to remit the fine. In the next year the court committed to prison two merchants for the same cause. A great crowd came to complain of this to the governor, declaring that if this was allowed, they would no longer live within the bounds; and at last, on the governor's intervention, the merchants were released.

The capture of Madras by the French in 1746 was held to have dissolved the Mayor's Court; and in 1753 a new court was established under the same name, but with certain changes in its constitution and powers. Vacancies were to be filled by the Council instead of by co-option; and the aldermen were to choose two persons on the first Tuesday in December of each year, of whom the Council was to elect one as mayor. Nor was the court in future to hear suits arising between natives, unless both parties agreed to accept the jurisdiction of the court. This was in great part the result of a petition that had been sent home in 1736, stating the grievances of the natives and proposing that their differences in future should be settled by arbitration among themselves, or, in the last resort, by the decision of the head-men of the castes concerned. The governor of that time, Richard Benyon, had tried to bring the mayor and aldermen of the day to agree to this.

" I invited them to supper," he says, " on purpose to talk with them, and began with telling them I was very confident they had only their labour for their pains; that it could not be very agreeable to them to sit sweating several hours two days every week to hear such dry and formal pieces as were produced by the attornies . . . after which I told them I had thoughts . . . to form some proper courts among the natives for determining all differences between them . . . I did not doubt but all the contending parties would be satisfied without desiring to make any application to our courts, which were always attended with much loss of time, besides expence . . . and very material mistakes . . . by the ignorance of the interpreters, and not seldom by their knavery. . . ."

But the court of that time had refused to agree to any diminution of its powers. Now they were reduced, but no native courts were set up as Benyon had intended.

The new court was almost as disputatious as the old one had been. It demanded all the property which had been held by its predecessor; and claimed to own the court-house in which it sat. But the Council was now in a stronger position from which to assert its supremacy. Moneys paid into court were now all paid into the Company's treasury, so that the court could no longer pay its way by an abuse of trust; and when it criticised the appointments which the Council made to the bench, the Council tartly rejoined:

" Had you been as studious in reading the charter to learn the proper duty of the Mayor's Court as you have been forward in pointing out to the President and council what should be their conduct, you would have found that they are not in any degree subjected to your admonition in their choice of the members of the court; . . . and they will be careful never to appoint any person of an inferior character to those who already compose the court . . ."

In this serene and dignified atmosphere a worthy group of attorneys plied their trade. Their recorded professional offences were not numerous. In 1744 Henry de Veil, perhaps a relative of Fielding's fellow-magistrate, was fined 50 pagodas and required to dismiss his dubash, or chief native servant, apparently for refusing to conduct a suit without a greater fee than ordinary. The Grand Jury present barratry as common. An attorney refuses to give up the papers of a case to a client who is dissatisfied with his conduct. But for long years no lawyer practising in Madras had any professional qualifications at all. Several of them were young covenanted servants waiting until they should rise by seniority to a post with some pickings in it. Philip Francis Greenslate, after worrying his superiors for ten years with his neglect of duty, after being threatened with being sent off to Sumatra, and at last marrying an ineligible lady in the Black Town, is successively dismissed the Company's service, and admitted an attorney of the Mayor's Court. Another was Mr Isaac Merigeot, an adventurer who had lived on his wits in Madras for many years. When the court was in abeyance, he assisted Clive to supply the army with bullocks and provisions. "How could you think of recommending Merigeot . . .?" asks Lieutenant Repington of Clive. "That rascal has as much money as you have. . . . The Major [i.e. Lawrence] will certainly cut his ears if he comes this way." This, I suspect, explains why Merigeot returned to the Mayor's Court as soon as it was reopened. Another case more curious than reputable is that of Peter Dencker. He originally came out

to the East as a soldier on the Sumatra establishment in
1726. After serving his time and surviving that detestable climate, he settled in Madras, where he acted as
butcher to the garrison. In 1753 he too was enrolled as
an attorney, and when, in 1756, his effects came to be
sold, along with his betel-box and backgammon table, his
pipes and horsewhips, appear as evidence of his final profession his wig and gown and a book of law.

Later in the century matters improve. Robert Williamson in 1770 grounds his application to practise on being
" conversant with the laws of my country and the practice
of the courts at Westminster and Guildhall." I expect he
had been an attorney's clerk. The first real lawyer was,
I think, Charles Bromley, who claimed to have been
" regularly inducted in the profession of the law to the
several courts of record at Westminster." Thomas Johnson in 1773 is an attorney of the Court of Common Pleas
and a solicitor of the Court of Chancery. Edward Ellis
proves his admission as an attorney of the Court of King's
Bench in the Kingdom of Ireland. Pullein Spencer, who
first appears in 1784, had been sworn a barrister of the
Irish High Court of Chancery. When he died, his library
was found to contain a respectable collection of law books
—Wood's *Conveyances* and Hawkins' *Pleas of the Crown*,
Addington's *Penal Statutes* and Butler's *Nisi prius,* the
Statutes at Large, and Blackstone's *Commentaries,* and a
score of others now forgotten; and at the end of them
all, as if to show he was no dry-as-dust pedant, a little
volume entitled the *Sports of the Law.*

Their social status rises with their professional standing. The discharged soldiers and cracked linen-drapers
give place to the brother of the Solicitor-General, or to
Mr Stephen Popham, an Irish M.P. driven from his home
by debt. He came out secretary to Sir John Day, Advo-
cate-General in Bengal, but, quarrelling with his patron,

preferred to remain at Madras.   Their dispute is said to have nearly brought on a duel, and the circumstance inspired an epigram better than most metrical effusions in the Indian journals of the time:

" If the astonishing account is true,
 They met, they talked, they drew, and then withdrew."

Popham was an amiable man, a great reformer, with a constitutional incapacity for managing his own affairs. Mrs Fay, who stayed with her husband at his house on her way to Calcutta, describes him as

" one of the most eccentric of beings I have ever met with. Poor man!   He is a perpetual projector, a race whose exertions have frequently benefited society, but seldom, I believe, been productive of much advantage to themselves or their families.   He is at present laying plans for building what is called the Black Town to a great extent, and confidently expects to realise an immense fortune."

He had obtained a grant of a piece of waste ground opposite his house, and which had remained time out of mind an unwholesome nuisance to the neighbourhood.   This he proposed to raise, drain, and lay out in regular streets, with a central market, regular fish and meat shambles, the whole to be inspected and kept clean.   He gives a dismal but not overcharged account of the condition of the Black Town in his time:

" There is scarce a street . . . wherein there are not many puddles and holes of considerable depth, and some wells too without any wall to prevent the uninformed traveller from breaking a limb or losing his life.   Mr Ram, who acted as coroner, has said that the accidents of persons found in wells exceeded all others on which he sat as coroner. . . .   The streets also almost generally are too narrow, highly uneven, no fall for water, no foot-

PART OF THE BLACK TOWN.
After the aquatint of Thomas Daniell.

160]

way for passengers, no lamp for the safety of persons by
night, nor anything to give a stranger reason to believe
that an Englishman has any idea of police . . ."

But down to the very end of the century the attorneys
of Madras still included men who, to use the significant
phrase, had "turned lawyer." When the old Mayor's
Court was in 1798 superseded by the Recorder's Court
conducted by a barrister of standing, of the thirteen practising attorneys three had been military officers and one a
surgeon. One of these had too various a career to be
passed over in silence. In December, 1775, John (or
James) Stuart Hall was admitted an ensign on the Madras
establishment; in 1780 he became lieutenant, in 1786
captain-lieutenant, and in 1790 he was allowed to resign
the service. Such are the official outlines of his career.
As an officer I do not think he was a conspicuous success.
In 1781, in the course of the war with Hyder, he is said
to have committed an error of judgment which led to the
loss of 500 men and three guns, and so affected his commanding officer that he took to his bed with a bilious fever,
" which prevents me from being so explicit as I otherwise
should have been." This produced bad blood not only
in Colonel Nixon, but in the lieutenant as well. By ill-
luck both were in garrison in Trichinopoly, when the
paymaster, a covenanted servant named Norris, thought
that his chief native servant had tried to poison him; and,
as there were no civil courts, the man was brought for
trial before a Sepoy court martial. Nixon thought the
sentence altogether inadequate, and said what he thought
about the dubash in garrison orders, whereon Hall said
what he thought about Nixon and Norris in a paper which
was handed round the garrison. For this he was court
martialled, charged with clandestinely writing " a false,
malignant, and scandalous libell." But the court had

probably laughed too much in private over the libel to treat it very seriously in public. It found that Hall had written a paper containing a severe attack on the characters of the commandant and paymaster, " containing some few assertions unsupported by evidence "; that he had acted improperly in communicating it to others without Nixon's knowledge, but that the delay in his trial had deprived him of a variety of assistance, and he was sentenced to be reprimanded in general orders. Meanwhile Hall had signalised himself in other directions. David Young writes in 1780:

". . . Had Mrs Angus set out with Mr Hall (the gentleman that lived with Mr Angus) before you left Madras? If not, it must have been soon after. They went to Tanjore together, and I think Angus is well clear of her, don't you? . . ."

This Mrs Angus was Mary Frances L'Allemande, whom Angus married at Chingleput in 1777. " Mr Angus is married to the lady that he kept," says the incurable gossip Young, " and she brought him a young girl a few days after . . ." No wonder he thought her elopement a good riddance. However, when Angus died, later in 1780, Hall married the widow, who must have had the knack of making herself indispensable. In 1789 we hear more of Hall, then on half-pay and permitted to practise as an attorney in the Mayor's Court. General Horne forwards to Government letters from Lieutenant Hammond of the Company's artillery, complaining of his wife's misconduct with Hall, and desiring Government's intervention, I suppose by way of punishing Hall; Government, however, thought that his proper course was to sue Hall for damages in the Mayor's Court. After his retirement from the army, Hall not only practised as an attorney, but also acted for a time as editor or took some part in the

management of the *Madras Courier,* then lately founded.
On 15 September, 1791, the *Courier* published a story in
the manner of the day called "A Chinese Anecdote,"
which professed to describe the tyrannous administration
of a mandarin. The disguise was thin, and almost at
once Mr James Landon, of the Company's Civil Service,
complained that this satire must be aimed at his conduct.
Hall was required to declare publicly that he was not the
author, that he did not know who the author was, and that
when he published it he did not know that it had any personal bearing. He complied, but how many of his readers
believed him?

CHAPTER XI

HOUSES AND HOUSEHOLDS

IN spite of the white ant and all the other destructive processes of India, many of the houses in which our predecessors revelled long and died quickly have survived to our own day. Perhaps most of the buildings in the Fort, and several of those in the suburbs of the city date back into the eighteenth century, and preserve the type of dwelling that European merchants seem commonly to have built for themselves in the East. This has on the ground floor a series of small rooms, low-arched, dimly lit, ill-ventilated; above them on the first floor a large central hall, with suites of high, airy rooms on either side, and broad verandas before and behind. The rooms below were storehouses—go-downs, as they were called; those above, approached by a broad, easy staircase, were the living-rooms. In accordance with their respective purposes the first were heavily doored, strongly barred, securely shuttered, as a protection against thieves; while the walls of the second were almost all doors and windows, so as to admit the air, whichever way the wind might blow. Little glass was used. Indeed, early in the century, a house with glass windows was known as the " Glass House." The windows were closed either by venetian shutters—*jin-mills*—or by rattan screens. The oyster-shell windows of Goa and Bombay were unknown on our side of India.

ST THOMÉ STREET IN FORT ST. GEORGE.

(By F. S. Ward

Above all was a flat, terraced roof, that taxed, and still taxes, human ingenuity to prevent its cracking in the hot weather and admitting deluges of rain in the monsoon. Once papers relating to an estate lay under seal in an upper room in Vizagapatam; the winds blew; the rains descended; and the papers were ruined before leave could come from Madras to break the seals and open the room. This was the principal defect of such houses. Otherwise they were excellently adapted to the climate; and were built not only by the English, French, and Dutch on the Coromandel Coast, but even by factors in distant Smyrna and Aleppo.

What was peculiar to the Madras houses was the fine, white plaster, which you could polish up like marble, used for covering the high pillars of the verandas and the wide spaces of the walls. Every visitor noted and admired its lustre, which the larger, finer houses of Calcutta could not match; and in a few houses, in some churches, it may still be admired.

Rents were high, as they always have been in India. In the Black Town, where your neighbours might be noisy, and your surroundings nasty, you might get a house for 10 or 15 pagodas a month—say £48 to £72 a year. But in the Fort, owing to the limited space and the larger size of the houses, rents were higher. Hastings paid 108 pagodas a month. In 1778 and 1779 Jourdan offers his house next the Admiralty—so called from having been bought for the accommodation of the admiral when ashore —first for 750 and then for 900 pagodas a year; the latter rent was about 10 per cent. on its value. Some years earlier he had offered for sale either this or another house in the Fort for 8,500 pagodas. He thus describes it:

" The upper part contains an hall and seven rooms, none very large; the lower on the northern side 2 go-downs, together the length of the breadth of the house, and two small go-downs within these; the southern side, one go-down and two smaller ones, which serve for butlery etc.; to the eastward there are go-downs besides cook-room etc. The house shall be made over to you in a fortnight, and taken of you, if agreeable, for Mr Lewin Smith at 80 pagodas a month for six months . . ."

It looks as though the Commissary-General, Colonel James Capper, was justified in complaining in 1775 of the 25 pagodas a month allowed him for house rent. The Commissary-General in Bengal gets 600 Rs. a month, he says—

" a sum that may appear very considerable in Europe, where the interest of money is very low, but in this country, where 12 per cent is the legal rate of interest, no person of the rank which the Honourable the Court of Directors have been pleased to confer on me can live in a house of lower rent . . ."

The Council decided to double his allowance; and even then he was probably out of pocket.

All through the early part of the century a house in the Fort was necessary to every considerable family, not only for protection from possible enemies or marauders, but also for business which centred round the Sea-gate, the Customs House, and the governor's residence. Until the very end of the century the Fort was frequented for business and needed for protection. In every Mysore war except the last, " looties " raided the outskirts of the city and drove the inhabitants within the shelter of the walls. There were all the large offices, public and private; in 1803 eight out of ten houses of agency had their Madeira go-downs in the Fort. There were all the shops displaying the costly and ill-chosen imports from Europe; and there too or hard by were the places of meeting and amusement until the theatre was moved from the island to the Choultry Plain in 1790 and the Pantheon Rooms set up in 1793.

Nevertheless men had been glad from the first to escape from its narrow dusty streets into the open country beyond the walls. The governor set up a country house with garden and bowling-green on the banks of what then was a clear though sluggish river, now called the Cooum, much as in England men were building villas at Hampton and Richmond. Some seven miles inland lay St Thomas Mount, the traditional scene of the martyrdom of the apostle. There too houses began to spring up, week-end bungalows, for, though beyond the English limits, the place was popular both for the relative coolness of the air and for the fowling, hawking, and coursing which it offered. But it was somewhat too far from Madras for comfortable residence. It was plundered by Dupleix, it was plundered by Lally, it was plundered by our Mysore enemies; consequently, though it became the head-quarters of the Company's artillery, it was superseded as a place of residence.

West of the Fort, beyond the river that poured its intricate channels round the walls, lay the Choultry Plain, so called from the great white customs-post standing in the middle of it. This was much more conveniently situated for garden-houses than the Mount. Your chaise and pair, or even your palanquin with its six bearers, could easily take you into the Fort in time for business in the morning, or out of it in time for dinner in the afternoon. Here therefore sprang up the residential suburb of Madras. The movement had begun even before 1746; but it became rapid after the middle of the century, and towards its end was stretching southward to the banks of the Adyar. The Company at first tried to check this emigration, which it attributed merely to " the folly and

vanity of merchants in having the parade of country
houses and gardens." The council, in obedience to the
wishes of its Honourable Masters, resolved that no grants
of land should be made for such purposes except to those
of higher degree than that of writer. But the movement
went on none the less, and their gardens became the joy
and pride of the Madras residents. Nor were they really
an extravagant hobby. Even at the beginning of the
nineteenth century, the smaller houses could be rented at
20 pagodas a month.

The lively Hickey, who would have told us so much
had he decided after all to join the Madras Army, relates
how on his arrival he was conducted by a friend to his
garden-house. He found it a dreary-looking habitation,
with no furniture but a few rough chairs and tables,
and surrounded by an uncultivated waste which his host
was pleased to call a garden. But Hickey saw the place
under the worst possible conditions. He arrived in the
hot weather when all was bare and scorched; the last
gardens he had seen were those which slope greenly down
to the banks of the Thames; and the incursions of Hyder's
cavalry the year before had obliged everyone to remove
all furniture of value to the Fort. In happier days
garden-houses were better filled than when Hickey spent
his restless night upon a bare couch. Had he visited a
few years later the garden of Dawsonne Drake, of the
Company's civil service, he would have found a much
more luxurious welcome—the veranda with its rattan chairs
and couches from Canton; the drawing-room set out with
card-tables and arm-chairs of ebony and rosewood, the
floor of alternate black and white squares covered here and
there with Persian rugs, and the white walls hung with
mirrors and engravings; the dining-room with its well-
polished mahogany; the bedrooms with their mirrors and
wardrobes and bedsteads hung with mosquito-curtains. In

the cold weather Hickey would have found the garden covered with grass and gay with flowering trees. David Young writes to a friendly sea-captain going down the Straits:

" If you can find it convenient to get me some young plants of curious trees for my garden and some seeds, it will be the greatest present you can bring."

And Jourdan begs a friend on his way home to send him back from the Cape strawberry-plants, young almond and laburnum shoots, and any flower-seeds that can be got.

Furniture offered to the housekeeper a more difficult problem than either house or garden. Mrs Kindersley complains bitterly of its cost at Calcutta, where you had either to pick up all sorts of oddments never intended to appear together, or resort to " the blundering carpenters of the country," or send to Bombay, which meant waiting for three years or so. Matters, however, were better at Madras, where the artisans had long produced delicate woodwork. In 1731 the French Council at Pondicherry ordered at Madras chairs and tables for their factories in Bengal. But though furniture was made at Madras it was dear even there. A bill which has been preserved, shows the following items:

2 dozen Europe chairs	.	81 pagodas	(27s. each)
a dining-table in two part	.	15 „	(£6)
a couch	.	8 „	(£3 4s.)
a mahogany bureau	.	25 „	(£10)

The Madras inventories confirm the belief that the hanging punkah, which in the nineteenth century was so characteristic a feature of Anglo-Indian rooms, was not used by Europeans of earlier periods. It does not occur at all, for the " pair of punkers " of Laurence Bowden's inven-

tory were almost certainly large fans. Since it was by
origin an Arab and Persian device, and certainly used by
the Moghuls at Delhi, I may hazard the guess that its
introduction coincided with the growing acquaintance of
Englishmen with upper India from the last years of the
century.

The walls were generally covered, as they are now,
with whitewash, but in the finest houses the plaster might
be polished, and sometimes they were hung with " China
paper." Jourdan in 1771 asks for a square with which
to cover the hall of his garden-house; and in 1759 six
rolls of China paper hangings, six sheets to the roll,
were sold at Madras for 3 pagodas. I suppose this was
the sort of paper with which the great banker, Samuel
Bernard, hung the gallery of his mansion at Passy. " Ces
papiers de la Chine semblent avoir fait rêver tous les con-
temporains," says his biographer.

Of the pictures which hung upon these walls we know
little. They are enumerated with irritating vagueness.
Not much can be made of " 24 French pictures in crayons "
or " 20 Europe pictures." Mr William Roberts, by whom
the inventory-makers dealt more kindly than usual, had
a considerable collection of prints, including the King and
royal family, engraved portraits of Pope, of Chesterfield,
and of the Gunnings, Titian's " Loves of the Gods " in a
set of ten, and seventeen large prints after Rubens. Minia-
tures, as we should expect, were certainly common; and
family portraits, also as we should expect, rare. The only
undoubted reference I know of is that case of family
paintings sent out to Edward Croke, Begam Johnson's
father. As a matter of fact, the portraits on the walls
were much more likely to represent the existing generation
than even imaginary ancestors. The fame of the wealth
and generosity of nabobs—both the Indian and English
varieties—attracted many portrait-painters to the East

at this time; and of these several visited Madras. There was Katherine Read, whom I have already mentioned; she had a brother William, a surgeon on the Madras establishment, and a nephew, Alexander Read, an ensign in the army, but destined to be the first collector of Salem. She was employed during her short stay at Madras in painting for the Nawab. David Young, who of course knew all about her, for she came from Dundee, writes:

" The old lady is vastly liked by everybody, and has been visited by the young Nabob; I hear she is going to draw his picture, and she may have a chance to draw their ladies' pictures; if this should be her fortune, it will be a great thing for her . . . They live very retired. The old lady has not the least inclination for show, but rather too much inclined to the contrary in this country. . . . She loves to hear of her friends making money . . ."

But though employed chiefly by the Nawab, she certainly did some Europeans. Young was involved in a dispute with James Call, of the Covenanted Service, for whom Miss Read had painted a portrait of Miss Shutter. The portrait was damaged; and Young in vain attempted to persuade Call to pay for it. John Paxton, portrait-painter, was licensed to proceed to Madras for five years in 1776; in 1778 was living in Jourdan's house in the Fort George Willison, who had been introduced by George Dempster as " a very near relation of mine now at your presidency, Mr Willeson, painter, whom you will find an amiable modest man as well as an ingenious artist." In 1785 came out John Smart, miniaturist, and his daughter. Nor does this exhaust the list. There were Thomas Hickey, and George Chinnery, and Carrier Deah. But the oddest painter who ever set up his easel at Madras was infallibly the first complaisant husband of the second Mrs Hastings. The following passages from unpublished letters from Warren Hastings throw a queer light on this famous transaction:

" In my last," he writes to Surgeon Hancock, over whom he had nearly quarrelled with Clive, " I desired you to take the trouble to enquire for a lodging for a Mr Imhoff who proposes to try his fortune as a miniature painter in Bengal. . . . Mr Imhoff is a ship-mate of mine, an officer of some rank in the German service, sent hither with great expectations as a cadet with a family, and must have starved had he not happily been qualified to seek a livelyhood in a more profitable employment. He has had some success here, having taken off the heads of half the settlement, but he must soon be aground here . . ."

And after Imhoff had gone, leaving Marion behind him at Madras, Hastings thus addresses him:

" Dear Sir, I have received your favor of the 5th June, with Mrs Imhoff's picture enclosed, which arrived in perfect order. I am delighted with the picture, which independent of its likeness, I think is the best painting you have executed, at least of any that I have seen. I return you many thanks for it. . . . I think the resemblance more striking than it appeared when you had it here, and it is admirably finished. I hope I have not put you to any inconvenience in sending it, as I could have been well contented to have waited longer for it. If I expressed any impatience to receive it before Mrs Imhoff, I do assure you it was not in complaint, because I know how little leisure you had from business, and how necessary it was to establish a character for punctuality on your first appearance in a place where you was a stranger . . . I had the pleasure of writing to you the 12th of last month, and took the liberty to send you a little China paint and a stick of Indian ink which had been sent me from China. I hope they arrived safe. Mrs Imhoff tells me several of her letters have miscarried, and a box of bracelets which I forwarded for her to you . . ."

Hastings seems to have lived in the Fort; and drew the utterly insufficient allowances for house-rent and servants paid by the Company to its members of Council. Servants, as elsewhere, were expensive. Europeans were rare in that capacity. The governor might bring out with him a body-servant. Lord Pigot leaves £500 to his servant Joseph Nutting, and Samuel Chaplin came out as butler and valet to Lord Macartney. " As I had much leisure time," the latter writes, " during his Lordship's residence at Madras, he was so good to permit me to exercise my trade [as hairdresser] with the addition of keeping a shop in the Fort to vend Europe articles." Officers of the Europeans would have soldier servants; and an order of 1778 shows one private employed as a piper, several as grooms, postilions, and coachmen, others as gardeners, and one as keeper of a madman. Paul Benfield afforded a French cook, who died at Madras in 1778. But few households could afford such luxuries, and most confined themselves to Indian servants, who, then as now, were extravagantly praised or blamed. Their number always made their individual cheapness collectively dear. An English gentleman or considerable merchant must have twelve or fifteen, and this number could not be diminished.

" If you lessen the number but by one," says Mrs Kindersley, " they have a thousand tricks to distress you. . . . All are combined to oblige you to keep the number which they deem proportioned to your rank. As their master rises in life, they insist upon more cooks, more peons, more kissmagars, more bearers."

Even the humblest subaltern could not do with less than three. They spoke a broken English peculiar to themselves, in which English words and Tamil idiom and construction entered into an unholy alliance on their artful lips. About 1750 they were paid pretty much the same at Madras and Calcutta. In 1765 a butler at Madras got from 1½ to 3 pagodas a month, while one at Calcutta would get from 5 rupees upwards; but at Calcutta wages rose faster than at the southern presidency, for at the end of the century the Calcutta butler would be getting 10 to 25 rupees while a Madras one would still be content with 3 pagodas even on campaign. Sometimes these servants were known by curious nicknames. At the Madras tavern kept by Michael Fennel, the billiard-marker was called " Red-bonnet," while the butler was called " Lord Clive," probably for the same reason that Clive himself was addressed by his friends as " Dear Beauty." A certain subaltern's servant was " the Flamingo," for short " the Flam."

Besides these hired servants, slaves were not unknown, though they disappear in the later part of the century. Thus in the account sale of John Norris in 1756, five " black boys " and one " black girl " were sold, fetching from 20 to 37 pagodas each. In 1770, just before the famous decision that freed slaves as soon as they set foot in England, a slave-boy was sent to Mr. Hyndman, merchant in London, as his nephew had promised to do before his death. Mrs Turing in 1761 had several " Coffree girls " in her service. Jourdan, acting as executor to a friend's estate, writes in 1784:

" As to the slaves, I detest selling of men, but see no alternative. I wish H—— would take them, because then they would not be ill-used."

The prevalence of such sentiments probably explains why slaves disappear from the inventories.

In respect of food the inhabitants of Madras were at a disadvantage. Travellers like Bowry might say that they lived on the fat of the land, but he was used to a diet of salt junk, and indeed most verdicts were passed after four or five months on shipboard. So far as food went Madras ran a poor second to the moister province of Bengal. The fact is proved by the supplies of sheep, geese, and turkeys, which were sent down from the latter. Richard Harris leaves to Lazarus de Monte " whatever sheep, geese, turkeys, grain, etc., may come from Bengal this season." Hastings writes from Madras to Surgeon Hancock:

" I received . . . the 12 geese, the survivors of 24. Of these two died before I could distribute them. . . . The captain apologised for the loss of the rest, which he said was owing to a great mortality on board, having a great multitude of geese-passengers, who died by being too close stowed."

Jourdan acknowledges the kindness of a Bengal friend in sending down a sheep, a goose, and potatoes. The Northern Circars were another source of delicacies. Young writes to a captain at Coringa:

" As your vessel is so small, I do not like to trouble you; however if you can bring me a dozen of good large hens, I shall take it very kind of you, and also a maund of Yanam biscuits, if to be got, and a good fat goose or two for Christmas . . ."

Besides these the Company's shipping annually brought out, either on the officers' privilege or as private consignments from friends in England, eatables of many kinds —hams and tongues, casks of butter, cheese packed in lead, jams and preserves. The Company itself once sent out Cheshire cheeses packed in olive oil, observing that if the oil were not eatable on arrival, it could be sold for burning; this experiment was not repeated. The inventory of a shopkeeper, Thomas Leany, at Trichinopoly, includes 4 square bottles of capers, 4 bottles of cranberries, 10 quart bottles of fish sauce, 2 bottles of Carvey (?), 6 bottles of fruit for tarts, and 10½ round cheeses. China was another source of supply, sending hams and other things, besides tea, already in 1760 " almost the greatest want in life among superfluities." With these additional delicacies, with the fruit afforded by the Coast—pine-apples, mangoes, limes, oranges, pimple-noses, and the plantain —and with the chutneys for which Madras was famous, housewives made do with the flavourless beef, tough mutton, and stringy fowls that the country provided. The inventories suggest that many kept a stock of animals, doubtless in the hope of fattening them into a more palatable consistency. Major Achilles Preston had 3 turkeys and 12 ducks in hand; Captain d'Illens had a whole farmyard—2 cows and calves, a sheep, 3 goats and 8 kids, one hog and 7 large pigs, 2 geese, 3 turkeys, 35 ducks, and 13 fowls; and so had Robert George Lathom, of the Covenanted Service, who died in 1792.

Plate, never common, certainly became rarer as the century advanced. In the old days the governor had enjoyed the use of a fine set of plate belonging to the Company; but that fell as spoil to the French, and the Company refused to replace it. I should think it likely that the governor of that time, Pigot, had his own; but it is much less likely that any succeeding governor had. Really large fortunes were not common at Madras; and unless Paul Benfield used plate on fine occasions, no one at Madras ate off anything more valuable than porcelain. From this, however, the military officers must be excepted, not because they were unduly wealthy, but because on campaign plate had the advantage over china of not easily being broken, and over pewter of being easily cleaned. Several of them left one or two silver plates, and a silver tankard or so. An order of 1792, issued to the army before Seringapatam, announces that one of Captain Beatson's coolies has remained behind in camp, probably in order to sell his load, which consisted of a Europe mahogany box, containing: 1 plated teapot, 1 ditto milkpot, 6 silver teaspoons, 3 tin canisters, 6 cups and saucers, 1 sneaker, with some small bottles and other things. He at least did not campaign in great luxury. The plate which figures in the inventories is mostly of the ordinary sort—spoons and salt-cellars, tankards and teapots. Sometimes a silver sauce-pan is mentioned; and the most notable single article is certainly the silver hand-basin. This article is mentioned several times; with its companion ewer it was carried round before and after meals, to perform the service of the finger-bowl, of which I find no traces at Madras. Daw-sonne Drake was the only person to whom a large collection can be positively ascribed, and his plate so far as described offers no items of special interest. But if plate was going out of use, Madras was well placed to secure regular supplies of china-ware. It was regularly imported by every vessel from Canton or Macao. From a suit heard in 1757, it appears that in 1745 Francisco Manucci, in whom I suspect a son of the great Niccolao, sent to the Malabar Coast 20 sets of table china, costing 5 pagodas or £2 the set of 27 pieces.

In the thirsty Indian climate, beverages were various. Water was used as little as possible. At Salomon's sale in 1757 Orme bought "a filtering stone" for 3 pagodas 27 fanams, but this is the only occasion on which this desperate remedy is mentioned. Instead of purifying their water, men preferred to disguise its flavour. This explains the popularity of tea, and also of those hot, high-flavoured wines usually sent to India.   In the seventeenth century Canary was the wine most commonly sent out; but Shiraz wine was also largely drunk.   The English had their own wine-maker at Shiraz, and the Gombroon factory regularly supplied his produce to Madras down to 1740 or so.   It is described as somewhat thick, red in colour, and fiery in taste.   So popular was it that attempts were made to imitate it by the French at Bourbon in 1742, and by the English at Cuddalore in 1698 and at Bangalore in 1805.

When the troubles in Persia brought the wine exports to an end, the Company took to sending Madeira.   One of its ships would put in there annually to take on board a stock of wine for the use of the Company's servants in India; 150 to 200 pipes were sent to Madras annually by the Company, besides what might be brought on private account.   So popular did this wine become that foreigners began to compete for it at the public sales.

" As our Honourable Masters," say the Council in 1754, " out of their indulgent care are pleased to send a ship annually to Madeira to supply their own settlements with wine, it must be contrary to their intention that foreigners should be suffered to rob their servants of this advantage by bidding at the out-crys to an immoderate price; this was the case last year when several persons were employed to purchase a large quantity of Madeira wine for the Dutch, by which means it was raised in value beyond the reach of many of the Company's junior servants, whose allowances scarcely suffice to purchase the mere necessaries of life . . ."

It was decided therefore not to sell more than 50 pipes by public auction; all the remainder was to be issued to the Company's servants at 52 pagodas a pipe, which with allowance for leakage made 25 per cent. on the prime cost; no one under the degree of Junior Merchant was to have more than one pipe, and the rest no more than two, and that on condition that it was for their own private consumption only. The 50 pipes realised from 62 to 70 pagodas, one officer, Captain de Morgan, buying 14, and another, Captain Brohier, buying 6. They probably resold their purchases, or part of them. However, it was impossible to keep the price down to its old level. Wine, which in the 'forties had cost £12 to £14 the pipe, in the 'fifties cost £20 or £22, and in the 'nineties £35 or £40. At Madras the price was about 45 pagodas—£18— in 1745; it rose from 50 to 70—£20 to £28—between 1750 and 1759; and in the last quarter of the century ruled from 90 to 100 pagodas—£36 to £40. At any distance inland it sold at much higher rates—4¾ pagodas the dozen at Ellore in 1775, 4½ pagodas in camp in Mysore in 1790. These rates I reckon to be about 140 to 150 pagodas the pipe.

Madeira is, I believe, the only wine that improves in the climate of India; consequently it is the only wine of which large stocks were to be found in private cellars. The tossing of the sea-voyage was thought to be particularly good for it; so the eccentric Colonel Martinz of H.H. the Nawab's service would hang his pipes from the cellar roof, and periodically set them spinning, or give them a voyage round the Cape, as he called it. Calcutta firms would send pipes up country to Cawnpore to season. A present of well-matured Madeira from Madras was thus a present worthy of acceptance by anyone. Lieutenant Andrew Morris of the Company's Artillery desires of his executors

" that they may take the trouble of sending from Madras to London one pipe of the best Madeira wine to the Rt Hon the Earl of Courtown, to whom I owe the post of honour which I now enjoy (I mean my commission) and

I hope from many instances of his Lordship's goodness that he will honour my memory by accepting and drinking a glass of it thereto . . ."

Madeira was drunk, not only as a dessert wine, but also at meals mixed with water. In many inventories, besides claret, hock, and madeira glasses, I find others described as " wine and water glasses." What these were does not plainly appear. They were not tumblers, for those are separately enumerated. I fancy they must have been half-pint glasses on stems, not unlike those used for the familiar half-peg. But their use at all events was clear. Captain Eastwick, after a long residence in the East, horrified a merchant friend at Hampstead by mixing with water his prime London Particular.

Madeira was not the only wine that was drunk at Madras. Claret—called English, Rrench, or Danish, according to the flag of the importing ship—was to be had at anything from 16 to 64 shillings the dozen; hock is also found, though more rarely; champagne at 10 shillings the bottle; and Port which often partnered Madeira at dessert. But the real rivals of Madeira were not to be found in other wines, but in malt liquor and spirits. Even in the eighteenth century the Indian demand was recognised by brewers, as is still shown by " East India ales " and " India porter." Small beer, ale, and porter occur time after time in the inventories. A lieutenant at Arcot had 10 dozen of ale; a free merchant of Madras 4 dozen of ale and a cask of porter. The stock of liquor laid in for Admiral Watson included 6 casks of Europe beer. But this was expensive. Porter cost at least a shilling the bottle. The popular drink was the country spirit, arrack. It was cheap, cheering, and seductive. The highly respectable Mrs Cumberland in her country vicarage doted on it. But the danger of it was that one unaccustomed to it drank more than was wise. This with Madeira was the drink *par excellence* at Madras. Every social evening, whatever the drink at supper, was crowned with the appearance of the silver bowl and ladle, the decanter of arrack, the water, the limes, and sugar.

In this respect the nabobs were only following the customs of their native country. But in smoking they hopelessly violated all the canons of good breeding, and showed themselves to rise no higher than the level of the common-room. Only at the universities, as has been happily said, *lampada vitai tradunt*. The learned Dr Parr, on a visit to Lord Granville, was indulged with a pipe only " in a room somewhat apart from the rooms we live in." But in India men, and ladies too, smoked hard all through the century. Madras, setting out with its own traditions and customs, fell under the influence of Bengal in this respect as well as in the matter of government. At first the churchwarden pipe was used; but Captain Cope and his contemporary, Peter Dencker, were, I think, the last to use it. Achilles Preston is the only officer who owned the cheroots which in the nineteenth century became universal. But, about the time when Clive reconquered Calcutta with the sword, Calcutta retaliated by invading Madras with the hookah. In nearly all the later inventories one is almost sure to find it, silver-mounted or plain, with its foreign and barbarous accessories—snakes and cases and chillums.

CHAPTER XII

THE STANDARD OF TASTE

THESE houses with their fine large rooms, these households with their unnumbered servants, were inhabited by gentry who attired themselves with a magnificence to match. The costume of eighteenth-century Madras was as gay as, nay, gayer than that of contemporary England. They attended church, they went to concerts, balls, and dinner-parties, bright in silks and velvets. No one went to church without losing some ounces by perspiration; how much more then under the exercise of the dance or the dinner? The inventories reveal suits of all sorts and colours, from white to crimson, from green to scarlet, from alapeen to pompadour cloth gold-laced; breeches of all materials from buckskin to silk-web and dimity. A Company's servant sent ambassador to a country princeling submitted the following bill:

10 yards of Europe flowered [silk?] . .	80	Rs.
Brocade for a waistcoat	132	,,
Hatt with a point d'Espagne . . .	50	,,
A set of gold buttons	25	,,
Taylor's bill for making a suit of cloathes .	13	,,
	300	Rs.

Nor was this gaiety of attire limited to the courts of princes
or the bounds of Madras. Men would fig themselves
out in remote factories too, like Conrad's character who
in the wilds of Africa always dressed for dinner. But
the splendour of Madras paled before the gorgeousness
of Calcutta. Jourdan was commissioned by a friend in
Bengal to get some coats embroidered for him; they were
lost at sea; and then Jourdan sent up some lace. But
this was not fine enough to give satisfaction. " The lace
I forwarded to you," Jourdan writes, " I thought would
have made you a coat handsome enough for you [to appear
in] before the Mogul, but you, I find, are gayer than I
expected." Gayer too than was customary in London.
After only two years' absence in the East the volatile
Hickey wore such " gay India coats " as shocked his
friends, and they we may be sure were not models of
moderation. The thing seems to have been perennial, for
a century later after a short Indian service a man would
appear in Bond Street in neckties such as a bookie might
wear on the race-course. The occasions on which these
eccentric costumes appeared multiplied as the century went
on. At first they would come out on Sundays only, and
dissolve the too solid flesh of councillors nowhere but in
church. But as society became more numerous and co-
herent, balls and supper-parties, concerts and the theatre
exacted more frequent and continuous tribute from vanity
to the climate.

At all times, however, this gaudy and cumbersome
apparel was the uniform of pleasure or respectability, not
of ease or business. If the nabobs were inclined to overdo
their grandeur, so also at times they put off their dignity
with their silk coats and wigs. Early in the century
Muhammadan costume supplied them not only with sleep-
ing-suits, but also with a free-and-easy dress by day,
consisting of a long loose coat and loose trousers. Time

had been when, as a garrison order shows, officers and their men had appeared thus in church and on parade. An idle young gentleman at St David's was seen loafing about at midday "in long draws, a banian coat, and slippers." Something perhaps a little more elaborate was owned and worn by many early officers. Captain James Cope bequeathed "all my Moors clothes" to his dubash. The versatile Dencker had "a complete dress for a Moor-man." Captain Lee had four suits of Moors dress; Captain d'Illens had "a pair of Moorman's slippers, 3 ditto coats, and 3 ditto tapets and sash"; Captain Callender, who was lucky enough to show the white feather and lose his life in the same action, had two complete suits; and Achilles Preston had five. With him the list comes to an end. I do not find further traces of this practice, though in the nineteenth century in Northern India Government had specially to forbid it in civilians.

Analogous to this was the practice of chewing betel. In the earlier part of the century, it was quite a usual thing for Europeans to do. Pyrard de Laval used and liked it. La Farelle, who commanded the Pondicherry garrison about 1730, was disgusted when first he saw ladies with red-stained lips and teeth, but found it a healthful and agreeable practice which he missed on leaving India. Nor was it confined to the French. Most of the men who served as fellow-subalterns with Clive had their betel-sets and spittoons. Cope had an elaborate one —large and small salver, rose-water bottle and betel-box, weighing 49½ oz. But these articles vanish from the later inventories, along with the evidences of native costume.

The approved dress for the transaction of business consisted of a starched white cap instead of the wig; a plain cotton shirt; breeches of dimity, gingham, or nankeen; white cotton stockings; and a white sleeved waistcoat. This would be the mode for the sales at the Sea-gate, the counting-house, the Company's offices, or the courts of justice. It was convenient and cool; but had the great disadvantage of looking extraordinarily shabby after a few hours' wear. You had to be constantly changing it. Hence the amazing numbers to which these articles run. A lawyer, for instance, owns 71 pairs of breeches and 81 waistcoats. But these testify more to cleanliness than ostentation. And indeed the nabobs were cleaner than their English contemporaries. Lord George Sackville regrets that an intended guest requires a cold bath, particularly " as we have not the least convenience of that sort here "; she had therefore better send her bathing-tub down to Knole by waggon; and General Dyott, driven to bathe by the dirt aboard ship, found it so agreeable that he resolved to continue the practice ashore. If he did he must have been the cleanest general officer in Europe. But in India the climate compelled frequent and complete washing, lest worse followed; and I fear the nabobs' ablutions were more a matter of comfort than of self-respect.

Such exotic customs, such ill-judged gaiety of clothes, such big houses and so many servants, ensured a reputation for tasteless and exorbitant expense. From early times the Company had suspected its servants of imitating " the vain and ostentatious pomp of India." Early in the century it writes:

" We hear from several hands that many of the people at Fort St George are gotten into a more expensive way of living than formerly, and that our young covenant servants, though they have not wherewithall to support it, will vie with those in better circumstances in the like unjustifiable pageantry of pallenkeens, horses and other disbursements; and even in private houses the profuseness vastly exceeds that of former times."

" We particularly recommend it to you," they write

again, " to check the expensive manner of living and the strong bias to pleasure which at present too much prevails among our servants in general, as otherwise we can never expect to find . . . industry and diligence . . ."

Clive himself, who should have known, said that the Company's servant spends three fortunes while he gets one. There are plenty of cases of their lavishness and unrestrained generosity. Clive himself is the outstanding example. Here is another on a smaller, more ordinary scale. Jourdan desires the use of a young friend's house near Masulipatam.

" If the advantages you can make of the money," he says, " will render it convenient to you, I will advance you the money you have laid out on it, on the condition that on my leaving of Masulipatam you shall take it back for the same sum, or if it will be more agreeable to you to take 10 or 12 pagodas per month it shall be on those terms. . . . I think it ridiculous of you to lend your house in the manner you do, because your fortune is at present too small to admit of it; and, although it be but a trifle, yet a trifle here and another there greatly add to your necessary expenses; moreover there is no knowing how things may turn out in the Company's service, and it therefore behoves you to be as saving as decency of appearance will justify . . ."

But as against this there were plenty of cases where a hard apprenticeship to poverty was preceding the hard-won acquisition of wealth.

" You seem to think," writes Thomas Munro to his sister, " that [Indian officers] live like those satraps that you have read of in plays; and that I in particular hold my state in prodigious splendour and magnificence—that I never go abroad unless upon an elephant, surrounded with a crowd of slaves—that I am arrayed in silken robes, and that most of my time is spent in reclining on a sofa listening to soft music, while I am fanned by my officious pages; or in dreaming, like Richard under a canopy of state. But while you rejoice in my imaginary greatness, I most likely am stretched on a mat, instead of my royal couch; and walking in an old coat and a ragged shirt, in the noonday sun, instead of looking down from my elephant, invested with my royal garments. You may not believe me when I tell you that I never experienced hunger or thirst, fatigue or poverty, till I came to India —that since then I have frequently met with the first three, and that the last has been my constant companion . . ."

In fact the nabobs were of many sorts, and not all bred to one type.

In the nature of things there could not be at Madras anything at all like learned society. There were no persons of leisure. The chaplains were almost the only men who had attended a university. In 1787 the two private schools of the place were kept by retired soldiers. In 1790 this may have been changed for the better. In that year John Holmes, A.M., announced the opening of an " accademy " where children would be taught reading, writing, arithmetic, history, the use of the globes, French, Greek, and Latin; and in the next year we have a seminary for young ladies, modelled on Miss Pinkerton's in Chiswick Mall. But though in these new institutions the teachers may have known a little more than reading, writing, and the manual exercise, the excellence of the instruction cannot be taken for granted. Nevertheless it would be wrong to assume that the nabobs were all illiterate vulgarians. Many of them no doubt read nothing and cared to read nothing. But against them may be set Major Madge, or Major Caillaud, who could write to Orme in 1757:

". . . What makes me so angry and disgusted with magazines, I had nothing else to read up in the Madura [country]. I took few books with me, except some *du métier*, to have less baggage. And to have something to read to set me asleep, I found some volumes of magazines among the Sepoy sergeants. You cannot imagine with what gout on my return I read over some good authors . . ."

Nor, in spite of the many perils attending the lives of books in India, would he have found any difficulty in obtaining access to some excellent literature in Madras. Many volumes might be destroyed by cockroaches, white ants, or ignorance. The garrison at Tellicherry being short of cartridge-paper, the Council there ordered all the printed books in the place to be sent into store. But Madras was, I think, always well supplied. In earlier days it had possessed a library that was more than respectable. Among the early acts of kindness shown to Clive at Madras, " he considered as one of the most important his admission, soon after his arrival in India, into an excellent library belonging to the governor." However, this was not, I think, the governor's private library, but the Library of Fort St George. It had been founded in 1664 by the purchase of a retiring chaplain's books, and had been augmented from time to time both by presents from the Company and bequests from the inhabitants. For a long time the Company made a practice of sending out such new books as it thought suitable; and in 1754, when the library had been unhappily scattered by the French occupation, the Council proposed that the custom should be renewed, asking for certain specific works " and as many more on all other parts of literature as you may think proper. We hope it may be an inducement to your servants to employ their leisure hours in reading and study." But now times had changed. The Company agreed to send the most useful of the law books wanted, and a pair of globes, but, they said, times were too bad to think of forming a library. Chance has preserved a copy of the catalogue of the old library, before it suffered dispersion, much as it must have been in the days when Clive solaced his young home-sickness in its seclusion. The catalogue is divided into two parts. The first contains the library proper, as it had grown by gradual accretions. It shows few books on Oriental languages, but these few included practically all that had been published at that time. In Greek and Latin, we have the principal classical authors and a host of fathers. In English, first and foremost, innumerable theologians, for those were days when men discussed the relative merits of Sherlock and Stillingfleet, and loved to perplex themselves with doctrinal subtleties. Modern literature was represented by Blackmore's intolerable epic of *King Arthur*; Cowley's works, which Clive, if he looked into them, must have found monstrously tedious; a translation of the *Lusiad*, which he would have thought more interesting; Drayton's *Polyolbion*, in which he would have read no more than related to his native Shropshire; *Hudibras*, the fourth part, which he enjoyed, regretting the absence of the other three; Sidney's *Arcadia*, which I suspect he cared little for; and Shakespeare, a most welcome relief; scarcely any other plays; and a romance called *Don Fenise*. What I think occupied most of Clive's leisure hours was neither the *belles lettres* in the library nor yet the law-books— Shepperd's *Guide for Keeping Courts-leet and Courts Baron*, Maleyne's *Lex Mercatoria*, Molloy's *Jus Maritimum*—but the histories—Plutarch's *Lives*, Baker's *Chronicle*, Raleigh's *History of the World*, and above all the travels, from Hakluyt and *Purchas his Pilgrimes* down to Herbert in Persia, Bernier in Hindustan, and Lasalle in America.

The second part of the catalogue contains the books that had belonged to Thomas Consett, and it suggests a man of exceptionally wide knowledge and attainments. He was the son of an ecclesiastical lawyer of some eminence in his day, and came out to Madras as a chaplain, dying there in 1730. He possessed a number of Hebrew works; his Greek and Latin included the principal classics, and even later writers, such as Erasmus and the memoirs of du Thou; besides English theologians, he read Milton and Prior, Addison's *Travels* and the *Polite Gentleman*, the *Ladies' Tales* and *Parismus a Romance*. The art military is represented by Vauban and the *Compleat Captain*; commerce by the *Compleat Compting-house or the Misteries of Trade and Exchange*. If you add books in French, German, and Dutch, with books and manuscripts " in the Slavonian and Russian languages " which the compiler was unable to catalogue, you have represented a considerable range of reading, combined with diversity of interests and an unusual gift of tongues. Such was the library in which Clive and other Company's servants amused their leisure, to which the chaplain resorted to settle a point of doctrine or the governor a point of law.

Besides this there were private collections of books such as the inhabitants chose to have at hand for their guidance or diversion. The earliest of these is the library of Thomas Eyre, who had been of Council when La Bourdonnais took Madras and who died a few years later. This manifests the same serious turn as the official library. We find Stillingfleet, Hoadley, Clarke, and Drelincourt on his shelves, with the *Grounds of Religion*, the *Connection between Sacred History and Profane*, and several volumes of unspecified sermons. Bacon and Locke are his philosophers, Butler and Pope, Blackmore and Garth his poets, besides which he had the essays of Steele and Addison, one or two tiresome romances, a few plays, a life of Mahomet, and a history of Rome. For the later part of the century many book-lists occur in the inventories. Dawsonne Drake's inventory includes sundry chests and trunks containing 1,600 volumes ranging from duodecimo to folio; and John Hubbard's will provides that the best of his books are to be retained by his executors, and lent or given to the persons who will make the best use of them. To give such lists in detail would be insufferably tedious; but their general character does not lack interest. Their principal defect from the contemporary standpoint is the lack of Greek and Latin. Just once or twice you find a Virgil, Horace, or Homer in the original; but it is clear that, while many as a matter of duty or inclination purchased such translations of the classics as could be got, few could read Latin, still less Greek, with facility. Many had left school too young; others had distinguished themselves by their idleness. And the consequences of this ignorance of the classics was incomparably more important in the eighteenth century than it would be to-day. But even so they must not be exaggerated. Intimacy with the classics was the test of a liberal education in England; but even there many contented themselves with less, and that with less excuse; the men who gathered round the gaming tables of White's, the correspondents of George Selwyn, nay, the ornaments of the court and the orators of the House of Commons, often depended more on their native vivacity or talent than on the soundness of their learning.

Whatever their classical defects the nabobs would seem to have been familiar with some great and not a little good literature. On many book-shelves you would find Shakespeare and Milton, Swift and Pope; the essayists from the *Tatler* to the *Rambler*; minor poets like Pomfret and Akenside. For classical history, they had Rollin, Plutarch, and Gibbon; for English history, Mrs Macaulay,

Hume, and Smollett; for the history of their predecessors in India the judicious Orme, the laborious Cambridge, the moral Raynal, besides the lively pamphlets of Holwell and Scrafton. Officers carry with them on campaign *Tom Jones*, *Don Quixote*, or *Gil Blas*; *Clarissa* was less popular in India than in England. Temple and Clarendon, Camden's *Britannia*, and Montaigne's *Essays*, Spencer, Johnson, and Raleigh, all appear. Every now and then we strike a wider range of reading—Boileau, Molière, and Montesquieu in French, Camoens in Portuguese, Ariosto and Tasso, Machiavelli and Guicciardini in Italian. Then too the type of reading evidently changes. Minds become more secularised, especially those within the reach of French literature. Tillotson and Stillingfleet are replaced by Voltaire and Rousseau, by Hume, and Adam Smith and Gibbon. New books which achieved a fair degree of fame or notoriety were sent out by friends or brought out as a speculation, with noteworthy promptitude; and new doctrines were assimilated with a curious rapidity. If some nabobs never read at all, and all were innocent of Latin, I think a more than normal proportion of them were well read as things went in those days. The main reason was that life in India, in those days at all events, afforded a good deal of leisure, when it was too hot to go out and partake of violent sports and a book offered an almost inevitable form of amusement; and then, just as Caillaud read magazines at Madura because he could not procure anything better, so also the bored civilian or officer would resort to Addison or Gibbon because he had exhausted all the lighter literature within his reach.

Printing was practised in the East Indian settlements earlier than one would have expected. In 1717 there were presses at Batavia capable of producing a book in Dutch, Portuguese, and Chinese. The Jesuits too had a press

at Pondicherry in early days; and when that place was
taken by the English in 1761, the press was brought up
to Madras, along with a printer from Pondicherry, and
employed to produce a manifesto containing our reasons
for demolishing the French settlement. It also printed
a journal of Caillaud's siege of Vellore. But this press
was closed down by the Company's orders, seeming but
a useless piece of expense. The next did not appear
till more than twenty years afterwards, and then was
owned by private persons. In September, 1783, Richard
Johnston, captain of the 13th Foot, was permitted to come
out to join his brother-in-law, Sir John Burgoyne, commanding the 23rd Light Dragoons then at Madras. He
doubtless expected military preferment; but, finding Burgoyne involved in furious disputes with the civil powers,
and his patronage consequently valueless, he sold out and
sought a living in other ways. In August 1785, he was
allowed to publish a weekly newspaper and to set up a
printing office in Fort St George. Thus was born the
first Madras periodical, called *The Madras Courier*. Its
first number appeared in October, price 1 rupee; and it
enjoyed the advantage of being carried postage free.
Johnston himself only owned a half share of the press,
the capital of which at the time of his death was reckoned
as 16,300 pagodas or just over £6,500. He had probably
been the first editor as well as founder and manager; but,
a couple of years before he died in 1791, the editorial
duties were taken over by a less shadowy person. This
was Hugh Boyd, to whom injudicious admirers ascribed
the *Letters of Junius*. He had lived in London in the set
of which Burke was the centre, and came out to Madras
in 1781 as one of Lord Macartney's private secretaries.
He was one of Lamb's Great Men, who lay all the rest
of mankind under contribution. Every friend who became
involved in his private affairs had reason to regret it, but

few could resist the seduction of his manners. He secured various posts at Madras. He became, for instance, Master Attendant of the Port, a position involving the privilege of providing the vessels that put in with various kinds of stores. Men had made comfortable money at this post, for the ship's captain who was so unwise as to buy elsewhere would be likely to wait long for the boats he needed to unlade and lade again his vessel. Boyd had sought the job as eagerly as might be expected from an intriguing person in an intriguing age. He finally secured it by the influence of Macartney with the directors. Another post he owed to his friendship with the Burkes—that of Deputy Paymaster to the King's troops in India. But in spite of all these advantages his affairs were greatly embarrassed at the time of his death. His connection with the *Courier* is unflatteringly mentioned in the Roebuck-Abbot correspondence. Abbot writes to Benfield, on 16 May, 1792:

". . . The share that we have in the press is only in the property, not in the labour. There is an editor who has the whole and sole management of it, and Hall sometimes assists for his amusement. The property in Boyd's hands was in jeopardy, and [poor?] Mrs Dick Johnston, whose all is in that concern, applied to us for relief. There was no possibility of affording it but by becoming really or nominally proprietors. Maule and Colonel Capper particularly pressed this matter on us, and, knowing that by the concern we could not lose, we did not hesitate in purchasing one-eighth share for 3,000 pagodas. By that, and lending some money and taking up Mrs J's shares that were mortgaged, we were enabled to [save?] the press out of Boyd's clutches. He still continued editor for some time, till he took huff at some trifle and gave it up. Notwithstanding it might be made a very lucrative concern, for the printing, exclusive of the *Courier*, is about 5,000 pagodas *per annum*. Yet we shall take the earliest opportunity of getting rid of our share, as it does not seem to meet with your wish that we should be engaged in it . . ."

In 1795 the paper was being edited by James William Chater, who had come out in 1782 lieutenant on H.M.S. *Magnanime*, and who filled his leisure with selling Madeira and arrack. In the same year a rival to the *Courier* appeared in the *Madras Gazette*; editor Mr Emmanuel Samuel. He also had had a various career. He had been a Company's surgeon; he had been enrolled an attorney of the Mayor's Court; and for a time had been a part-proprietor of the *Courier*.

Of the outside contributors little is known. Hall wrote occasionally for the *Courier*, I suppose when some incident of official life permitted him to vent his bile; and Boyd was a smooth and practised writer; but apart from them little literary talent existed at Madras, and the *Courier* was not much better than the *Swillingford Patriot*. There was a poet in the Madras Army, Lieutenant Thomas Underwood, but his verses would have disgraced the Poet's Corner of a country newspaper. A rival rhymester faithfully describes it as " damned doggerel." Mr. Eyles Irwin, of the Company's Civil Service, publishes " St Thomas's Mount, a poem," but that is not much better. Nor was the place much more fortunate in its writers of prose. Apart from the works of Orme and Dalrymple, none of which were produced at Madras, our nabobs have no nearer literary connections than affording a reluctant refuge to Sterne's Eliza. The presence of a large number of officers, and especially of engineers, however, ensured that there should be a few who knew how to paint. This accomplishment, which was much commoner in the eighteenth century than to-day, was possessed by Achilles Preston, though I know of no product of his brush; and Captain Trapaud of the Madras Army was an accomplished colourist, in spite of the unkind remarks of Captain Elers, who compares his pictures to scene-painting. Nevertheless, when all allowances have been made, Madras was not the place in which to seek a high degree of culture. Men were too engrossed with the day's business, too anxious to make their fortunes and go home, too ill-prepared by their early education to develop high-brow tendencies. In comparison with good English society they were decidedly second-rate. But they were just as good as a great many of their critics, and much cleaner.

CHAPTER XIII

THE LADIES

TIME had been when the English factories were void of Englishwomen. And even when the Company relaxed its restrictions towards the end of the seventeenth century, the terrors of the long and uncertain voyage, the remoteness of Madras, the unlikelihood of return, all tended to limit the number that went out. However, in spite of all these difficulties the number grew. Wives joined their husbands; daughters accompanied their parents; the Company itself sent out in 1678 three unmarried women, " having neither relations nor recommendations to any person in this place "; others went out as a private speculation, like Mrs Anne Miller, who, as a friend wrote to Governor Pitt, " goes out to your parts to make her fortune; her father is a vyntner and an honest man, but has many children. . . . I have no knowledge myself of her, but my wife's midwife desires this favour of me." As the fame of the Indies rose in the course of the century, so did the number of ladies who sought husbands there.

" DEAR BEAUTY," writes that madcap, Dalton, to Clive in 1752, " by this time I reckon you are able to give one an account of the new-arrived angels. By God, it would be a good joke if your countenance was to smite one of them and you was to commit matrimony . . ."

The good joke came off, and early in the next year Clive married the sister of a brother-officer, bestowing on Mr Fabricius, who performed the ceremony, " so great and undeserved a present whereby you have made us quite amazed and ashamed." The wedding made no small stir in that little world. Clive's friend, Repington, says:

" Georgy Gardiner has wrote the Major in capitals that you was married to Miss Maskelyne last Sunday, on which we all sincerely congratulate you. 'Tis much better in my opinion than going home . . . You have generously obliged a man who loves you, made a little family happy, and are a gainer into the bargain . . ."

And the Old Cock himself records his opinion, " 'Twas a wise step." Once in India, there was small difficulty in a lady's getting married. Foote's Nabob offers as a favour to send thither the sisters of the girl he proposes for. Miss Sophia Goldborne describes how the newly arrived ladies were met at the church door the Sunday after their arrival by a crowd of gentlemen eager to hand them from their palanquins; and if Miss Goldborne is apocryphal, her narrative is well within the canon. A young miniature-painter after a couple of years catches a gentleman high in the service with a large fortune. Take an authentic case from Madras. Along with Miss Read the painter came her niece, Miss Elena Beatson. On 7 September, 1777, the faithful Young writes of her, " Miss Beatson is as fine a young lady as ever I seed come to this country, and as well accomplished as any, of age, and draws finely . . ." Only five weeks later, " Miss Beatson is to be married to Mr Oakley soon." Then on 24 October, " Miss Beatson was marry'ed a few days ago to Mr Oakley, as good a match as she could have got on earth or I am mistaken, and he has settled £10,000 upon her. Is not this good luck? " It was indeed, for Oakley was a rising young civilian, destined to become Sir Charles and the governor of Fort St George; and I fear her good fortune turned Miss Elena's head a little. She began to look down upon her sparing and perhaps shabby aunt.

" She [Miss Read]," Young writes not quite a year later, " has been very ill-treated by Miss Beatson since her marriage, and the old lady has taken it so much to heart that it has been in a great measure the cause of her complaint . . ."

And when the news of her death arrived, Mrs Oakley hardly condescended to wear black.

Nor was the Indian market open only to the young and blooming. Mature experience had its value also. Ladies who lost their husbands had no difficulty in replacing them. I have already mentioned the repeated marriages of Miss Frances Croke. A kinswoman of Dawsonne Drake's, Hannah Butterworth, ran her a good second with three marriages in eleven years. Lieutenant Matthias Calvert thus describes his marriage and prospects:

" I now beg leave to inform you that among the different ladies that came from England last year, there was one Mrs Williamson, widow to a nephew of the present colonel Williamson of the Artillery; she come to Madras with her daughter, the last of which is married to a captain in the Company's service, and I have married the mother. She is a woman endowed with qualifications that might make any man happy—at least she does me. . . .

" I do suppose when there is a peace, our regiment will be called home, granting what officers and men chuse to stay in the country leave; if so, I have already a promise from Mr Pigot and General Lawrence of rank and pay as captain; but if I could raise 30 or 40 men, I should have a company, which will make the ods of about 600 pagodas a year by what they call off-reckoning . . ."

With such attractions to offset the dangers of the voyage, the thirty-five Englishwomen of 1700 increased more than tenfold in the course of the century, though the exact number in 1800 cannot be exactly stated, owing to the abandonment of the invidious particularity of the earlier lists. With them came all that women's world of toilets and fashions which played so large a part in the eighteenth century. Their cheeks broke out into patches. Rouge, Venus Bloom, Mareshall Powder, repaired the ravages of a trying climate on a delicate complexion. Lavender and Hungary water, Eau de Mille Fleurs, Bergamot, hair-dyes and restorers, could all be bought in the tiny shops of Madras, or even at Trichinopoly, along with powder-puffs, hair-cushions, and false hair to turn over them. Nor was the hairdresser, the great high priest of the toilet-table, absent. Two Europeans followed that calling at Madras in 1787—Macartney's late valet, who attended impartially to gentlemen's wigs and ladies' hair, and another who attended to nothing but ladies' heads.

Unfortunately very few lady's inventories are included in the will-books. Indeed one could expect only inventories of widows or independent women, and of those only when fully recognised as Englishwomen. The only ones which help us in the present case are three in number—those of Eleanor Cope, widow of Captain Cope, of Mrs Bromley, widow of the lawyer, and of Anne Page, ambiguously but perhaps precisely described in the burial register as " mistress." And when we turn to these, we find a further limit imposed on their usefulness, for they were made by men who shrank from committing themselves to technicalities. The principal articles of Mrs Cope's wardrobe were a silk brocade gown and petticoat, a white satin sack half trimmed with gold, a checked lute-string nightgown, a pink satin quilted petticoat, 4 gowns of white morees, 20 coarse dimity petticoats, 14 ditto bedgowns, and 24 shifts. Mrs Bromley's includes, besides a considerable number of petticoats and shifts and other things, 2 chip hats, a gauze dress hat, and 3 muslin silver-flowered dresses and petticoats. Mistress Anne Page's is less distinguished. None of her gowns was worth a separate entry, and the enumeration of her abandoned garments has a sordid mean appearance. One imagines that of her two fans one must have been soiled and the other broke. Yet in spite of this defect of evidence we know that the ladies of Madras outvied the men in brightness of array, to say nothing of the loads of diamonds with which affectionate husbands testified to their sincerity of love.

Perhaps I do them an injustice, but I think their average below the men's. Every man had serious work to do; but they had nothing except to oversee their servants. If the men were in general of doubtful social rank, they were still more dubious. At all events the men's motive in marriage was seldom mercenary; theirs generally was; and above all the men mixed with all ranks of Indians, while they seldom saw any but their servants, and so their attitude and influence were never healthy.

However, to speak the truth, the choice lay between them and worse. Their rivals were those dark-eyed girls whose early charms promised a premature, unlovely age, shrill, sluttish, and obese. At the beginning of the century they bore Portuguese names; at the end they bore English ones; at the end too they had usually been educated in England; but in either case they commonly exemplified the evils of an early upbringing amid a crowd of Indian servants—and so lazy that they would call someone to pick up the handkerchief that they had dropped. Owing to the problems which marriage with their class often involved, ever since 1719 it had been a formal rule that no Christian inhabitant of Madras should presume to marry without the governor's consent, " many of the young gentlemen in the Company's service being of good families in England, who would be very much scandalized at such marriages as were likely to be contracted here without the consent of the President." Just the same rule, and for the same reason, prevailed at Pondicherry, while the Dutch even set up a sort of court before which the parties had to prove the suitability of the marriage. The chaplain who consecrated unauthorised unions was liable to dismissal. Clive dismissed one for this reason in 1765, and so late as 1817 a chaplain's allowances were suspended for a like offence.

That some such control was needed is shown by a number of marriages that took place in spite of it, and some of which one would have thought could hardly have happened outside the pages of Congreve. For example Mr Eric Dieurstedt was a musician at Madras who ultimately became the organist at St Mary's and took part in concerts with the gentlemen of the Company's service. In 1762 he wished to marry Christina de Silva; the governor refused permission; the marriage could not therefore be solemnised at Madras, or at St Thomé which lay within the English limits. The couple therefore went to Covelong and were married there. The man thus had every opportunity for reconsidering his position, which needed it. The bride had come down from Bengal in 1749 to join her brother, the butler of George Mackay; she had become Mackay's mistress, and had been turned off when he married in 1756. The colonel of Engineers at Madras some years later married in January, and his lady presented him with his first-born in the following March. Another officer was sentenced by court martial to be cashiered for seducing an unmarried girl and then procuring her marriage with a brother officer; and in Bengal was an officer married to a woman who had been kept in succession by Colonel Forde, Captain Pye, and Captain Broadbridge. A friend of Jourdan's either made himself a similar convenience or else illustrates the ease with which such transactions could be carried out. Jourdan writes: " I imagine your brother has written to you of his marriage to a young lady, an acquaintance of a gentleman with whom he has a concern in a voyage to China." But Jourdan had heard her well spoken of.

Marriage with persons of unknown antecedents was apt in that age to produce the kind of situation in which the novelist delighted, with its surprises and discomfiture. Thus the will of Captain John Mackain disowns and disinherits the child commonly known as John Mackain, born during his absence at Manila; what became of the wife is shown by the verdict of a coroner's jury that sat on the bodies of Ensign John Ramacles and Mary Mackain, shortly before the return of the troops. It found that Ramacles had murdered the woman and then killed himself. Other cases are mentioned in the wills. Theodore Ivy Tanner, senior merchant in the Company's service, says:

" And whereas Frances Mary, my wife, having behaved to me with infidelity and having committed adultery with Alexander Cuthbert, late of Madras, whom I am now prosecuting to the end of obtaining a divorce from the said Frances Mary, I do give unto her one shilling, with the view and intent that the same shall be a bar of all dower or thirds, . . . and I do also give unto a female child born of the said Frances Mary in adultery with the said Alexander Cuthbert, and named Anna, one shilling and no more . . ."

The will of Captain Samuel Baker Evance, who, you may remember, had got into trouble over his Sepoys, deals with the same situation as Tanner's in a spirit of moral indignation. " And whereas my wife, Lucy Evance (whether for just cause or not a just and impartial God will hereafter judge between us) refused to live with me and has for a considerable time past lived publicly, in open violation of all laws human and divine, with James Daniel, a man of infamous principles, by whom she has had children," like Tanner, he leaves her one rupee in bar of dower or thirds.

The last case of the sort which I will here cite is that of a woman named Sophia Barrett. She was the daughter of John Croley, a sergeant promoted to commissioned rank in 1758, by his mistress Jenny Campbell. Croley himself did good service, and was at last killed before Madura in 1764. It was, I think, in acknowledgment of his services that his son, another John Croley, born of the same mother as Sophia, was given a commission in the Company's service; but I know no good of him. He was broke in 1784, and eight years later was still living in Madras. Sophy thus enjoyed but an indifferent up-bringing. In 1775 she married Cottrell Barrett, who kept a tavern at Madras and who could afford to give her a harpsichord and at all events some diamonds; nevertheless in 1782 or 1783 she eloped with one Captain Landeman, after which her husband was frequently heard to express himself in terms of the highest detestation respecting her conduct. In 1792 she thus wrote to her brother from Calcutta:

" I am extremely sorry I have not had the pleasure of receiving a letter or hearing from you for these three years past. Let the consequence be what it would, you never ought to forget corresponding with your own sister. . . . I never was in want of dutiful esteem and regard in enquiring of you and sister Nancy with every ship-captain that arrived from Madras. Let me advice you never to forget that you are our eldest brother and of consequence you ought to esteem us and give us friendly advice in corresponding. Nothing can give me greater pleasure than to hear from you. Please to let me know what business of life you are in, whether still a lieutenant in the army or not; you might have been made a captain by this time. Believe me sincerely that I am grieved at your situation and of your choice in a wife, for you might have married a European lady . . .

" I must now inform you of my situation, which is really very disagreeable . . . After leaving Mr Templeton the attorney, he promised to settle 5,000 rupees on me when he went to England but the gentleman who had the agreement run away to Bombay, and I never received a pice from it, by which means I have been obliged to sell every valuable thing I had to support myself; and want of health prevented me from accepting the offers of some great gentlemen at this place and up the country. I am at present very ill, neither have I any ready money about me but what a friend of Templeton's assists me with—a few rupees now and then. I have often wished to come to Madras, but never can meet with a good man in that way who I could entrust myself with.

" I am informed by some ships captains that my husband Barrett is dead, and has left me the sum of 350 rupees per month as long as I live and a house which my little boy John was christened and born in, which I think the best house he had at Madras. I hope you'll inquire about the circumstances and desire Mr Popham the attorney and Mr Ledsham the sheriff to remit me a copy of his will and any letters that he might have wrote for me before his cruel death. Likewise please desire him to remit the sum of 400 pagodas, which is the allowance for four months, that I might pay my debts and provide myself with some decent linnen, and then I hope to be in my own country, enjoying the true felicity of embracing my relations and happy in their company after an absence of ten long years . . .

" P.S. . . . Pray who is Betsy and Fanny, my step-daughters married to? Perhaps they have entirely forgot me. I suppose Barrett has left all my diamond things and valuable joys to them, and my harpsichord which I regret parting with . . .''

This singular letter was forwarded by Croley to Barrett, who was still alive, with the equally singular comment, " I only mean that it should make you laugh a little." After Barrett's death, which really took place later in the same year, this lady of many episodes claimed a share in the estate.

Compared with these dingy marriages, some at least of the many irregular unions that were formed appear refined and respectable. The will of Henry Littleton, a Company's officer, bears high testimony to the virtues of his mistress, a Brahman woman called Raja. The original will leaves her all his property and attests that all her jewels are hers entirely, having been made out of the proceeds of her houses at Srirangam; and repeated codicils confirm his first dispositions. Or take General John Pater's mistress, Arabella Robinson. She was the daughter, I expect the natural daughter, of a Company's officer and lived with Pater for twenty years at least; and on her epitaph he described himself as " her ever-grateful and affectionate friend." Her death which occurred in 1809 was the occasion of a characteristic incident. The chaplain of Masulipatam, where the general was quartered, re-fused to bury her in consecrated ground. Pater then buried her in a field, but over her grave he built the church of St Mary's which he presented to the Company. And the Company, accepting this munificent gift, ordered its consecration and use. So poor Arabella lies in sacred ground in spite of the chaplain.

Another case in which the lady was on the upward grade appears in the Roebuck papers. Sir John Call was interested in a girl called I think Anne Shaw, who had been the mistress of Captain George Mackay (a son of the George Mackay previously mentioned); and he desired his correspondents Roebuck and Abbot, to make her certain offers, the exact nature of which does not appear. They report as follows:

" Mr Roebuck has had a long conversation with the person you requested might be spoken to relative to her unhappy plan of life. He represented in as strong terms as he was capable of doing the impropriety of a woman possessing her knowledge and education continuing in such a vagabond system, of the remorse she must feel at a future day when she would probably be in a situation of want, and of the necessity of her altering her mode of life if she had faith in her religion or had a spark of shame left. She replied she had been unfortunate, and had suffered much from the fickleness of man, that she was the mother of five children by Captain Mackay, but that now she had found an attachment which she must await the issue of before she could avail herself of your indulgence towards her, that Mr Selby, who commanded the packet, was attached to her, that she could not say but hoped he would marry her, that she had from him at present 50 pagodas a month, and that she expected he would come out to his situation in Bombay as soon as he was released or exchanged by the French. . . . We shall make further enquiries from another quarter before we close this. . . . We understand he is absolutely engaged by a deed of contract to marry her. He is a man of some £1,000 property . . ."

Of course David Young, the general friend, had much to do with the ladies of his seafaring friends while they were absent. This must have been the most thankless of his many tasks. " Victory will take anyone's advice sooner than mine," he writes. " She is the most stubborn girl I ever saw." Or again:

" Bett is making the damndest noise that ever I heard from morning to night; we can have no peace with her; she quarrels with her servants in such a manner that I believe she will get none to stay with her; and when I gave her her monthly allowance, she kicked up such a dust that I could not still it. . . .   I shall have a fine time till your return if she goes on at this rate . . ."

Sometimes, with that curious inconsistency which passed with many of that century for virtue, bequests are coupled with moral advice.   James Buller, mariner, leaves to a slave-girl, Nolly, her freedom and 15 Arcot rupees a month, provided she becomes a Protestant Christian. William Stevenson, engineer, leaves a third of his estate to Maria Victoria for the benefit of their child, provided she does not continue her lawless course of life.   John Adam Kisselbach, captain of engineers, not only bequeaths to his servant Mary 4 pagodas a month so long as she leads a regular life and attends church every Sunday at Vepery, but carries his morality into the next generation, by leaving to his children (called Smith) 2 pagodas a month each for life subject to their not turning out bad. *Video meliora proboque*, I suppose they said.

As a rule, however, much larger provision was made than the pittance just mentioned.   It was a common belief that provision must be made.   Charles Lamb, who had a distant relative married in India, seems to have been told so; and Jourdan lays down the doctrine most uncompromisingly.   To a friend acting on behalf of a lunatic officer's relatives he writes:

". . . As the family for whom you are empowered to act cannot before a statute of lunacy indemnify me by law, I cannot give up any effects unless by decree of court.   But as it has ever been my wish to act for the best, I will in January advance 1,000 pagodas for Mr Blake Eyre's and your passage. . . .   If you can get him

to England, a statute of lunacy will easily be procured
. . . I must however observe to you that there is a
grown-up boy whom you must take home, or a sum
must be left in India to provide maintenance for him, and
something must be done for the woman . . ."

However that may have been, the wills show clearly that
there was a well-established custom of making such provision as was possible. Captain William Oliphant, regretting that he has not much to leave, gives all to his
natural child; " I can make no further provision for the
child's mother than allowing her a subsistence for a few
months till she has time to provide herself with another
protector, which, as she is a well-behaved girl and of a
good person, she can find no difficulty in doing." Where
money was available it was freely given. Lieutenant-
Colonel George Stewart leaves to his four natural children
£2,000 each to the eldest boy (at school at Northwich in
England) and to the girl, and £1,500 to the other two
boys. Major Thomas Gordon directs that his three illegi-
timate sons receive a good education and be brought up
to some creditable profession. Hew Stuart, who had
risen to the rank of Council in Sumatra, leaves £12,500
to his children by " Inche Rassow who lived with me
many years." Whatever slaves are thought fittest to
accompany John Stuart, one of the sons, to England are
to be freed. Joseph Garrow leaves £5,000 to his natural
son " whom I call Joseph," the interest being applied to
his education " which I desire may be as good as he is
capable of receiving."

Usually these children bear their father's name. Often
they are confided to the care of relatives at home. Lieutenant Robert Macmurdo appoints a Writer to the Signet
and his aunt Barbara Douglas guardians to his two natural
children. Lieutenant-Colonel George Brown's son Archi-

14

bald was left 5,000 pagodas and was to be sent home to
the testator's father when four years old. Old Mrs
Powney's will provides for two natural children belonging
to a deceased son. And the natural son of Robert Hughes,
of the covenanted service, was brought up by his uncle,
the Principal of Jesus, Cambridge.

All this was in full agreement with the customs of the
age. Consider how many characters of mysterious or
dubious birth figure in the pages of Fielding and Smollett,
or even in those of Scott and Marryat. The novelists were
not unfaithful to their time or exaggerating for the sake
of romantic interest the frequency of such blotted pedi-
grees. They were much more frequent at Madras and
the other English settlements in India; but that was due
to special reasons, not to any extraordinary degree of
vice in the English settlers. In the first place there was
the very small number of appropriate English brides. In
the second the official discouragement of marriages with
poor girls of mixed and especially of Portuguese blood.
In the third the blunt fact that the maintenance of a
mistress was much cheaper in India than in England. In
England, the class from which nine-tenths of the nabobs
came, the middle class, could not afford such luxuries.
Kitty Fisher's favours were reserved for the peerage. But
when they got out to Madras, they found that they could
do as well as their betters. The cause which had made
the middle-class so much more moral than the rest of
the community was no longer operative. Accordingly the
mistress became a recognised institution. Attached to
many of the old houses at Madras are much smaller,
separate bungalows. Now we let them off separately;
yesterday they were used to lodge guests when they arrived in unusual numbers; but the day before yesterday
they were the abode of the bachelor's lady.

CHAPTER XIV

SOCIAL INTERCOURSE

ORIGINALLY, when the Company was still discouraging its servants from carrying their wives out with them to India, the social life of its little factories was framed on the collegiate model, such as you would have found at the Merchant Adventurers' factory in Middelburg or the Levant Company's factory at Aleppo. It was a system of common life and common work; everyone attended prayers in the chapel and sat down to the general table in the hall. But expansion, and especially the influx of European women, broke down this monastic mode of life. Married servants received diet money in lieu of commons. The governor ceased to preside and set up a separate table of his own, frequented by the senior servants and distinguished visitors. The general table, at which the youngsters were thus left to their own discretion, became the scene of disorders that sometimes demanded a file of musketeers to keep the peace. At last in 1722 this general table was abolished, and all servants got diet money instead. This was designed as a measure of economy; for at the same time a fixed allowance was made for Governor Elwick's table, and this was not nearly enough to maintain it " in the manner it was in his predecessor's time "; nevertheless, being " unwilling to reduce any part of the grandeur of his post," he resolved for the future to make good the deficiency out of his own pocket. This institution was the centre of early social life at Madras. The ensign on guard at the Sea-gate took the foot of the table and said grace. Ships' captains, any other voyagers of equal quality, and visitors from foreign settlements, were invited as a matter of course; and the principal residents had a standing invita-tion, of which, I fancy, they were not expected to make too regular a use. The future Mme Dupleix partook of an uneasy dinner there, when in 1728 she and her sister made their Rabelaisian expedition to Madras. Some forty years later, in Hickey's time, the governor sat down to table at 1, and at 3 would dismiss his guests with the toast, " Gentlemen, a good afternoon." But you had to know how to carry your liquor. Captain Henry Eglinton Connor, of His Majesty's 96th, was broke for misbehav-ing in his cups at the governor's house in 1761, having by so doing violated the promise he had passed when pre-viously released from confinement.

On special occasions, at Christmas or the King's birth-day, the governor greatly extended his hospitality. Thus we read in the Fort St George orderly book on 24 Decem-ber, 1761, " The governor expects the favour of the officers' company to breakfast, dine, and sup with him to-morrow." On the King's birthday he gives a dinner and an entertainment, or a dinner and a ball, at the Admiralty House. When he entertains at his garden-house outside the Fort, St George's Gate is to be left open till all his company are safely in; if they are later than half-past 11, the key-sergeant is to attend at the gate, but not to lock it, until all the palanquins have passed; and the same rule is to be observed whenever any gentleman shall desire the favour of the gates being left open. In like manner the mayor would signalise his election by an entertainment or a ball at the Admiralty House. The commander of the squadron too might entertain the whole settlement on special occasions; or the Nawab might give a grand display to celebrate the marriage of one of his sons, or on the occasion of his investing Sir John Lindsay with the insignia of the Bath. I fear these festivities were not always quite harmonious. One of the Nawab's balls was followed by a duel between Ensign Leighton and Mr James Capper, caused among other things by Capper's saying to the other that Lieutenant Dee had behaved very ill, as military gentlemen mostly do. Indeed the civilian always resented the soldier's airs of superiority, and the soldier always grudged the civilian his allowances and station; so that in mixed companies a little liquor would often kindle a flame between them.

Besides these extraordinary festivities, there were regular concerts and assemblies at the Admiralty House at least as early as the 'sixties. In 1761 a prisoner before the court of Quarter Sessions was charged with burglary there " one concert night "; and in 1765 John Francis Edwards began a prosecution against Colonel Faizan for writing to the governor that Edwards, who had been appointed the master of the ceremonies at concerts and assemblies, was the worst man in the settlement for debauchery and criminal practices. Another scrap of evidence suggests that the concerts were subscription affairs. The inventory of James Hughes, described as " First Musician to the Concert," includes among other items " subscriptions received from sundry persons." This Hughes, who died at Madras in 1758 or 1759, is an intriguing person, a man of education and refinement. How he drifted to Madras I do not know; he died poor, his assets just sufficed to pay his debts; but he read Homer and Pascal, Horace and Livy. Did the maxims of Seneca and the philosophy of Lucretius fortify him against the outrages of fortune? And did he comfort himself as well as

charm others with his music? Caillaud, the most culti-
vated officer of the Madras Army, and but newly come
from Europe, writes from the wilds of Trichinopoly,
" P.S.—'Tis just come into my head that I would give
20 pagodas to hear Hughes play a solo. Alas! Alas!
Alas! "

There were other musicians too besides Hughes. Of
one we hear that he came out in 1759 and later turned
shop-keeper; of another, that he was a Bohemian. Both
I suppose belonged to the Governor's Band. That institution dated back, in all probability, to the seventeenth
century. Collet, we know, kept " a very good concert
of music " about 1720. This band was certainly lent to
private parties, as at Calcutta, where Clive, having recently
gone up country, was delighted that his *locum tenens* had
refused " the music " to the gentlemen who asked for it
with a view to " an insolent celebration of my departure. . . . I doubt not but you will at all times positively
refuse the musicians to any of those who have declined
paying me that deference and respect which it was their
duty to pay me as governor." This was in 1766, in the
course of his second vigorous government of Bengal; but
nine years earlier, before the battle of Plassey and when
he still expected to return to Madras, he had recruited and
sent thither some musicians probably intended to form a
band at Fort St David's. " I have received your consign-
ment of fiddlers," Orme writes to him from Madras.
" I pay them. They get victuals with the Governor's
band." But beside such professional musicians as found
their way to India, there were many amateurs. The taste
for music must have been nearly as wide-spread as in the
days of Pepys. The inventories show us " parcels of
music books," flutes, English and German, violins, including one Cremona which fetched £24 12*s.*, harps,
and harpsichords, and spinets, and, in 1778, even the

newly invented pianoforte. This last was a troublesome instrument. The only man in the place who could tune or repair it was the organist, Eric Dieurstedt, whose queer taste in a wife I have already mentioned. It was brought out by the purser of the *Princess Royal*, East Indiaman, and was left unsold in the charge of David Young. He reports at last:

" I have got your piano-forte repaired, which cost 40 pagodas, a most extravagant bill, but it was of no use till it was repaired, and Mr Dursted [*sic*] was the only man that could do it in this place, . . . and after all I was obliged to sell it at prime cost £65, and glad to take it, as I was afraid the hott land winds might have put it out of order again . . ."

In the shops were to be found considerable quantities of music and song-books; and the only shopkeeper of Trichinopoly kept by him bundles of fiddle-strings.

Amateur theatricals made another very popular form of amusement. At Calcutta this began early. In 1758 the Company was asking whether the theatre there could not be turned into a church. The first reference to a theatre at Madras hitherto quoted dates from 1778; but that was by no means the beginning. In 1766 there was already a theatrical society, possessed of considerable funds, for it had lent nearly £2,400 to the Nawab. Among the inventories I find in 1770 a collection of plays stitched in blue paper, and in 1778 a book called *The Companion of the Playhouse*. In that year tickets cost 2 pagodas each, for Young writes to one of his customers, " I cannot find that I received any money from you . . . except 4 pagodas for two tickets for the play lost at cards." In 1778 a temporary theatre was in use. It stood on the island outside the Fort. This was pulled down in 1783, and I do not know where plays were given between that year and 1791, when "the little theatre on the plain was already open"; but I expect they were given pretty regularly. The sort of plays that were presented were comedies like the *Minor* or the *Provoked Wife*, tragedies like the *Revenge*, or ballad opera like the *Waterman* or the *Padlock*. Tom Underwood, the poetaster, himself produced a farce and a tragedy, which he advertised for publication by subscription; but as the tragedy was thought a farce, I infer that the farce was damned.

Concerts and plays, however, were but occasional amusements compared with the perennial pastime of gambling. That was the pet vice of the century. Rodney himself (men said) had been superseded by the lucky admiral who had won great sums of Fox at hazard. Francis won a handsome competence at the whist-tables of Calcutta. No similar record exists for Madras, where indeed "the rhino" (as Sir Charles Bunbury would have said) was less plentiful. But all the Council with one exception was once dismissed by the Company for gambling; cards and card-tables were as common at Madras as elsewhere, though we cannot count the sums staked at them. Hickey was set down to whist at pagoda points, when his disgusted partner, Jack Whitehill, advised him to confine himself to things he was more fitted for. But the dismissal of Governor Floyer was the last outburst of the Company's moral censorship. In earlier days they had taken a more active part.

"It is with great concern," the directors wrote in 1721, "we hear the itch of gaming hath spread itself over Madras, that even the gentlewomen play for great sums, and that Captain Seaton makes a trade of it to the stripping several of the young men there. . . . Discountenance it in all our covenant servants and other dependents, and civilly acquaint the gentlewomen we desire they will put a stop to all high gambling."

And in 1728 they strictly forbade all manner of gaming whatsoever. With the expansion of the English interests and the increase of the English establishments, the Company's servants, civil and military, ceased to be so closely looked after. If they would study Hoyle's " History of the Four Kings," as an indignant merchant called that famous book of games, the Company was now busy with larger things and no longer interfered. At the taverns the most popular games were backgammon and billiards, as had been the case ever since Lockyer's time at the beginning of the century. There was a billiard-room at the Mount, at which Daniel Morse owed an account at the time of his death; there were three tables at Whittle's Tavern in 1776. You might even find one in private houses like George Savage's, with its " 11 masts, 6 ques, and 2 balls." At the Cape too you would find the same amusement on the way out. George Bruce played a game there with one of his Scotch cadet friends, afterwards drinking a bowl of " zangree " for the sake of talking with the landlady's daughter, so pretty a girl that Bruce resolved to play another game when he passed the Cape homeward bound. He could not keep his vow, for he was shot before Conjeeveram in the war with Hyder.

But in spite of their billiard-tables, the taverns of Madras left no little to be desired. As soon as society became articulate in a newspaper, the satirist at once commemorated them. Now the landlord of the Griffin Inn (" Griffin " was the slang of the time for a new-comer) celebrates his stale beer, sour claret, and rotten hams; now a writer in heroic couplets describes the host, by turn obsequious and insolent, his bill invariably extortionate, his company mostly discreditable. They are such cut-throats, says an officer who knew them, that a man needs the wealth of the Indies to pay their bills. But many bills, no doubt, went unpaid. David Young says in a letter to one of his gentlefolk friends of Dundee:

" It is hard for one to come here who has nowhere to go to or a friend to assist him. Those that have not are obliged to go to a tavern, where at least it will cost them a guinea a day, and they are led into so many bad habits and expenses that they get into debt so much that they can scarce get out of it again."

And the same complaint is repeated officially at the end of the century. Had Shenstone lived in the East, he would perhaps have been less enthusiastic about the welcome of an inn.

All the same, there were places worse off than Madras. Batavia, for instance, was a much greater city, the capital of the Dutch Indies, abounding in wealth and trade. Yet owing to Dutch policy, there was but one tavern. It was the Red Lion, and at the beginning of the century had been kept by an old witch from Flores called Black Moll. Hamilton thought well enough of it, but country captains of his time were not too particular. It was built in the deadliest part of the deadliest city in Asia. A Madras visitor, James Strange, who was there in 1786, says:

" It is surprising that in a place of such resort as is Batavia there should be but one inn for the reception of . . . strangers . . . The government draw a considerable revenue from the profits arising from this tavern, which is farmed out from year to year. The expense of bed and board appears at first sight by no means unreasonable, being no more than 2 dollars a day; but the several items which follow this charge make it amount in the whole to an extravagant sum. . . ."

He arrived there in the evening, and found 40 or 50, covers laid for supper in a spacious hall; and his first impressions were not unfavourable; but next morning he learnt that in the previous five weeks seven persons had died in his bed, which had not been aired all that time. On inquiring for another room, he found that in one a man had died of a putrid fever 48 hours before his arrival, and that the others were commonly known as the Tavern Sepulchres. He therefore slept on a billiard-table till his departure.

Madras was at least better off than this, probably because there was choice and competition. The Madras taverns were divided into two classes—punch-houses and houses of entertainment. The difference was that the latter were confined by their licences to receive only commissioned officers, ships' officers, and others on the footing of a gentleman. They were usually kept by retired soldiers. Two houses of entertainment were specially licensed in 1760; and I expect it was one of these to which, under the name of the " hotel," General Smith invited all the officers of the garrison to dinner and supper on New Year's Day, 1771. In the later part of the century, one of the chief taverns at Madras was Whittle's, so called after its proprietor, John Whittle, who, perhaps, for all the difference in the spelling called cousins with his namesake the governor. An inventory of the tavern contents shows, besides the three billiard-tables, which I have already mentioned, 48 chairs, 9 standing and 8 camp-beds, 8 looking-glasses, 68 dinner-plates, 18 soup-plates, and a larger amount of silver than one would expect—a coffee-pot, 2 salvers, 4 salts and spoons, 12 table spoons, a punch-strainer, and a marrow-spoon. Another well-known tavern was that called the Madras Coffee House, originally kept by John Jackson and Cottrell Barrett, and later on in the hands of Edward Rylance. In 1799 the chief ones were the Navy Tavern, the King's Arms, and the Old London Tavern, all on the esplanade of the Fort. They were distinguished by being allowed to remain open till midnight. Besides these was a tavern in the Fort itself, called therefore the Fort Tavern, which advertised in the cold weather " Soups every morning, and dinners dressed on the shortest notice, and the very best wines." Also in the Fort was the Exchange Coffee Tavern, which was opened in 1792, in quarters under the newly-built Exchange (now the officers' mess). The enterprising proprietor announced that he was going to run the coffee-room on the same plan as the New Lloyd's in London, by maintaining a register of the arrival and departure of ships, and taking in the newspapers of India and Europe.

The standard charge for food and lodging was 8s. or a pagoda a day; but he had need to be abstemious who paid no more. If a guest wanted to hire a horse or a carriage, it would cost him another pagoda at least. And his liquor would probably come to as much too. A bottle of porter was over 3 shillings; a bottle of beer about half a crown; a bottle of Madeira or port, 6 shillings; a bottle of claret, 8 shillings. At most places you would not get more than three bowls of arrack punch for a pagoda. Such rates afforded profits running from 100 to 300 per cent. A specimen or two of tavern bills will illustrate both the charges and the consumption of those days. Here is the bill which Joseph Shearme ran up at a common punch-house about 1770:

1 bowl punch	.	.	.	.	6 fanams
Supper .	.	.	.	.	8 ,,
Breakfast	.	.	.	.	6 ,,
1 bowl punch	.	.	.	.	6 ,,
1 sneaker of grog .	.	.	.	3 ,,

Dinner	12	fanams
Punch at dinner	5	,,
4 bowls of punch	24	,,
Lodging (one day). . . .	6	,,
1 glass sherbet	1	,,
1 bottle [country] beer . . .	14	,,
Shrub liquor	4	,,
1 bottle syder	16	,,
Tiffing	4	,,
1 bottle port wine	30	,,
Shrub sangree	3	,,
1 bottle madeira	30	,,
1 bottle claret . . 1 pagoda	—	,,
3 dram cordials	6	,,
1 bowl milk punch	12	,,
3 bottles Tenerif wine . . .	36	,,
1 bottle arrack	7	,,

[6 pagodas 29 fanams]

Not bad going for a day and a half at a place frequented by persons not on the footing of a gentleman.

Among other miscellanea of the Mayor's Court papers is an account book, belonging to a tavern which I cannot identify, for about the last six weeks of 1780. It must have been a largish place of its kind, for on 9 November seventeen guests were living there, though that number seems to have been exceptional. On successive days Lieutenant Villars entertained first four and then nine gentlemen to dinner and supper. The first cost him nearly £5, the second £12 16s. The first night they drank about two bottles of mixed liquors a head, and the second night not quite three, so that while both were festive, neither was outrageous. On Christmas Day Lieutenant Gascoyne ordered a dinner to be sent out to him, but whether to his quarters in the Fort or whether to the scene of a picnic I cannot tell.   The bill was thus:

Dinner for 17	25 pagodas	21 fanams
24 bottles of claret	24 ,,	
12 bottles madeira	8 ,,	24 ,,
21 bottles porter	9 ,,	
4 pints cherry brandy	1 ,,	21 ,,
1 bottle brandy	— ,,	31 ,,
1 case-bottle of gin	1 ,,	
9 coolies hire	1 ,,	9 ,,
	71 pagodas	**25 fanams**

That is as near as may be £29 for a Christmas dinner.   A couple of days later the lodge dined there ten strong. Their dinner cost a pagoda each.   They drank 12 bottles of claret, 7 of madeira, 11 of country beer, 1 of brandy, and a bowl and a half of punch—say something over three bottles apiece.   They also broke three long glasses, and their bill came to 30 pagodas 34 fanams—£12 6s.

While social life at Madras was thus becoming more active and gradually learning to revolve round definite centres, it was also becoming more mobile.   As the century progressed, the slow-moving palanquin, borne by its four boys, with two in reserve, was gradually being replaced except for long journeys by wheeled carriages.   Lockyer about 1700 noted that the English were beginning to use chariots to take the air in.   But at first these were pretty well confined to the governor and the Council.   In 1749 Admiral Boscawen marked his sense of Governor Floyer's politeness during his sojourn on the Coast by sending him a chaise and furniture from Europe on his return there. A couple of years later the Nawab, eager to be in the forefront of fashion, asked for a chaise and pair. About 1754 one-horsed and pair-horsed chaises were becoming popular; and Dupleix carried back with him to France the *beau carrosse* in which he had driven about Pondicherry. At first I suppose these came from Europe. In 1776, as some specially handsome ones had arrived, the Council resolved to buy a chariot, a vis-à-vis, and a phaeton, as presents for the Raja of Tanjore. But the Madras artisans speedily learnt how to copy them; and Madras-built coaches became not only common, but also acquired some reputation in India. A ship being about to leave Madras for Masulipatam, Jourdan in 1769 writes to one of his friends there, " I shall send the chaise for Jogee [?] and one for you by the above conveyance. A Europe chaise is seldom as good as a country one and always very dear . . ." They were sent, like the household furniture made at Madras, even as far as Calcutta. David Young writes to a friend in 1780, " Your bandy [the local term for carriage] is finished but not yet guilt; it will be ready to send in a few days . . ." After learning of its safe arrival, he writes again, ". . . I . . . am glad the bandy pleases you so well, and hope you will find it as good as it looks . . ." In revenge for this, however, some ten years later I find at Madras " an elegant bandy with a top built in Bengal."

The cost of keeping a horse was at this time reckoned at about 6 pagodas a month. There were several markets from which they were procured. Small, hardy, and fast ponies might be obtained from Pegu across the Bay; others were fetched from Manila, but those of any size were mostly bespoke. Jourdan writes:

" I have a pair of Manilla horses which I could let you have, but Mr Holford tells me they will be too small. I have ever since the arrival of the —— endeavoured to get a good pair, but those of a size that would suit you were marked at Manilla for particular gentlemen who bespoke them."

At this time the only great horse-fair in Southern India was held at a place some distance north-west of Hyderabad, and the latter place was regarded as the main centre of the local horse-trade. Jourdan asks his brother to get him a couple of mares cheap and handsome, and is willing to give 700 rupees for the pair, for, though he could get them for 500 at Hyderabad, it was expensive to bring them down to Madras. 1,000 rupees is the highest price I have noted as given for a horse; but that price was no doubt often exceeded. 400 was reckoned an average price for a serviceable animal.

In a country where Englishmen had horses, there was naturally hunting, though it were after no nobler an animal than the jackal. The first reference to this has been thought a letter of 1776 asking for a yearly draft of 20 couple of hounds for the " Madras Hunting Society." But jack-hunting was certainly followed twenty years earlier. In the Mayor's Court papers of 1753 is a horse-dealing case, in which the seller demands specific performance of the contract, while the buyer claimed to have bought the horse under warranty of soundness. The horse in question, it appears from the evidence, was that ridden by Pigot on an occasion celebrated by Orme, when in 1751 Pigot and Clive saved themselves from a body of the enemy by the superior speed of their animals. When the plaintiff recalled this incident as a proof of the goodness of the horse, the defendant rejoined that that was before it " was sprained by Mr Pigot in a fox-chase." Hunting saddles occur frequently in the inventories; there are four for instance in 1768; and I think that hunting, though perhaps in a rough and ready form, was popular

THE ASSEMBLY ROOMS ON THE RACE GROUND AT MADRAS.
After the aquatint of Thomas Daniell.

round Madras. In 1791 Roebuck writes to a Calcutta friend:

" Will you excuse me troubling you with a trifling commission, which is to procure for me any number of half-bred hounds, from one couple to six couple. They are dogs bred in this country from the Europe fox-hound and a half-bred country dog, and they live better than the Europe hounds. . . . The dogs are for the Madras Hunt, and I have undertaken to procure them. The fleeter they are the better, as our present dogs are very fast . . ."

Roebuck must have been reckoned a doggy man, for only a couple of years later I find him ordering two pointers from Pondicherry for a friend in Bombay. The jack was coursed as well as hunted. Watts escaped from Murshidabad just before Plassey on the pretext of a coursing match; and leashes of greyhounds occur in the Madras inventories. Even in the nineteenth century Sir William Denison got some rattling good gallops when he got near enough to the jack to slip a greyhound.

The origins of racing at Madras are as obscure as those of hunting. I expect many scratch races were run long before the sport was in any way organised. The Fort St George orderly book of 1773 contains the first reference known to me. Colonel Lang there announces that not more than half the officers off duty can be allowed to be absent at one time to attend the races at the Mount; but in order that " they may partake of the diversions day and day about, and for the convenience of such as have not accommodations at the Mount, the gates will be ordered to be opened every morning at 4 o'clock."

The earliest-mentioned form of field-sport, however, was none of these, but hawking. So early as 1654 the Agent, as the first governors of the Fort were called,

15

went hawking by the Mount. In 1771 Warren Hastings, during his short stay upon the Coast, did the same· Captain Fletcher had sent him a present of hawks from Ongole, which Hastings thus acknowledged:

"I return you many thanks for your genteel present. . . . I have been twice abroad with the hawks, and hope I may find an inducement in them to use the exercise of a morning ride, which I much want. They seem to be well trained, and the chief man, as well as his bird, very intelligent and expert in their respective professions. The only difficulty is to meet with game for them. The Carnatic yields none but kites, crows, and paddy-birds. The two former will not be catched, and the latter are hardly worth catching. These however afford me sufficient entertainment."

To big game I find hardly a reference. Not for lack of game. After the Second Mysore War the Carnatic was teeming with tigers, and no doubt many an officer in the up-country garrisons went after them, either on elephants, which were common enough too in the south in those days, or with his muzzle-loader on foot. The records of shikar belong almost entirely to the nineteenth century.

However, among the stray references is one that I wish to mention, for it introduces as well the concluding topic of this chapter. In 1794 Captain Alexander Macpherson and Mr Dawson Logan were stationed at Ambur, in hilly, jungly country where you could easily flush a brace of tiger before breakfast. They were out shooting together, and got on the track of an animal which Macpherson said was a tiger. Logan denied it, and that with so much heat and persistence that the other was at last obliged to inquire the meaning of his behaviour. A duel followed, in which Logan was shot. And if there are few records of shooting tigers, there are plenty of shooting men.

It is very natural, for the manners of the age with

something less of their external formality, and something more of their underlying crudity, had followed the European into Asia. In the warm latitude of Madras where men ate the heavy meats of England seasoned with the hot spices of the East, and washed them down with long drafts of wine and spirits, few constitutions could resist the combined influences of climate and diet; and ill-health bred ill-temper. You became very touchy on your own point of honour, and rather careless about other people's; and when you were inflamed by wine and anger, your conduct might pass all bounds of decorum. Even among the polite French two councillors could fall to fisticuffs after dinner. A councillor at St David's was himself chastised for taking the liberty of chastising another man's servant. On another occasion Ephraim Isaacs, inhabitant of Madras, lost his roundel—the umbrella which in the days before the topi was carried over one's head by a servant whenever one went out in the sun. Isaacs at last found it in the possession of an officer's servant, whom he seized and sent to the justice for punishment. Unluckily the justice was out, and the servant was brought back to Isaacs' house. Half an hour afterwards, according to the petition which Isaacs submitted to the Company, the officer, Caleb Powell,

" came into your memorialist's house, and . . . your memorialist in a polite and friendly manner invited the said Powell to sit down, but the said Powell . . . flew into an outrageous passion, and . . . assaulted your memorialist by raising his closed hand over your memorialist's head, and dared your memorialist to go out of his own house, and offered him a shilling so to do. . . . [And when Isaacs complained to Governor Pigot,] the said governor, with an air tending to ridicule rather than pity or redress his grievances, laughed at your memorialist . . ."

That was, I am sure, very wrong in the governor of the
settlement; but Isaacs was a regular sea-lawyer, who had
made himself universally disliked in the place, and he
had after all suffered no material damage, and, not being
a gentleman, could not be supposed to have suffered any
moral one.   In another case a chaplain complains of ill-
treatment.

"What ignominy can be greater," he rightly asks, "or
what reproach more severe, than to be kicked?   The order
and tranquillity of a place may be broken by passion and
inadvertency, but will hardly be re-established by monitors
like Mr Pybus, who cannot govern his own passions. . . .
He has truly exalted himself to a degree of authority
never yet assumed by any governor of a settlement, I
mean, that of threatening to kick a clergyman . . ."

The commandant of a station justifies his ordering into
arrest an officer suspected of shooting another in a duel by
stating that on the former's face he saw plainly the mark
of a blow.   Moreover, if conduct was rough so also was
language.   There was once an eloquent sea-captain, whose
finer flowers of fancy must be left blossoming in a decent
obscurity, but who continued by the space of two hours
"cursing and swearing, dam'ing and sinking all the Company's servants," because one of them had abused his
confidence after drinking too much burnt cinnamon in his
round-house.

"Full many a gem of purest ray serene
     The dark unfathomed caves of ocean bear."

Perhaps not many of the nabobs could have entered into
competition with him with any prospect of success; but
when their blood was up, they had a decided habit of direct
speech, and a love for making their sentiments known to
the world.   "By God, Sir," says Ensign Brooke to Ensign

Pearson, " you are a dirty scoundrel and your name shall be posted up at the Sea-gate to-morrow." A writer, Thomas Wallace, posts a man at the gate of the Fort Square with orders to show to everyone the following paper:

" To the Gentlemen of this settlement.
    " This is to notify that Mr Cecil Smith, writer on this establishment, has behaved himself as a coward and a scoundrel in his late transaction with me."

Lieutenant John Hollond posts Mr Emmanuel Samuel, successively surgeon, attorney, and editor, as in his opinion " an infamous coward and a detestable poltroon." You could not expect an attorney to let such an opportunity escape; and the lieutenant, prosecuted before the justices in Quarter Sessions, was fined 15 pagodas for libel.

In these conditions frequent duels were inevitable, and the way in which the official attitude towards them changed is not a little curious. Originally they were strictly prohibited. Company's servants accused of striking and challenging another would be summoned before the Council, reprimanded, fined, and ordered in future to live in amity together. Even the captain of the garrison was expected to accommodate himself to mercantile ideas of conduct; and was fined and ordered to give security in 500 pagodas for fighting a duel. Indeed something of this spirit never quite died out, for, when the mercantile feelings of the Government began to wane, they were reinforced by the later humanitarian ideas of the later part of the century. From time to time efforts are made to prevent a particular duel or to discourage duelling in general. Colonel Champion in Bengal required two officers to give their parole not to fight; a lieutenant of the 36th is reprimanded in orders for striking another without sufficient provocation; and in 1787 the Commander-in-Chief announces that he will not recommend for promotion those who have been proved to be the aggressors. But the growing custom of the service must have far outweighed any such occasional and uncertain discouragements as these. In 1768 an officer is reprimanded by the Governor and Council for being beat by and receiving ungentlemanlike language from Mr Woodbine in the King's barracks; in the next year another is broke for allowing himself to be kicked and struck; in 1770 the officers at Ellore decline to do duty with one who has been accused of being a liar; and some years later Lieutenant Yeoman, of His Majesty's 52nd, was broke for being beaten and violently turned out of a tent. In all these cases the offence lay, not of course in the indignity suffered, but in the neglect properly to avenge it.

Nor were courts martial so inconsistent as to inflict the smallest penalty for killing your man unless your conduct had in other respects fallen short of the standards of the time. Thus Lieutenant Bowen, tried for shooting Lieutenant Bell, was duly acquitted, but as " several circumstances appear in the proceedings extremely unfavourable to the character of Lieutenant Bowen," he is released from arrest but ordered to quit the army to-morrow. But such a thing was most unusual. A much more common finding, as in the case of Ensign John Demaria in 1782, was that the accused acted from necessity and self-defence; or, as in the case of Lieutenant Campbell ten years later, that " as it has not appeared in evidence that the said deceased was wilfully, maliciously and premeditatedly murdered . . . , the Court is therefore of opinion that the prisoner is not guilty."

Nor was the court of Quarter Sessions much more rigorous than the courts martial. Just as in the early days the merchants had tried to impose on the soldiers their ideas of conduct, so now the soldiers infected the merchants with their ideas of honour. Thus in 1781 a quarrel arose out of gaming; the lie was given; blows were exchanged; and a duel followed. The seconds, anxious to avoid bloodshed, had proposed that their men should be posted at the usual distance back to back, to turn and fire immediately on the signal. But the aggressor would have none of it, and even insisted on the distance being shortened from 12 paces to 8. His inveteracy ended in his own death. The survivor and his second were put on their trial for murder. The first was found guilty of manslaughter, and admitted to bail until he should appear to plead the King's pardon. The second observed in his defence that " it would have been inconsistent with that profession which I have embraced to forego the requisition of my friend and brother-officer in the defence of his honour and his life," and that " my innocence depends upon the merits of my principal's conduct." He was acquitted. As a rule such cases fell through for lack of evidence, though the juries differed much as to the circumstances in which they would acquit or convict of manslaughter. In two trials in 1784 there was no direct evidence at all, and in both of them the circumstantial evidence was equally convincing. But in the first the prisoner was acquitted; in the second, convicted of manslaughter. I think, however, that towards the close of the century there was a slight though uncertain rise of sentiment against the practice of duelling. At all events in 1788 and in 1805 two trials took place which were much less make-believe than usual. In 1788 a duel was fought between two officers of a Hanoverian regiment then stationed at Madras. I fancy more lay behind the incident than was allowed to appear. At all events the alleged cause—a dispute over the dignity of " the Abbot of Lockum in Hanover " and whether he was entitled to style himself " I " or " we "—sounds as if it might have been employed to cover some more intimate resentment. Several witnesses were called and examined and cross-examined, even the jury asking questions. The evidence was full of prevarications. For instance that of the surgeon who accompanied the party ran much as follows:

Did you accompany the party? Yes.—Where did they go? They entered a grove of trees beside the Poonmallee Road.—What did they do there? I do not know.—Why is that? Because I remained behind to watch a passing palanquin.—While you remained behind, did you hear any sound? Yes, I heard a report.—What was it like? It was like a pistol shot.—What did you do when you heard it? I followed my companions into the grove.— Had you taken your surgical instruments with you? Yes, but I never go out without them.—What did you find on entering the grove? I found the deceased lying on the ground.—In what state was he? He had a wound in the left breast.—Was that wound the cause of his death? I cannot tell.

However, another witness bluntly declared that the prisoner alone discharged his pistol, on which the deceased dropped his to clasp his breast; and yet, for some reason which is hard to divine, in spite of the interest of the jury and their hostility to the prevaricating surgeon, the accused was found not guilty.

The other case to which I referred was tried in 1805 before the Supreme Court which had by then been set up to replace all other tribunals in the city of Madras. Two officers of the 34th Foot were on trial for the murder of Captain Bull of the same regiment. He had been ordered on detachment; and certain officers had made themselves so disagreeable that he had withdrawn his name from the detachment mess. The officers then threw dice to decide which of them was to call him out and which was to act as second. Bull was shot, and public feeling ran high. Elers, who was present at the trial, says that all the jury but one were for a verdict of guilty, but that one managed to bring the rest over to his side. They were absent for an hour. On their return, a strained and awful silence filled the court. " Not guilty," says the foreman. " Not guilty! " exclaims the Chief Justice, who was trying the case. " Not guilty! A most merciful jury! Prisoners, had you been found guilty, you never would have seen the sun rise again. . . ."

So that however resolute judges might be to bring the custom of duelling to an end, public sentiment still supported it though at last with weakening effect. One curious memorial of a duel still survives in the presidency. On one side of the parade ground at the now abandoned station of Arni stands a tall column 65 feet high. It bears this inscription:

" Sacred to the memory of Colonel Robert Kelly, who departed this life in the vicinity of Arnee September 29, A.D. 1790, aet: 52. This monument was erected by Lieutenant-colonel Urban Vigors as a mark of respect for a gallant soldier."

The story runs that Vigors in conversation with his wife called him an old woman, that Mrs Vigors repeated the phrase to Mrs Kelly, who insisted on her husband's obtaining satisfaction. Such a story of feminine spite is not impossible in eighteenth-century Madras; but I am glad to think that Vigors changed his mind about the colonel.

CHAPTER XV

THE HOMEWARD VOYAGE AND SOME REFLECTIONS

MADRAS is an expensive place to get away from. Captains of East Indiamen know the advantage of their position and make the most of it. For a section of the great cabin containing two windows Colonel Champion in Bengal has to pay 2,000 rupees. Mrs Barclay is willing to go as far as a thousand pagodas—£400—for a passage for herself, a European servant, and a black one. Colonel John Wood, for himself and family, pays £1,000 for a passage which he never takes because he finds a shorter, quicker way out of Madras by dying there. As is still the case, everyone says that foreign ships are much cheaper and more comfortable to travel on. And sometimes, when you have agreed with the captain and paid him, you may find the whole thing upset by some member of Council who has resolved to go home at the last moment, and who claims a superior right to decent accommodation. Matters go so far that the Company at last intervenes, and ordains that persons going home on sick certificate shall only be required to pay certain fixed rates, running from £200 for a general officer to £70 for a writer, lieutenant, or ensign.

You have to provide the same furniture—bed, chair, and table—for your cabin that you did on the outward voyage; but otherwise your kit is very different. Then most of your baggage was composed of cool clothes for tropical wear; but now you want only so much as will suffice for the voyage, and all the rest you give away to your servants. On the other hand, you have accumulated a mass of curiosities—carved tables and cabinets, silver and brass ware, shawls and images, which you mean to give to your friends or to use yourself. This too runs to unreasonable quantities, and in one ship the passengers' baggage takes up no less than 63 tons of space. In future they are to be limited to five tons if they are members of Council or general officers, and so on down to one ton for the writer, lieutenant, or ensign. Like Jos Sedley, you probably travel home with a servant or two to look after you on board, and to be sent back by the next returning Indiaman.

How different too your feelings and your company from those of the outward voyage! Then you were nearly all young and in the pink of health, looking forward to the wonders of the East. Now you return mature, sallow, disillusioned. The wonders of the East, like the wonders of other places, are not so wonderful as you had dreamed. You will have a liver-complaint which you will sedulously doctor. At table you will notice one or two of your fellow-travellers and wonder whether they will see the voyage out. Probably they won't. There will be no young misses aboard to provide the ship with harmony and discord. You will play your steady rubber of whist when the weather permits, and gossip about the past with the skipper and one or two old friends. You will air your old grievances, though they are in no danger of growing musty, and agree what a damned shame it was for Hollond to keep Tudor out of the Board of Revenue, or for Oakes to come poking back where he was not wanted. Above all you will talk of how the place has changed since first you knew it.

And indeed Madras which we leave in 1800 is very

different from the half-dismantled, wholly neglected place at which we disembarked fifty years ago. Hardly anything is the same, except the unresting surf, and the English flag that still flutters on the flagstaff bastion. Fort St George has been new-designed and rebuilt from top to bottom. It has become the strongest place of arms in the East. The Black Town no longer presses against its northern side. All round it stretches the broad esplanade. But for the gallows and Captain Powney's forty-foot monument nothing rises to intercept the fire of the guns just peering over the crest of the glacis. It is provisioned for a twelvemonth. It has secret cisterns full of water. It contains great magazines of powder, shot, and shell, securely protected from the fire of any enemy. It is the head-quarters of an army of 60,000 men, to say nothing of a brigade or two of King's troops. Any expedition that the French with all their vigour and genius could equip at the Mauritius would now hardly dare to land before it. Pondicherry, once so dangerous a rival, is in English hands and will never again gird itself with the panoply of war. The French flag, though it once flew for a time where the Union Jack now waves, has been struck in all South India. Nowhere from Cape Comorin to the Kistna will you find an organised body of French troops. The last parties of them have just been driven from Hyderabad or captured in Seringapatam. The only thing that could seriously threaten our position is a great fleet and army from Europe; but how could they escape the ships that watch for them? In five years Trafalgar will be fought, and then no fleets will be left to dispute our supremacy at sea.

And ashore no native power remains in the south to question English authority. The Nawab whom we were fighting for in 1750 has lately died in his palace at Chepauk; you can see its banded minarets rising just south of what we used to call the Governor's Garden but now Government House. There he built his home, to be near the guns of Fort St George, and adorned it with spoils from the famous palace of Dupleix. But the splendours of his durbar, like those of the French governor's little court, were almost as transient as the images in the great gilt mirrors that reflected both. Muhammad Ali has died and been laid to rest at Trichinopoly, beside the headless corpse of his early rival. He has been succeeded by the son whom he strove long and earnestly to disinherit; but already papers have come to light seeming to prove that neither father nor son were unswervingly faithful to their allies, and next year his son too will be dead and all his dominions will have passed into the Company's control.

More than this, on 4 May last year, the long struggle with Hyder and Tipu, his son, was brought to a final and dramatic close after long vicissitudes. In two wars we had hardly held our own. In the third we had left half our work undone. But after the fourth nothing remained over. Our columns swiftly gathered at the enemy's capital, and what followed was short, bloody, and decisive. The gunners breached the walls; the storming party was told off; and within sixty minutes of the time when the forlorn hope sprang from their trenches, more than half the garrison of the fortress had fallen, and the rest, utterly broken and demoralised, were herding together like a flock of sheep. At the appointed hour of that great and terrible day the most persistent and dangerous enemy of the English was delivered into their hands. No neighbouring power remains that can dream of disputing with success the pre-eminence achieved in these last fifty years.

But all this has been bought at a price. How fat that graveyard on the Island has grown with English bodies.

There alone since our arrival we have seen more than 7,000 buried; and how many more lie scattered at a score of cantonments, on a hundred battle-fields, and along every road that our armies followed? Think of all the hope, fear, wrath, horror, and desire that disappeared with them! Well, they must all have died somewhere; and we know at least what they bought with their blood—a blank in the Great Indian Lottery. Poor things, they should of course have had higher, nobler ambitions. They should have thought more of their country's mission, more of their imperishable souls, more even of their mortal bodies. They should not have snatched so hastily at pleasure, or drunk themselves into a fugitive contentment. They should have been wise, virtuous, and fortunate. But one thing or another they lacked; and there they now lie, uncounted save by the Recording Angel, who has a long score against them, and so is sure to hold them in memory.

But meanwhile their companions go on without too much thought of them. If the luck of the roster puts you on a funeral party to-day, you will be on a guard of honour to-morrow, and your friend in the Artillery fires minute-guns and salutes with equal indifference. On no other terms could Madras have become the capital of the South, and capital it is, though but a provincial one. How it has grown in these fifty years! Its Indian population, which used to be reckoned at 40,000, is now a quarter of a million, and of the Europeans four or five hundred families think themselves entitled to be asked to Government House and admitted to the Assembly Rooms. The governor was formerly able to entertain all the eligible part of the settlement at the Admiralty House in the Fort; but we have long outgrown that. Our present governor, Lord Clive, son of the conqueror of Bengal, invites us to the Exchange or the Pantheon; he is about to enlarge the Government House, and add to it the Banqueting Hall, expressly for the purpose of his greater entertainments. We have ceased to live in the Fort, though we still own 52 houses there. We now stretch down the Mount Road, beyond the Cooum, where in 1753 were only three garden-houses besides the governor's, with a Sepoy guard to protect them. There are Pater's Gardens, Dent's Gardens, Mackay's Gardens, and many others, each with its wide grounds, out to Blacker's Gardens on the Long Tank. North of the river are Haliburton's Gardens, and the Pantheon, and Casamajor's Gardens. Along the Poonamallee Road another string leading to Landon's Gardens and the house of Attorney Disney. Southwards too by Sulivan's Gardens to Moubray's Gardens on the banks of the pleasant Adyar, and General Brathwaite's mansion at its mouth. In all perhaps nearly a hundred great houses thinly scattered over an area four miles by two, for we like elbow-room, both in our homes and round them.

And when we set our minds to it what entertainments we give! Wayte and Ellis, living together in a house on the bank of the Long Tank, give a masquerade and ball. They build a temporary ball-room, as no room even in their house is large enough for their guests, and illuminate their gardens and the borders of the tank with thousands of little lights. Dancing begins at midnight, and supper is served at three. Again the same two and eighteen others give a grand masquerade. Thackeray's uncle is of their number, and represents Death by his costume, while another of the hosts is the Devil. This ball was given at the Pantheon, and the whole place was gorgeously decorated. Changes of costume were the rule on that occasion. Before supper the hosts retire to reappear dressed as Knights of Malta; and many of their guests figured under more than one character in the course of the night. There was no dancing till after supper, but then it is said to have been continued by some at least till 8 next morning.

Madras indeed is at its zenith. Never before has it been so large, so prosperous, so important. Trade flourishes because the Company has resolved if possible to dominate the markets of all Europe in Indian produce, and its orders for goods are almost unlimited. Victory has given everyone confidence in the future. No one foresees the depressing years that are ahead, when the growth of machinery at home shall render Indian manufactures unsaleable, and when the growth of the English territories in the north and the rise of new enemies shall have transformed the political balance and rendered Madras a place of little weight. Then Madras will know poverty once more; house after house will close its doors and suspend payment; the Supreme Government will neglect it, will try to enforce on it methods of administration already tried and found unsuitable, will demand from it a disproportioned share of its scanty revenues; and will ignore the talent in its services. It will become a presidency apart, and those who do not know it will say that it lives upon its former glories.

The earlier age was the age of merchants; the coming one will be the age of administrators; but these fifty years we have just passed have been the age of the soldier. No one else has been so important. He has been the person who really counted in our little world. He has given force and validity to our negotiators' demands, he has given the tone to our society; he has brought a certain group of virtues and vices into fashion, and infected the civilian with his ideas. This he has been able to do partly because he has been much the largest element at our balls and concerts, partly because the circumstances of the time have made his services specially indispensable. We have been involved in wars of importance in twenty-nine years of the last half-century. If we take into the account lesser expeditions, against Tanjore, Ramnad, Sivaganga, and the many chiefs of our northern hills, who would never pay their revenues with regularity, I hardly think there can have been a year in which our officers and men were not risking their lives somewhere in the field. War was the normal state of things, and peace the lucky exception, when you could get leave to Madras and have as good a time as that city could afford. You were ready enough to pay whatever might be demanded in pain or death; but if you were going to buy life as dear as that, life while it lasted had to be brisk, stirring, and pleasureable. At all events till you were the colonel of a regiment or highish up in the Company's civil service, you found your delight in the adventurous much more than in the comfortable. You were so accustomed to stake all you had against the devil, and had seen so many pay their last forfeit, that you were indisposed to guide your social life by different principles. The possibility of losing your prize-money would not keep you from the gaming table, or the likelihood of confronting an injured husband's pistol deter you from intrigue.

But on your arrival home you find a very different atmosphere from that which you left behind you fifty years ago. Then a nabob was a rare but not an unpopular animal. Governor Pitt could found a family without exciting any unfavourable notice and could be offered, though he was too wise to accept, the government of Jamaica. Governor Harrison's daughter could become my Lady Townshend and keep all London diverted with her wit and gallantries. Governor Saunders could come home and become High Sheriff of Bucks. But now, though the worst has passed, people are still inclined to look askance at you. You join an Anglo-Indian club, and your society is composed very much of people of your own service. The fact is that your mode of life has rather

16

scandalised good people at home. In London licence is permissible only in the upper classes. Just as a peer cannot be tried by the same tribunal, or even hanged by the same kind of rope, as other men, so also he and his associates claim and are allowed the privilege of damning themselves genteelly without being cut or scolded. But at Madras people without such pretensions to birth and breeding as will pass muster at St James's have tried to arrogate to themselves the same privileges. They have not only broken the moral laws, but defied the social conventions. It is an unnatural thing that persons who, had they remained in England, would have kept a shop, or become country apothecaries, or at best have been city merchants, should presume to stake their guineas, keep their mistresses, or punish insults to their imagined honour in the manner of gentlefolks.

The other difference was that in the nabobs' magnificence and gaiety and vice there was an element of falsity and make-believe. They lacked the polish of the real thing, and were fine gentlemen rather after the manner of Smollett. You could see it in their dress, their language, their amours. Their embroidered coats had not the fit and hang of Piccadilly. Their tone was apt to be loud and violent. They lacked the air with which Grafton would conduct Nancy Parsons from her box at the Opera, and the ease with which Q would consult Lady Rochford about stockings for the Zamperini. Indeed how should they acquire it? Madras was an outpost of empire, not a school for manners. And under the decorations of high life lay that preoccupation with the business of making a fortune which was so inconsistent with gentility in contemporary eyes. Not content with the state of life to which they had been called, they were aping the style of their betters and even seeking to accumulate enough to continue their flagitious course of conduct in England.

'Twas flying in the face of Providence and the Catechism.

Thus under the combined assaults of the beaux for their lack of taste, and of the moralists for their lack of virtue, and of the scholars for their lack of learning, the poor nabobs fell under a load of opprobrium which exceeded their deserts. They were condemned alike for their sins and for their follies. No plea was allowed in mitigation of sentence on account of their temptations and achievements. But were they really worse than their brothers and sisters, worse than their companions at school, worse than some of their very critics? If they were all as bad as that debauched adventurer, Mr Sheridan, they were not much to boast of. And some of them were as bad. Some of them too only came to Madras after having come to grief at home. Of them not much can be expected. Again, great men found India a cheap way of paying off their obligations. Dozens of their more disreputable dependents came ashore expecting to make their fortune, or rather to have it made for them, in a couple of years. There was Colonel Cooper, for instance, who arrived in '81. He was a natural son of Lord Holland, and so half-brother of Charles James Fox, who sent him out with warm recommendations. Macartney would do nothing for him, and sent him up to Bengal, where Hastings gave him £800 a year with nothing to do for it. But although he was a drunken fellow, indecently quarrelsome in his cups, I have no doubt that Hastings was blamed for not sending him back wealthy and reformed. But if we set aside these burdens imposed by politicians upon the Company, the nabobs were not very much worse than other people. At the lower end of the scale I expect more went to the devil than would have gone in England; but at the other end more rose to the height of their opportunities. Their circumstances, in short, developed in a high degree both the strength and weakness of their age. Beside their tough moral fibre, their condonation of many evils, their flamboyancy of taste, must also in plain justice be set their self-reliance, their high spirit, their gift of command, their love of adventure. And when I read Burke's indiscriminate invective I cannot but remember "those eighteen upon whom the tower in Siloam fell and slew them; think ye that they were sinners above all men that dwelt in Jerusalem?"

APPENDIX

CHAPTER I

p. 2. *Major Rennell.* He tells the story of his voyage out in a letter to Burrington dated 30 September, 1760 (Home Miscellaneous Series, No. 765, India Office).

Officers' trade. Curious detail is preserved in the manifests bound up with the dispatches from England at the Madras Record Office.

p. 6. *Routine of life.* See the pamphlet entitled *Journal of the Boscawen's Voyage,* 8vo, 1760.

CHAPTER II

pp. 11 etc. *Madras in 1750.* In general see Love's *Vestiges of Old Madras,* and Wheeler's *Madras in the Olden Time.*

p. 16. *De Morgan's Letter.* See Fort St David Consultations, 22 June, 1747.

p. 17. *Council's Letter.* See Public Dispatch to England, 26 September, 1741.

p. 18. *The Ignorant Superannuated Swede.* He was Peter Eckman. His letter, addressed to the director, Gough, of 2 November, 1748, occurs in the Miscellaneous Letters Received, 1747–48, No. 152 (India Office).

Francis Hugonin. His letter occurs in the same series, 1741, No. 224.

p. 19. *Chaplains.* In general see Penny's *Church in Madras.* *Francis Fordyce.* See Forrest's *Life of Clive,* i. 81 etc., and Miscellaneous Letters Received, 1749–50, No. 5.

p. 20. *Letter of 1695.* See the *Le Fleming MSS.* (Hist. MSS. Com., 12th Rept., App. vii, p. 338).

p. 23. *Petrus Uscan's Will.* See Madras Will-book 1756, under date 29 June.

CHAPTER III

p. 27. *The Nawab's Presents.* The list mentioned occurs among the Carnatic Records at the Madras Record Office.

p. 28. *John Whitehill.* See Wright and Sclater's *Sterne's Eliza.*

p. 30. *Letter from the Company.* 23 January, 1754.

p. 31. *Reply from the Council.* 10 November, 1754.

p. 32. *Jourdan's Letter.* This, and further details regarding him, are taken from his correspondence in the Mayor's Court Records.

p. 34. *The Floyers.* For some details regarding this family I am indebted to the Rev. J. Kestell Floyer.

p. 35. *The Bourchiers.* See a paper by Sir William Foster in the *Indian Antiquary*, October, 1911.

p. 37. *Edward Croke.* See my *List of Marriages at Fort St George* and the (unpublished) registers of baptisms.

p. 38. *Letter from Chambers.* 9 March, 1788, ap. Br. Mus. Add. MSS. 39403, f. 209.

CHAPTER IV

p. 39. *The Company's Officer.* The principal authority on the subject of this and the next two chapters is Wilson's *History of the Madras Army*; but it touches very little on the aspects with which I am particularly concerned.

p. 40. *Pigot's Medal.* See Public Dispatch from England, 13 March, 1761, para. 136.

p. 41. *The Fidelity Medal.* Madras G.O.G. 24 April, 1786.
Coote's Letter. Madras Military Consultations, 21 July, 1760.

p. 42. *Patterson's Certificate.* Letter from Brathwaite, 17 December, 1793, ap. Military Consultations of the same date, pp. 5408–10.

p. 44. *Alexander Delavaux.* See Fort St David Factory Records (India Office), vol. x, pp. 181 etc., and Fleming to the Board of Trade, 10 April, 1751 (P.R.O., C.O. 152–27).

p. 45. *Hickey's examination.* See his *Memoirs*, i. 124–5.

Cadets' uniform. G.O. by Sir Hector Munro, 10 February, 1780.

Appointment to commissions. Army Order, 19 June, 1772.

Ensigns on probation. Madras Military Consultations, 30 October, 1775 (pp. 1448-9).

p. 46. *Cadets kept in garrison.* Loc. cit., 4 February, 1780 (pp. 138-9).

Cadet Company. G.O.G. 15 July, 1800, and 11 August, 1801.

p. 47. *John Dalton.* Many letters from him are to be found in the Orme MSS. at the India Office.

John Caillaud. See letter from Colonel Draper to Council, 28 March, 1759, ap. Military Consultations of date.

Laverock's petition to the Company occurs in the Miscellaneous Letters Received, 1757, No. 28.

Thomas Madge. See Cotton's *Inscriptions,* p. 25. The Captain E. H. Madge there mentioned was, I think, one of his natural sons. His will occurs in the Will-books for 1773, under date 16 November, and his inventory in the Will-book of the next year, under date 2 August.

p. 48. *Hyde Parker's letter.* Miscellaneous Letters Received, 1749-50, No. 7.

Arthur Nelson's certificate. Madras Public Miscellany, vol. i, p. 77.

The relations of King's and Company's Officers. See Orme to Holdernesse, 30 July, 1757 (Orme MSS., Various, 17, p. 341): R. Smith to Lawrence, 1760 (loc. cit. 27, p. 50); Military Dispatch to England, 1 August, 1759; Coote to Council, 1 July (Military Consultations, 3 July, 1760); Coote's Journal, 3 July, 1760 (Orme MSS., India, viii, 1953); and Military Consultations, 28 July, 1760.

p. 51. *Peter Eckman's inventory.* Will-book, 1760, 2 January.

Crompton's inventory. Will-book, 1765.

De Morgan's will and inventory. Will-books for 1760 and 1761.

p. 52. *Raillard's death.* See Orme, ii. 501, and Smith to Council, 20 June, ap. Military Consultations, 5 July, 1759.

Wolfe on military education. See Beccles Willson's *Life and Letters of James Wolfe.*

D'Illens' inventory. Will-book, 1757.

p. 53. *Leigh's will* occurs in the Will-book, 1761.

The principal inventories of books belonging to deceased Officers are the following: d'Illens, ut supra; Bullock, 1765; Corneille, 1766; Dixon, 1767; Madge, 1774; Kempson, 1776; Gordon, 1779; Manoury, 1782; Moorhouse, 1792.

p. 54. *Call's letter.* To Maskelyne, August, 1759 (Orme MSS., Various, 26, p. 16).

Letter from a Company's Officer. Robert Bannatyne to ——, 11 April, 1759 (Will-book, 1759).

p. 55. *Jolland's will.* Will-book, 1773.

The captain who sent away his brother the cooper was Edmondes (Young to McCullock, 15 September, 1777, Mayor's Court Records).

CHAPTER V

p. 57. *Officers' pay.* See G.O.G., 23 September, 1788, and Army Order, 3 October, 1788 and 4 October, 1789.

p. 58. *Caillaud's letter.* See Miscellaneous Letters Received, 1764, No. 356.

p. 60. *Off-reckonings.* See Wilson's *Madras Army,* i. 52 etc.; Public Consultations, 25 August, 1755; loc. cit., 21 November, 1758; Army Order, 27 December, 1768; G.O.G., 30 October, 1784; and Army Orders, 15 December, 1788, and 21 July, 1792.

p. 61. *Wood's trial.* See Army Order, 21 December, 1769, and Palk MSS., p. 121.

Arrack profits. See Jourdan to Colonel Tod (August, 1771), Mayor's Court Records; and Army Order, 11 November, 1789.

p. 62. *Early Officers' trade.* See Malcolm's *Clive,* iii. 83; de Gingens, Public Consultations, 30 January, 1744;

Wardlaw and Turnbull, Fort St David Consultations,
1 August, 1747; Harrison, Will-books, 1755; Pye,
Mayor's Court Pleadings, 1757, pp. 131 etc.; Hume, loc.
cit., 1763, pp. 74–5; Pascall, loc. cit. 1774; Greenwollers, Will-book, 1766.

p. 63 *Officers' money-lending.* Pascall, Military Consultations, 17 May, 1762, p. 120; Bowman, Public Dispatch
from England, 25 November, 1775; Butler, G.O.G.,
31 October, 1789.

Later trade. Gordon, Will-book, 1778; Calvert,
Mayor's Court Pleadings, 1772; Beatson, Young to Read,
2 November, 1782 (Mayor's Court Records); Browne,
Mayor's Court Pleadings, 1780; Read, Young to William
Read, 12 October, 1779 (Mayor's Court Records).

p. 65. *Prize.* For Wellington's definition of plunder see
Broughton's *Recollections*, v. 202. Letters patent of
14 January, 1758 are printed in the Company's Charters,
p. 460. Orders under this, Public Dispatch from England, 8 March 1758; for the *Santissima Trinidad,* see
Army Order, 12 August, 1768; for Pondicherry prize
see loc. cit., 24 November, 1788; for Negapatam prize,
loc. cit., 20 June, 1789; for Cornwallis's prize-arrange-
ments, Army Order 10 June, 1790; its distribution on
the batta basis, loc. cit., 28 February, 1791; for the
Seringapatam prize, Wellesley Dispatches, i. 710, and
ii. 40; also *Madras Mail,* 4 May, 1915.

p. 68. *Sepoy Abuses.* See Wilson's *Madras Army,* i. 234;
Spears, Military Consultations, pp. 18 and 39; Saunders
to the Secretary to the Company, 9 September, 1757;
and Orme MSS., India, xii. 3122. Alesieu, Wilson,
op. cit., i. 177 etc.; Hudson, Will-book, 1769; Collins,
Army Order, 11 May, 1771, and 21 July, 1772; Evance,
loc. cit., 17 December, 1772, and 7 October, 1774;
Calvert, Military Sundry, No. 43, and G.O.G., 29
August, 1776; for orders of 1787, Military Consultations, 10 August, 1787, pp. 444–50.

p. 70. *Neglect of duty, etc.* Army Order, 17 August, 1768;
Garrison Order, Ellore, 9 December, 1775; Love's

Vestiges, iii. 74; Army Order, 16 May, 1769. For West see Army Order, 16 May, 1769, and Military Sundry, No. 43; similar misconduct, Army Order ut supra, and 13 July, 1787; fancy uniforms, Army Order, 21 October, 1775; Madge's nephew, Palk MSS., pp. 84, 98, 115, and 119; Moody, Army Order, 22 October, 1773; Mitchell, Roebuck to Fairlie, 10 February and 13 December, 1794 (Mayor's Court Records).

p. 71. *Drunkenness.* Military Sundry No. 43 (Roberts); Army Order, 21 June, 1782; loc. cit., 22 December, 1791; and G.O.C.C., 12 September, 1802.

p. 72. *Desertion.* Love's *Vestiges*, ii. 71 etc.; Hitchcock, Edward Raddon to (? John Pybus), 1768 (Mayor's Court Records); Watkins, Military Sundry, No. 43.

CHAPTER VI

p. 74. *Recruits.* Lockyer, *Trade to India*, p. 26; Foster's *Factories in India*, ix. 18; Long's *Selections*, p. 152; Miscellaneous Letters Received, 1758–59, Nos. 141, 142; Memorandum, 11 December, 1752, ap. Newcastle MSS., Br. Mus. Add. MSS. 33031, f. 10; Bengal to Madras, 26 January, 1759, ap. Military Consultations, 28 February, 1759; Miscellaneous Letters Received, 1763, Nos. 142, 144, 146, 207; Military Dispatch from England, 31 January, 1776; Duke of Buckingham, Court, etc., of George III, iv. 51–2.

p. 76. *Recruitment of foreigners.* Public Dispatches from England, 15 December, 1752, and 29 December, 1756; Wilson's *Madras Army*, i. 62–3; Public Consultations, 17 June, 1752; Military Consultations, 1752, pp. 23 and 28; Public Dispatch from England, 19 December, 1755; Military Dispatch to England, 10 November, 1757; memorandum, 18 April, 1771, Public Record Office, C.O. 77–22.

Recruitment of deserters. Fort St David to Fort Marlborough, 13 February, 1748 (Letters from Fort St David 1748); Fort St David Consultations, 30 June, 1748; loc. cit., 19 February, 1750; Public Consultations, 30

October, 1753; Wilson's *Madras Army*, i. 70, 121, 140, 286; Caillaud to Madras, 30 May, 1757 (Military Consultations, 6 June, 1757); Orme MSS., India, xiii, 3581; Bengal to Madras, 5 April (Military Consultations, 6 May, 1786, p. 852).

p. 77. *Re-enlistment.* Military Consultations, 1752, p. 33; Army Order, 23 September, 1769; loc. cit., 1 and 9 August, 1788.

p. 78. *Enlistments from Royal Forces.* Lawrence to Council, 8 October, 1749 (Letters to Fort St David 1749); Military Dispatch to England, 10 November, 1757; Wilson, *Madras Army*, i. 213 etc.

p. 79. *Messing.* Wilson, op. cit., i. 52 etc.; Military Dispatches from England, 19 December, 1755, and to England, 21 November, 1756; Army Orders, 10 June, 1762, 11 February, 1766, and 24 March, 1770; G.O.G., 16 August, 1776; Army Order, 23 February, 1787; G.O.G., 10 December, 1798.

p. 80. *Field-diet.* Country Correspondence, 1749, pp. 31 and 42; Orme MSS., Various, 287, pp. 111, 395; loc. cit., 288, pp. 65, 85, 97, and 103; Orme MSS., India, ii. 488; Military Consultations, 1753, pp. 25, 26, and 104; Public Consultations, 26 February, 1753; Love's *Vestiges*, ii. 486; Military Consultations, 1755, p. 43; Correspondence with Adlercron, 20 April, 1756; Military Consultations, 30 November, 1758, and 3 December, 1759; Army Orders, 22 February, and 2 and 6 April, 1791.

p. 82. *Arrack.* Army Orders, 24 July, 1765, 29 September, 1781, 1 May, 1782, 29 November, 1783, 17 December, 1788; Military Consultations, 8 March, 1776; Army Orders, 4 April and 9 June, 1782, 24 May and 6 June, 1783, 26 May, 1790, 27 March, 1791, 16 February, 1792.

p. 84. *Training.* Fort St David Consultations, 29 February, 1749; letter from Clive, 19 July (Military Consultations, 1756, p. 236); Army Orders, 22 September, 1709, 21 July, 1781, 23 February, 1786.

p. 85. *The Conjee House.* Cuthbertson, Management of a battalion of infantry, pp. 150 etc.; Sime, Military Course, p. 173; Army Orders, 15 July and 1 October, 1770, and 22 December, 1772.

p. 86. *Desertion.* Army Order, 5 April, 1782; Correspondence with Adlercron, 1755, No. 19; loc. cit., 1756, No. 3; Army Orders, 2 July, 1781, 4 December, 1787, 1 and 2 December, 1788, 5 June and 9 July, 1789, 25 September, 1790; Correspondence with Adlercron, 1755, Nos. 37 and 38; Military Consultations, 1756, p. 203; Army Orders, 12 and 15 December, 1773; Military Consultations, 12 June, 1775.

p. 88. *Murder-trials.* Quarter-sessions proceedings—John Owen, 22 November, 1794; Timothy Grady, 15 April, and Michael Finey, 30 September, 1795.
Soldier-settlers. Public Sundry, No. 41. For Young's correspondence, Mayor's Court Records.

CHAPTER VII

Penny's *Church in Madras* contains much matter on the subject of this chapter.

p. 93. *Danish missionaries.* The letter referred to occurs in Fort St David Letters Received, vol. iii, and is dated 17 May, 1749. From misplaced tenderness no one who has referred to this letter has mentioned its damning conclusion.

p. 94. *Clive's marriage.* It was solemnised by Fabricius, and therefore probably did not take place, as Sir George Forrest supposes, at St Mary's.
Kiernander's second marriage. A caustic reference will be found in the *Letters of Asiaticus.*

p. 95. *Robert Palk.* For the depressing influence of Mr Palk, see Orme MSS., Various, 27, p. 150.

p. 96. *Salmon.* See minute by Wynch, ap. Military Consultations, 1 May, 1775.
Browne. Public Dispatch to England, 14 February, 1776.

Wells. His will occurs in the Will-book for 1792, p. 228. He did not, I think, return to sea as Mr Penny supposes.

p. 103. *Douglas.* His will occurs in the Will-book for 1783, p. 296.

Powney. His will occurs in the Will-book for 1740, under date 16 September.

p. 104. *Mitchel.* See Wheeler's *Madras* (ed. 1882), p. 342.

CHAPTER VIII

p. 108. *The alleged healthiness of Madras.* See *Letters of Asiaticus*; Lockyer, p. 23; Jourdan to [Stevenson], 15 April, 1767 (Mayor's Court Records); *Cumberland Letters*, p. 22; Orme to Payne, 2 November, 1756 (Orme MSS., Various, 28, p. 55).

p. 109. *Batavia.* See *Stavorinus* (ed. 1798), iii. 399.

The health of middle-aged arrivals. See Long's *Selections*, p. 63.

p. 110. *Health of newly arrived troops.* See letter from Bagshaw, 30 October (Public Consultations, 31 October, 1754); Howes to Saunders, 31 October, 1754 (Madras Military Bundles). The muster-rolls mentioned occur in the Fort St David Consultations, 31 March, 1742.

p. 112. *Manucci.* See my edition of the Mayor's Court Proceedings, Madras, 1915.

Voulton. See Orme, i. 274, and the Orme MSS., Various, 17, pp. 274–6.

Private soldiers as doctors. Public Consultations, 1688, p. 2; Public Miscellany, No. 1, 21 July, 1755; Gaupp to Pigot, 29 June, 1756 (Madras Military Bundles); Long, *Selections*, p. 282.

Cadets, etc., as surgeons. Military Miscellany, No. 2, 18 August, 1772; Public Sundry, No. 21, p. 148.

Bulkeley. See Hedges' *Diary*, ii. 320 etc.; Kellett, Public Consultations, 6 November, 1756.

p. 113. *Browne's case.* Wheeler, *Madras* (ed. 1882), p. 150.

Andrew Munro. Public Consultations, 6 May, 1754, and Mayor's Court Pleadings, 1755, pp. 391 etc.

p. 114. *James Wilson.* Miscellaneous Letters Received, 1749–50, No. 4.

Gilbert Pasley. Military Consultations, 16 February, 1761, p. 154; Public Miscellany, No. 1, p. 51; Mayor's Court Pleadings, 1778, p. 730; Jourdan to Monckton, 4 March, 1768 (Mayor's Court Records); Cottoh's *Inscriptions,* p. 26; Chambers's will (Will-books, 1769); Ardley's will (ibid. 1772); Ross's will (ibid. 1774); Cam's and Richardson's wills (ibid. 1776); Pigot's will (ibid. 1778); Richardson's will (ibid. 1779); Young to John Taylor, 13 February, 1780, and to Captain George Burrington, 28 September, 1781 (Mayor's Court Records); Love, *Vestiges,* iii. 177.

p. 116. *T. S. Hancock.* Br. Mus. Add. MSS. 29096, ff. 162–172.

p. 117. *James Potter.* Army Order, 11 April, 1772.

p. 118. *Davis's letter.* Madras Army Records, series I, No. 28.

Reorganisation of 1786. Army Orders, 14 April, 1786, 25 October, 1787, and 2 September, 1788.

p. 119. *Medical attention in the Field.* Coote's letter, 24 January (Military Consultations, 26 January, 1760); Davis's letter, 2 July (Military Consultations, 5 July, 1781, p. 1692).

p. 120. *Provision of diet.* Lockyer, p. 21; Public Dispatch from England, January, 1752; Miscellaneous Letters Received, 1749–50, No. 35; Public Consultations, 10 October, 1759; Wilson, *Madras Army,* i. 153 etc., Army Order, 10 March, 1791.

The Madras Hospital. Public Consultations, 1688, p. 54; loc. cit., 8 July, 1754, and 28 November, 1758.

p. 121. *Hospital Discipline.* Army Orders, 15 September, 1768; 4 December, 1770; 6 April, 1771; 2 September, 1772; and G.O.G., 17 February, 1794.

p. 122. *Surgeon Blackadder's suspension.* Army Order, 9 May, 1792.

p. 123. *Inoculation, etc.* Army Orders, 26 December, 1787, and 22 January, 1793; Public Consultations, 21 January, 1803, p. 109.

Destruction of pariah dogs. Army Orders, 10 March, 1770; 24 April, 1772; 3 April, 1789 (Walajabad). *The snake pills.* Military Consultations, 16 September (pp. 2586 etc.), 30 September (pp. 2901–2), and 28 October, 1788 (pp. 3293 etc.).

CHAPTER IX

p. 126. *The Carvalhos.* Will-books, 1782 and 1791 (wills of Francisco and his wife).

p. 127. *Yta y Salazar.* Miscellaneous Letters Recieved, 1756, No. 8.

John Powney. Will-book, 1740.

Samuel Troutback. Love's *Vestiges,* iii. 398, and Young to Wedderburn, 29 October, 1781 (Mayor's Court Records).

p. 129. *Respondentia.* Lockyer, p. 17; Counsel's opinion on respondentia bonds (enclosure to Public Dispatch from England 7 May, 1746); Mayor's Court Pleadings, 1770–72, pp. 272 and 310; 1774, p. 54; 1775, p. 213; 1782, p. 374; 1784, pp. 370 and 632. Jourdan to Holford, February, 1770 (Mayor's Court Records). Dawsonne Drake's inventory (Will-book, 1783, pp. 3 etc.).

Manila trade. Mayor's Court Pleadings, 1743, pp. 169–170; Jourdan to Dalrymple, 23 January, 1767; to Monckton, 2 April, 1768; to Crawford, 9 April, 1771; to the same, 19 April, 1771; to Hare, 3 June, 1771 (Mayor's Court Records).

p. 131. *Trade to Achin and Kedah.* Bowrey, Countries round the Bay of Bengal, p. 286. Marsden, History of Sumatra, p. 399. Jourdan to Monckton, 18 February, 1767; to Captain David Scott, 22 March, 1768; to Harrop, 6 January; to ——, 13 January; to [Holford?], 12 April; to ——, 13 April, 1767. Public Consultations, 21 January, 1768, pp. 42 etc. Jourdan to Holford, 5 and 18 April; to Crawford, 21 September, 1768. Jourdan to Casamaijor, 27 July, 1769. Public Sundry, No. 21.

p. 135. *The Nawab's debt.* Jourdan to Brown, 22 November, 1777; to Benfield, 23 May; to A. Ross, 2 June, 1778. Young to Alexander Watson, 14 February, 1777.

p. 137. *The Second Mysore War.* Young to Fannin, 14 September, 1781, and 30 January, 1782; to Captain Patrick Mouat, 13 August, 1782; to William Hamilton, 16 October, 1782.

p. 138. *Lautour.* Public Sundry, No. 41.

p. 140. *Marine Insurance.* Mayor's Court Pleadings, 5 June and 18 September, 1744; 1764, p. 375; 1781, p. 1014; 1772, p. 503. Jourdan to Crawford, 20 May, 1769; to Higginson, January, 1779; Young to Knox, 19 August, 1778; Mayor's Court Pleadings, 1784, p. 166; Daly to Tudor, 30 March and 22 April, 1791; Roebuck to Call, 29 April, 1791.

p. 141. *Roebuck and Abbot.* Letter-books of the firm in the Mayor's Court Records.

CHAPTER X

p. 149. *Pirates.* The first commission for trying pirates is in the Madras Record Office. A new commission was issued at the beginning of each reign.

Chartered Courts. The charters for the courts of 1726 and 1753 are printed in the collection of the Company's charters, London, 1772.

p. 150. *Criminal Procedure.* The procedure of the courts is detailed in a Sundry Book, Public, No. 8.

p. 151. *Court of Quarter Sessions.* The proceedings of the Quarter Sessions survive in 13 volumes at Madras, covering the years 1761 to 1798, but even for that period they are very incomplete.

p. 155. *Mayor's Court.* The proceedings of the Mayor's Court are much more voluminous. The pleadings alone comprise a large number of volumes and are nearly complete from 1753. For its relations with the Council see Love's *Vestiges,* ii. 233, and 273 etc.; my *Calendar of the Madras Records,* 1740–44, p. 418. For the native oaths, see Wheeler's *Madras,* p. 530, and Love, ut supra.

p. 157. *Benyon's letter.* See Miscellaneous Letters Received, 1754–55, No. 84.

Letter to the Mayor's Court. See Madras Public Consultation, 23 November, 1757.

p. 158. *Barratry.* See Records of the Town Hall Court, 27 March, 1744, and Quarter Sessions, 12 February, 1784.

Greenslate. See Public Dispatch to England, 10 March, 1755; Public Consultations, 20 March, 1759; and Mayor's Court Misc. Proceedings, 2 June, 1761.

Merigeot. See Orme MSS., Various, 288, p. 158.

Dencker. His inventory occurs in the Will-book for 1756, under date 25 May.

p. 159. *Pullein Spencer.* His inventory occurs in the Will-book for 1793, p. 271.

p. 161. *J. S. Hall.* See Military Consultations, 14 July, 1781, p. 1872; Public Sundry, No. 33; Young to Scott, 10 March, 1778; and to Mitchell, 26 April, and 28 September, 1780; Military Consultations, 10 March, 1789, pp. 776–7; and Love's *Vestiges*, iii. 441.

CHAPTER XI

p. 165. *Madras plaster—chunam.* See Mrs Kindersley's Letters, pp. 77–8.

House-rents. Jourdan to Williams, 4 March, 1778; to Willeson, 26 January, 1779; to Raitt, March, 1769. Military Consultations, 15 August, 1775.

p. 167. *Garden Houses.* Hicky's *Memoirs*, i. 174–5. Drake's inventory, Will-books, 1783, pp. 3 etc.

p. 169. *Gardens.* Young to Deckers, 4 August, 1777; Jourdan to Wynch, 12 February, 1776.

Furniture. Mayor's Court Pleadings, 1767, p. 454.

Punkahs. Bowden's inventory, Will-books, 1793, p. 631.

p. 170. *China paper.* Account sale, sloop *Favori* (Public Consultations, 4 December, 1759); Jourdan to Jameson, 15 August, 1771; Clermont-Tonnerre, *Samuel Bernard*, p. 100.

Pictures. Inventory, William Roberts, Will-books, 1760.

17

p. 171. *Miss Read.* Young to Wedderburn, 3 December, 1777; and to James Call, 16 February, 1779.

George Willeson. Dempster to Jourdan, 22 April, 1776; Jourdan to Willeson, 27 July, 1778.

John Smart. Public Sundry, No. 41.

Thomas Hickey. Two interesting articles appeared on him in the *Madras Mail* for 28 June and 24 August, 1911.

Imhoff. Hastings to Hancock, 4 July, 1770, and to Imhoff, 6 July, 1771 (Brit. Mus. Add. MSS. 29125).

p. 173. *Samuel Chaplin.* Public Sundry, No. 41.

Soldier-servants. Army Order, 30 June, 1778.

p. 174. *Servants' wages.* Public Sundry, No. 16 (18 June, 1770); Army Order, 7 May, 1790.

Slaves. Norris's account sale, Will-book, 1756; Main's inventory, 1770; Jourdan to Stevenson, 10 April, 1784.

p. 175. *Food from Bengal.* Harris's will, Will-books, 1737; Hastings to Hancock, 28 February, 1770 (Br. Mus. Add. MSS. 29125); Jourdan to Kellican, 15 April, 1775. Young to Dawson, 26 November, 1781.

p. 176. *Thomas Leany.* Inventory, Will-book, 1791.

Tea. Caillaud to Amyatt, 8 February, 1760 (Orme MSS., India, xii. 3069).

p. 177. *Beatson.* Camp Order, 4 March, 1792.

Manucci. Mayor's Court Pleadings, 1757, p. 387.

p. 178. *Madeira.* Public Consultations, 3 June and 17 June, 1754; Ives' *Voyage*, p. 3; Milburn, *Oriental Commerce*, i. 4; Ellore Orderly Book, 11 June, 1775; Roebuck to Nailer, 21 October, 1790; Morris's will (Will-book, 1792, p. 515).

CHAPTER XII

p. 182. *The ambassador's bill.* Tellicherry Diary, 19 April, 1747.

p. 183. *Extravagant costume.* Jourdan to Robert Crawford, 1 March and 7 October, 1768.

Hickey, *Memoirs*, ii. 283.

Native attire. Wheeler, *Madras*, p. 680. Cope's will

(Fort St David Consultations, 19 May, 1753). Inventories—Dencker (1756), Lee (ibid.), d'Illens (1757), Callender (1759), Preston (1766), Dewar, *Hand-book of the Records of the United Provinces*, p. 369.

p. 184. *Betel.* Pyrard de Laval, ii. 363. La Farelle, *Mémoires et correspondance*, p. 40. Account-sale, Cope, Will-books, 1755.

p. 185. *Style of life.* Public Dispatches from England, 8 January, 1718, and 24 January, 1753. Jourdan to Westcott, 4 November, 1772. Gleig, *Memoirs of Sir Thomas Munro*, i. 73.

p. 187. *Private schools.* Public Sundry, No. 41, William Joseph Rutter and Benjamin Goard. Love, *Vestiges*, iii. 442–3.

p. 188. *Books, etc.* Caillaud to Orme, 19 June, 1757 (Orme MSS., Various, No. 52, p. 90). Catalogue of the Library at Fort St George (Home Miscellaneous, No. 260, India Office). Inventory, Eyre (1753).

p. 193. *Richard Johnston.* Public Sundry, No. 41. Inventory, Will-book, 1792, p. 421.

Hugh Boyd. L. D. Campbell's Memoir. Hugh Boyd's *Will* (*Madras Mail*, 12 May, 1911). A lively description of him occurs in Hickey, iv. pp. 8 etc.

CHAPTER XIII

p. 197. *Mrs. Anne Miller.* Hedges' *Diary*, iii. 175.

Clive's marriage. Dalton to Clive, 1 July, 1752 (Orme MSS., India, ii. 488); Fabricius and Breithaupt to Clive, 22 February, 1753 (Orme MSS., Various, No. 288, p. 125); Repington to Clive, 25 February, 1753 (loc. cit., p. 101); Lawrence to Clive, 11 March, 1753 (loc. cit., p. 49).

p. 198. *Miss Sophia Goldborne.* "Hartley House."

Miss Elena Beatson. Young to Wedderburn, 7 September; to J. and D. Webster, 15 October; to Wedderburn, 24 October, 1777; to the same, 15 October, 1778; to W. Read, 12 October, 1779.

17*

p. 199. *Lt Matthias Calvert* to Colonel Morris, 23 February, 1763 (Br. Mus. Add. MSS. 5939, f. 5 verso).

p. 200. *Cosmetics, etc.* Inventory, Angus Mackintosh (Will-book, 1790, p. 414); Thomas Leany (Will-book, 1792, p. 438); Mrs Bromley (Will-book, 1790, p. 237).

Hairdressers. Public Sundry, No. 41, Chaplin and Stuart.

Ladies' wardrobes. Inventories, Eleanor Cope (Will-book, 1756), Mrs Bromley (ut supra), and Anne Page (Will-book, 1797, p. 98).

p. 201. *Governor's consent to marriages.* Wheeler, *Madras,* p. 384.

p. 202. *Eric Dieustedt.* Mayor's Court Pleadings, 24 May, 1764, and 1765, p. 360.

Unfortunate marriages. Young to Charles Maule, 12 March, 1778; G.O.C.C., 2 June, 1797; Adams' Orderly Book (Br. Mus. Add. MSS. 6049, f. 23). Jourdan to Crawford, 18 July, 1769.

p. 203. *Mackain.* Will-book, 1772, 28 July; Quarter Sessions Proceedings, 17 April, 1765.

T. I. Tanner. Will-book, 1790, p. 373.

S. B. Evance. Will-book, 1782, 5 November.

p. 204. *C. Barrett.* Sophia Barrett to John Croley, 12 April, 1792 (Will-books, 1797, p. 168).

p. 206. *Littleton.* Will-book, 1776.

Pater. Missionary Register, 11 November, 1794, baptism of Sapphira, aged 4, daughter of Major John Pater and —— Robinson.

Cotton's *Inscriptions,* p. 230.

p. 207. *Anne Shaw.* Roebuck and Abbot to Call, 16 October, 1794.

Victory, etc. Young to Kent, 25 March, 1780; and to Deckers, 4 August, 1777.

p. 208. *James Buller.* Will-book, 1774.

William Stevenson. Will-book, 1765.

Adam Kisselbach. Will-book, 1797, p. 226.

Charles Lamb. Letter to B. W. Procter, 19 January, 1829.

Blake Eyre. Jourdan to Hughes, 6 August, 1784.

p. 209. *Captain William Oliphant.* Will-book, 1798–1800, p. 128.

Lt-col George Stewart. Will-book, 1797, p. 446.

Major Thomas Gordon. Will-book, 1798–1800, p. 26.

Hew Stuart. Will-book, 1783, p. 64.

Joseph Garrow. Will-book, 1792, p. 458.

Lt Robert Macmurdo. Will-book, 1781.

Lt-col Brown. Ibid.

p. 210. *Mrs Powney.* Will-book, 1780.

Robert Hughes. Caldwell, *Tinnevelly,* p. 194.

CHAPTER XIV

p. 211. *The Governor's Table.* Love, *Vestiges,* ii. 169, 424; Guet, *Jan Begam,* p. 40; Hickey, *Memoirs,* i. 169; Garrison Orders, 31 October, 1761; 24 December, 1761; 3 June, 1768 and 1769; 14 May, 1766.

p. 213. *Leighton and Capper.* Garrison Order, 7 September, 1771.

Concerts and music. Quarter Sessions, 15 January, 1761, and 18 July, 1765; Hughes' inventory, Will-book, 1759; Caillaud to Orme, 2 October, 1755 (Orme MSS., Various, No. 293, p. 55); Clive to Verelst, 29 March, 1766 (Home Miscellaneous, No. 739); Orme to Clive, 5 May, 1757 (Orme MSS., Various, No. 293, p. 20); Young to Scott, 10 March, 1778. Perhaps I may add that one of the foregoing references entirely disposes of Lord Curzon's statement (*British Government in India,* i. 224) that the history of the Governor-General's band begins with Lord Wellesley.

p. 215. *Theatricals.* List of the Nabob's creditors, ap. Mayor's Court Pleadings, 1768; Inventories, Main (1770), Frere (1778); Young to Linnear, 21 October, 1778; Love, *Vestiges,* iii. 150, 219, and 407.

p. 216. *Gambling.* Public Dispatch from England, 26 April, 1721; Lockyer, p. 23; Bruce's Diary, 6 April, 1777;

Inventory, Daniel Morse, Will-book, 1762; George Savage, Will-book, 1791, p. 378; Mayor's Court Pleadings, 1776, p. 644.

p. 217. *Taverns.* Love, *Vestiges,* iii. 444, 452; Dalton's *Memoirs,* p. 51; Young to Miss Ann Fletcher, 1 July, 1777; Hamilton, New Account, ii. 137; Strange's Narrative (Public Sundry, No. 37); Public Consultations, 29 January and 12 February, 1760; Garrison Order, 29 December, 1770; Mayor's Court Pleadings, 1776, p. 644; Shearme's bill, Mayor's Court Pleadings, 1770–72, p. 258; Account Book, 1780.

p. 222. *Carriages.* Lockyer, p. 27; Invoices, ap. Public Dispatches from England 1749; Ives' *Voyage,* p. 21; Public Consultations, 1 July, 1776; Jourdan to Crawford, 18 July, 1769; Young to Ferguson, 18 April and 28 July, 1780; Inventory, Robert Mitford, Will-book, 1790, p. 379.

p. 223. *Horses.* Public Consultations, 15 August, 1758; Jourdan to ——, 20 May, 1771; Military Consultations, 1780, p. 3344, and 1782, p. 3598; *Hyderabad Gazetteer,* p. 292; Jourdan to his brother, 6 November, 1775.

p. 224. *Hunting and racing.* Playne's *Southern India,* p. 420 etc.; Mayor's Court Pleadings, 1753, p. 5. Roebuck to Henry Abbott, 24 December, 1791; Denison, *Varieties of Vice-regal Life,* ii. 145. Garrison Order, 27 December, 1773.

p. 225. *Hawking.* Hastings to Fletcher, 15 May, 1771 (Br. Mus. Add. MSS. 29125).

p. 226. *Duelling.* Quarter Sessions, 3 May, 1794; Fort St David Consultations, 15 June, 1747; Miscellaneous Letters Received, 1758–59, No. 132; ditto 1757, No. 18; Madras Letters Received, 1688, p. 23; Garrison Order, 10 December, 1770; Military Consultations, 1 March, 1792, p. 1058; Quarter Sessions, 5 May and 22 September, 1794; Public Consultations 1687, p. 88; Love, *Vestiges,* ii. 36; Champion's Journal, 1 July, 1765 (Home Miscellaneous, No. 198); Army Order, 18 May,

1787; 22 March, 1769; 21 May, 1770; 25 July, 1792;
17 November, 1791; 21 June, 1782; 18 May, 1792;
Quarter Sessions, 18 April, 1781; 8 October, 1784;
7 July, 1788; Elers' *Memoirs*, p. 171; Cotton's *Inscriptions*, p. 136.